Sports
Geography

Sports Geography

JOHN BALE

University of Keele

LONDON   NEW YORK

E. & F.N. SPON

First published in 1989 by
E. & F.N. Spon
11 New Fetter Lane, London EC4P 4EE

Published in the USA by
E. & F.N. Spon
29 West 35th Street, New York NY10001

© 1989 John Bale

Typeset in 10/12 Palatino by
Scarborough Typesetting Services
Printed in Great Britain by
St Edmundsbury Press Limited
Bury St Edmunds, Suffolk

ISBN 0 419 14390 4

British Library Cataloguing in Publication Data

Bale, John, 1940–
Sports geography
1. Sports 2. Geography
I. Title
796 GV706.8

ISBN 0 419 14390 4

Library of Congress Cataloging-in-Publication Data

Bale, John
Sports geography.

Bibliography: p.
Includes indexes.
1. Sports 2. Geography I. Title
GV706.8.B35 1989 796 88–35617

ISBN 0 419 14390 4

CONTENTS

ACKNOWLEDGEMENTS

I am grateful to the following for permission to reproduce passages, illustrations and tables contained in this book:

Bob Jones for Fig. 2.4b, the University of Texas Press for the quotes from the text by Al Reinert in *Rites of Fall: High School Football in Texas*, photographs by Geoff Winningham, text by Al Reinert, copyright © 1979, on page 17, Hal Gilman for the passage on page 29, Eric Dunning for Table 3.1, R. Harisalo for Fig. 3.1, Tony Mangan for the passage on page 70, Peter Toyne for Fig. 4.4, *The Guardian* for Figs 4.7, 5.8, 6.14 and *The Guardian*, David Frost and Matthew Engel for Fig. 4.15 and the passage on page 173 respectively, *The Tampa Tribune* and Richard Mudry for Fig. 4.8, *The Miami Herald* (and Rex Walford for drawing my attention to) Fig. 4.9, Jorge Gaspar for Fig. 4.10, John Rooney for Figs 4.13, 8.1, 8.6 and 8.7, William Schaffer and Lawrence Davidson for Table 5.3, Wes Dow for Fig. 5.6, the *St. Petersburg Times* for the passage on page 127, the *Sydney Morning Herald* and Daniel Moore for Fig. 5.8, *The Observer* for the passages on pages 134 and 153, *The Fresno Bee* and Wanda Coyle for the article on page 245, *The Economist* for the passage on page 151, the City Museum and Art Gallery, Stoke-on-Trent for Fig. 6.7, Bob Adams for Figs 6.9 and 6.11, Collins Publishers and Simon Inglis for Fig. 6.16, A. G. Macdonnell and Macmillan Publishers for the passage on page 180, 'Gren' for the inspiration for Fig. 7.2, H. C. Marais for Fig. 7.9, Ernst Jokl for Tables 7.2 and 7.3, Paavo Seppänen for Tables 7.4 and 7.5, Brian Rodgers for Fig. 7.16, Robert Campbell and D. S. Chen for Table 8.1.

Every effort has been made to trace copyright holders but I apologize for any unintended omission or neglect.

. . . in the next great Atlas to be produced by English mapmakers . . . a map of the distribution of games throughout the world might be included. The inferences to be drawn from it are not within my power to draw; but they might be curious.
Edmund Blunden, *Cricket Country*, 1944.

Sportsworld is a sweaty Oz you'll never find in a Geography book.
Robert Lipsyte, *Sportsworld*, 1976.

He was in love with travelling, with running, with geography.
John Updike, *Rabbit Run*, 1964.

PREFACE

In the preface to an *Introduction to Sport Studies** Harold Vanderzwaag and George Sheehan explained that the selection of sub-disciplines which made up each chapter of their book was undertaken in a somewhat arbitrary manner and was based largely on the content of courses being taught in the USA in the mid and late 1970s. The philosophy, sociology, history and psychology of sport were all dealt with but the geography of sport was not. They accepted that sports geography is another avenue for studying sport but they failed to embark on its exploration, believing that at the time there was a paucity of published work in this area.

The present book is written to show that this is no longer the case. It seeks to fill a substantial lacuna in the sports studies literature and is an initial attempt to draw together the principal foci from the existing literature on the geography of sports. It represents over a decade of academic involvement in the geographical dimensions of sport and a lifetime's activity as a sports enthusiast and participant.

When I started studying sport I tended to use it to teach geography. I found that allusions to sport, a pervasive feature of modern society, helped motivate my students and make my geography classes more interesting. I realize now that I was tending to devalue sport by reducing it to the level of a teaching gimmick. Sport is worthy of academic study in its own right and its geographical dimensions provide special insights not included in any other of the 'disciplines'.

This book is primarily intended for those following introductory sports studies courses in higher education. At the same time geography students might be interested in a book which deals with location, landscapes and regions, among other things. For geographers I hope that *Sports Geography* provides examples and insights of well-known geographical themes. In addition, a wide range of social scientists may use this book as a source of reference.

This book is not an encyclopaedia or gazetteer. Instead it is concerned with ideas, using specific facts to illustrate recurring themes in a variety of geographical contexts. Believing that geographers are essentially concerned with places I have included in each chapter vignettes which try to capture sport–place associations in an evocative way. The inclusion of

* Published by Brown, Dubuque, Iowa, 1978.

several extracts from daily newspapers (and not always from the sports pages) serves to remind us that a geography of sport is all around us! I have tried to assist the readers of this book by providing detailed references and suggestions for further reading. Those using the book as a source of reference will be able to ignore the student-centred learning experiences, discussion topics and suggestions for projects, included as an Appendix, but all readers will probably benefit from having a good atlas close at hand, given the global nature of the illustrative material.

Many people have helped in the writing of this book. In particular I would like to thank John, Sandy, Dick, Pat, John and Jane for extravagant hospitality and good times while I was ostensibly involved in the academic study of sports in alien climes. As this book is a synthesis the names of a large number of other people are included in the pages which follow. Although I've never met most of them – and although they may never read this – I must thank all who have unwittingly provided ideas and information included in the maps, diagrams, tables and text in this book.

As in all productions of this kind thanks must go to the author's family. In my case my parents supported an early interest in sports; today Ruth, Roderick and Anthony continue to support an ageing geography teacher cum sports enthusiast in diverse ways. Despite the help of all these people, the usual caveat applies.

John Bale
Betley, Staffs

Chapter 1

INTRODUCTION

A well known professor of Geography once likened his subject to the city of Los Angeles in that it sprawls over a large area, merges with its neighbours and has a central area which is difficult to find![1] However, it did not take him long to alert his readers to the fact that geography is basically concerned with three themes, namely (1) the location and spatial order of terrestrial phenomena, (2) human–environment relationships, and (3) regional differentiation. Two recurring concepts in Geography are therefore space and place and the subject is popularly associated with 'knowing where things are' or 'knowing what places are like'. Because the academic discipline of geography is essentially a human creation its character and content vary among both individual geographers and national 'schools' of geography. Some scholars are more concerned with the physical than the cultural aspects of the world; geography in some countries is typified by a descriptive approach, while in others a more analytical approach is adopted. But while it is common to resort to the old saw that 'geography is what geographers do', the two recurring concepts of space and place are rarely far away from the geographer's task.

The broad umbrella of geography has produced a number of sub-disciplines. Among the most well known are economic geography, cultural geography, political geography and historical geography. In the case of economic geography, for example, the geographer will be concerned with the analysis of (1) the locational aspects of economic activities, (2) economic–environment interelations, and/or (3) regional variations in economic activity. Replace the word 'economic' by 'histori-cal' and we have the broad area of enquiry of the historical geographer. We could continue like this for a whole range of 'adjectival geographies' (from abacuses to zithers, according to one observer![2]) but the essential foci of space and place will remain. Beyond the recording of information the geographer is concerned with understanding, through analysis, the reasons for the locations of places and what they are like. Geographers are also concerned with making prescriptions for more optimal patterns of spatial organization, from the perspective of either increased profit or increased human welfare.

In recent years the adjectival geographies alluded to above, have proliferated, spawning a vast number of sub-fields. Geographers have hence brought their perspectives to bear upon a wide range of subjects and insofar as geography is concerned with the description, recording and analysis of phenomena on the surface of the earth, those phenomena associated with the pervasive cultural form known as 'sports' form a fully justifiable area for geographic study. Yet despite the ubiquity and significance of sports, the major fields of geography have only recently begun to accept the subject as a legitimate area for study.

The traditional neglect of sport in geography (and of geography in sport) is paradoxical for a number of reasons. First, sport is a major economic activity; it is therefore a legitimate area of economic geography. Sport is a principal component of modern culture, hence justifying its study from the perspective of cultural geography; and the physical environment undeniably affects sporting outcomes, making sports also amenable to physical geographic study.

Secondly, the traditional omission of sports geography from the main discipline is surprising when it is considered how important space and place are to both sport and to geography. We have already alluded to the centrality of space and place in the science of geography but these two concepts are also central to the study of sport. Sport and geography are both concerned with space and the way it is occupied; they both focus on the way people and objects move and interact in geographic space; regions form a central feature of the organization of sports; places are the means of identification for many sports teams; sport is affected by, and increasingly affects, both the environment and the landscape; sport is a world of hierarchy and territoriality. In short, sport – like geography – is a science of space. Indeed, in one sport (orienteering) where map, compass and route finding are all essential parts of the activity, it is difficult to know where the sport starts and the geography stops.

Despite its fundamentally geographical character, sport was not traditionally thought of as a subject worthy of serious geographic enquiry. In geographical writing sports may have been briefly alluded to in passing (a paragraph on English cricket was included in the monumental *Universal Geography** of the late nineteenth century humanist-geographer, Elisée Reclus[3]) and much excellent geographical work has been undertaken by scholars who would not claim to be geographers at all (the work on the Olympic Games by Ernst Jokl[4] comes to mind). But despite the fact that geography (more than many other academic

---

* His paragraph on cricket suggests that in his visits to England the game had made something of an impact on him since sports and games do not seem to feature in any other volume of his *magnum opus*.

disciplines) has treated sport as an epiphenomenon, being marginalized in economic, cultural and physical studies, there are signs that in the last two decades a sub-discipline called sports geography has arrived. Its arrival has been characterized by a number of indicators, typical of the growth of many sub-disciplines[5]. These are:

1. Programmatic articles calling for a geography of sport and suggesting the application of geographical ideas in a sporting context. Papers of this kind started appearing in the early and mid 1960s and are typified by those of Shaw[6] and Burley[7].
2. Empirical investigations of sport and sport-related topics from a geographical perspective. Much work of this type was pioneered by Rooney and his students [8–14] from the late 1960s onwards.
3. Theoretical essays addressing more fundamental geographical questions and problems in a sports context, exemplified by Wagner's view that sport is an admixture of culture and geography[15].
4. Books, monographs and dissertations which explore further the interrelations between sport and geography. By the mid-seventies the American writer James Michener was able to claim that it was sports-geographic writing which had proved the 'most intriguing' of the wide range of academic studies of sport which he reviewed in his monumental *Sports in America*[16].
5. Conferences and the establishment of journals dealing with the geographical character of sport, typified by geographers' regular contributions to annual conferences of their national associations (e.g. the Association of American Geographers has held sessions on the geography of sport since the early 1970s, though the same cannot be said for the equivalent Institute of British Geographers) and conferences convened by sociologists and historians, for example. In 1987 the international journal *Sport Place* was published to represent the sub-discipline.

Because sports-geographic writing has been undertaken in a wide range of disciplines and is found in often inaccessible and somewhat fugitive sources, the prime aim of the present book is to draw together the major themes from a scattered literature in a coherent form. Although sport (like geography) is rather difficult to define (see Chapter 2), we tend to use it in this book to describe the kinds of things written about on the sports pages of daily newspapers. In other words we are more concerned with top-class, achievement-oriented sport than with sport as recreation. However, because the distinction between these two levels of sport is blurred there is an inevitable overlap in terms of coverage and it must be noted that one reason for concentrating on serious sport is that recreational sport has received far more attention from academic geographers[17]. Integrating the literature on the geography of sport has been achieved by using broad theoretical frameworks (e.g. spatial diffusion, central place theory, spatial margins to profitability, regional multipliers, prospect-refuge theory etc.) in order to provide a structure, or skeleton, upon which the descriptive flesh of the real world can be draped. We do not seek in these pages to produce a theory of sports geography; if we have a conclusion it is that sport is becoming increasingly rational, more artificial, less like play and more like display[18]. We argue that the geography of sport, its locations and landscapes, reflect these developments.

Perhaps the most obvious way to examine the geography of sport is to think of an individual sport (or sport *per se*) as originating at points in geographic space, spreading outwards from these initial areas to embrace regions, nations and in some cases the world, and hence forming a kind of regional pattern. During this period of geographical diffusion, which is still taking place in many sports, profound landscape changes have occurred, be they in the countryside or the city. Some landscapes have become sportscapes, so momentous has been the impact of sport. Today sporting attributes, be they the distribution or density of clubs for participation or the ability to 'produce' star players, is far from evenly spread over the face of the earth. However, such distributions are not randomly arranged either and for this reason sports regions (areas identifying strongly with particular sports) can be recognized. Within the sports landscapes of the modern world facilities for sport, or the way in which sporting activity is arranged, may be far from optimal. Their geographical sub-optimality may derive from the perspective of the profit-maximizing sports entrepreneur or from that of the sports consumer. For this reason attempts can be made to produce geographically optimal or spatially equitable solutions to sports-geographic problems.

In brief, sports geography is concerned with the exploration of (a) sports activity on the earth's surface and how the spatial distribution of sport has changed over time; (b) the changing character of the sports landscape and the symbiosis between the sports environment and those who participate in it; and (c) the making of prescriptions for spatial and environmental change in the sports environment. Such explorations are undertaken at a variety of geographic scales, ranging from that of a sports stadium and the streets immediately around it to that of the world itself.

Chapter 2 shows how the geographical concepts of space and place are central to not only a definition of sport but also to an enhanced understanding of sport's significance. The spatial character of sport helps distinguish it from activities such as play, recreation and work while place not only influences sporting outcomes but also provides a social anchor to which clubs can relate. Chapter 3 examines the growth of sport, not simply historically but also geographically. Historians of sport are gradually recognizing that sports took time not only to grow but to spread from place to place. The spatial perspective adds much to our knowledge of the history of sport, how sports grew and how innovations in sports spread from their points of origin. Chapter 4 deals with locational changes of a rather different nature from those catalogued under the broad heading of geographical diffusion. At the present time sports clubs are involved in a number of locational adjustments. Some engage in re-location, be it to suburbs or to new regions; other clubs die out, a response perhaps to changing economic fortunes of the areas in which they are located; in other cases the balance of power in sport shifts from one region to another. Examples from several continents of the world are used to illustrate these themes.

The economic-geographical impacts of sport are introduced in Chapter 5 which discusses the contributions, both positive, in terms of income created by sports for example, and negative in terms of the kinds of 'sports pollution' which can be created by fandoms, the catchment area of a club's supporters.

Chapter 6 focuses on landscape impacts of sport. As sport has developed it has, in some cases, produced distinctive sportscapes – places designed specifically with sport in mind. In other cases the landscape impacts are temporary. Some of these bring benefits to the localities in which they are found; in other cases the impacts are negative. Likewise the sport landscape may enhance the quality of some people's lives but in other cases it can appear to be inhumane and dehumanizing. Each of these examples is considered with evidence from sports on either side of the Atlantic.

The focus of Chapter 7 is the idea of the sports region, i.e. an area identifying with a particular sport. Attention here is paid especially to the degree of congruence between sports regions as perceived in the mind's eye of the sports fan and the sporting reality, insofar as it can be objectively measured. Regional sports images may be stereotypes and it is incumbent upon the sports geographer to check their accuracy.

Chapter 8 deals with examples of geographical applications to problems in sport. For instance, where would be the best place to locate two new entries to the English football league? How should teams most efficiently organize their fixture lists? How should the frenzied recruiting of students in the American collegiate sports scene be rationalized? Should bonus points be awarded to teams whose results may be affected by rain?

The book concludes with a chapter dealing with the present state of sports geography and suggests new directions the sub-discipline might take. The aim of this book, as expressed earlier, is to draw together a scattered literature and in so doing introduce students to a new perspective on both sport and geography. The present book is an introduction but if it encourages either geographers or sports scientists to engage in further sports-geographic study it will have more than served its purpose.

REFERENCES

1. Haggett, P. (1979) *Geography: a Modern Synthesis*, Harper and Row, New York.
2. Hill, A. D. (1972) Geography and geographic education, in *Challenge and Change in College Geography* (ed. N. Helburn), AAG, Boulder.
3. Reclus, E. (1876) *The Universal Geography* (ed. E. Ravenstein), Vol.IV, Virtue, London.
4. Jokl, E. (1964) *Medical Sociology and Cultural Anthropology of Sport and Physical Education*, Thomas, Springfield, NJ.
5. Loy, J., Mcpherson, B. and Kenyon, G. (not dated, c 1980) *The Sociology of Sport as an Academic Speciality; an Episodic Essay on the Development of a Hybrid Sub-field*, CAHPER, Ottawa.
6. Shaw, E. (1963) Geography and baseball, *Journal of Geography*, **62**, 74–6.
7. Burley, R. (1966) A note on the geography of sport. *Professional Geographer*, **14**, 55–6.
8. Rooney, J. (1969) Up from the mines and out from the prairies; some geographical implications of football in the United States. *Geographical Review*, **59**, 471–92.
9. Rooney, J. (1974) *A Geography of American Sport; from Cabin Creek to Anaheim*, Addison-Wesley, Reading, MA.
10. Rooney, J. (1987) *The Recruiting Game*, (2nd edition), University of Nebraska Press, Lincoln.
11. Harper, G. (1975) *Intercollegiate Lacrosse in the United States, 1879–1975*, master's dissertation (unpublished), Oklahoma State University.
12. Rupert, M. (1980) *A Geographic Analysis of Professional Baseball's First Year Player Signings, 1965–1977*, master's dissertation (unpublished), Oklahoma State University.
13. Goudge, T. (1983) Interscholastic athletic participation; a geographical analysis of opportunity and development. *Proceedings, US Olympic Academy*, **7**, 165–202.
14. Hegarty, C. (1985) *An Analysis of the Geography of United States Golf with Particular Reference to a new form of Golf, the Cayman Facility*, master's dissertation (unpublished), Oklahoma State University.
15. Wagner, P. (1981) Sport: culture and geography, in *Space and Time in Geography* (ed. A. Pred), Gleerup, Lund.
16. Michener, J. (1976) *Sports in America*, Random House, New York.
17. Patmore, A. (1983) *Recreation and Resources*, Blackwell, Oxford.
18. Stone, G. (1971) American sports: play and display in *The Sociology of Sport* (ed. E. Dunning), Cass, London, 46–65.

Chapter 2

THE GEOGRAPHICAL BASES OF MODERN SPORT

It was noted in the previous chapter that space and place are two basic concepts which are central to both sport and geography. This chapter is devoted to a review of the ways in which space and place impinge on sport, and vice versa. The significance of space in the organization and the actual definition of sport is considered, as is the symbolic significance of sport–space. We examine the pervasiveness of place-pride, the apparent ubiquity of the home-field advantage, and the links between sport, place and politics. But we first turn to a brief consideration of the nature and definition of sport itself.

Conventionally sport is distinguished from related activities by stressing the physical and competitive nature of sports. For example, Fig. 2.1 tries to distinguish sport from two of its near neighbours with which it is sometimes confusingly associated, games and recreation. Recreation can be regarded as any free-time activity which is pursued voluntarily for intrinsic rewards; we cannot be forced into recreation. Games are

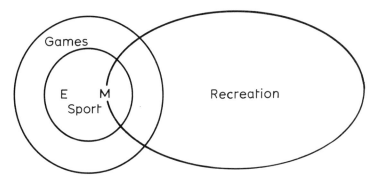

Fig. 2.1 Games, sports and recreation; E = elite sport; M = mass sport. (After Meier[1].)

goal-directed activities which have rules which limit the permissible means of winning. Rules (many of which may be of a spatial nature) prohibit more efficient means in favour of less efficient means; you are not allowed to run in a walking race or to kick the ball into play if it is over the touch line in soccer. Rules are accepted by all in order to make the game possible. All sports are games but their additional characteristic is that they [sports] exhibit physical prowess and skill. It is essentially the emphasis on the physical which is generally argued to distinguish sports from other games.

This is not to say, of course, that sport may not also be recreation. If sport is played for intrinsic rewards and is engaged in voluntarily then, according to our earlier definitions it must obviously be recreation. Much mass-participatory sport is clearly of this kind, people engaging in competitive physical activity for its own sake. It is much more difficult, however, to conceive of elite or top-level sport as being recreational in character. 'Players' at this level are more often professional and sport is more like work than play[2]. For many serious amateurs it is also difficult to think of sport as recreation. This is because for them sport, even at relatively modest levels of achievement, has to be done: it is often addictive and recreation is required to recover from the effort expended in training. It is not the level of performance that is important in defining non-recreational sport but the extent to which it is taken seriously. All mass-participatory sport is not recreation.

In addition to its physical quality, sport is also typically characterized

Table 2.1 Alternative views of modern sport

	Realist	*Liberal*	*Radical*
General characteristics			
Major actors	Places, nations	Individual	Class
Nature of relations	Conflictual	Cooperative	Contradictions
View of global order	Hierarchy	Interdependence	Imperialism
Major level	Inter-state	Transnational	Class conflict
Analytic assumption	Primacy of politics	No primacy	Primacy of economics
Intellectual roots	Power politics/ mercantilism	Functionalism/ pluralism	Marxism
Paradigm	International politics	World politics	World system
Particular characteristics			
Purpose of sport	Status/glory	Integration/order	Domination
Goal of sport	Victory	Participation	Alienation
Explanatory variable	National interest	Individual excellence	Class position

(Based on Shaw[5])

by competition, which is not a prerequisite of recreation or play (though those of a radical disposition might say that was a feature of work). The emphasis placed on winning (victory) in pure play is minimal or non-existent; in games a winner inevitably emerges, and in some games (e.g. world championship chess or darts) the significance of, and the emphasis placed on, winning can be considerable. However, in most games, and in most recreational sport, the play element is probably as significant as the emphasis on victory. In top class sport, however, the stress on victory approaches that level of importance which is placed on it in wartime. Many top-class athletes regard second place as a failure, sometimes breaking down in tears because they have not won.

We may therefore define sport by its physical and competitive character but it may be also interpreted as performing deeper, ideological functions which may not be so readily obvious to us until we strip away the superficial cover of the idealized picture which is so often painted. The image we hold of the nature of modern sport will depend in large part on our (formal and informal) political education. Trotsky believed sport diverted revolutionary fervour*; Lipsyte[4] believes sport is the most enjoyable way of using our bodies in public. Our perception of sport will depend on who we view as the main actors on the sporting stage. If we feel that the principal actors are universities, cities, regions or nations our perspective might be that sport is all about achieving status, glory, victory and increasing the local, regional or national interest. If, on the other hand, we feel that the principal actors are individuals (i.e. sportsmen and women) we may see sport as promoting integration and order through participation on the route to sporting excellence. A third view would be one which saw sport simply as a reflection of the class struggle, its purpose, therefore, being the domination or hegemony of the major power groups in society, the alienation of athletes and the maintenance of existing power relations in society.

Further views of modern sport are shown in Table 2.1. While these perspectives alert us to alternative interpretations, it should also be pointed out that dangers exist in generalizing about sport *per se*. The gamut of sporting activities is extremely wide; some sports verge on slaughter (boxing), others on ballet (ice-dance). To expect to find deep structural similarities in these might be unreasonable.

Just as sport may be so multi-faceted (work–play, freedom–constraint, recreation–athletics, process–product are only some of the continua on which sports can be located) that no single theoretical framework can be used to describe it[6], so no one philosophical position has characterized geographical approaches to sport. Indeed, existing work on sports

* Quoted in Allison[3].

geography embraces both empiricist and humanist, both positivist and structuralist philosophical positions* in order to tackle particular themes and problems. It is important to stress that two of the basic geographical concepts which lie at the very heart of the subject – space and place – also lie at the heart of sport. Although we have noted that conventional definitions emphasize its physical and competitive nature, we spend the remainder of this chapter stressing that the two fundamental geographical concepts not only help define sport but are also central to a full understanding of it.

2.1 SPACE AND SPORT

Sport is almost invariably characterized by rigorously enforced spatial parameters whereas recreation, leisure, games and work are not. Rules specify precise spatial limits on sports activities. Recreation does not require carefully defined spatial contexts, such as 400 m running tracks, pitches (as in soccer) of not more than 90 m in width, wickets (in cricket) of 22 yards in length. Neither does it require specified courses, pitches, routes, greens and rinks (see Fig. 2.2). Even sports like orienteering, cross-country running and skiing, and canoeing possess artificially imposed spatial and temporal limits. As Philip Wagner[8] says 'There is nothing natural about a sports event'.

The kinds of spatial boundaries described above are obviously explicit boundaries, written into the rules and regulations which define the area of sporting activity. A number of implicit boundaries also exist which are unmarked but readily recognizable. An attacking defender or a goal-keeper who wanders into the centre of the field are examples of athletes straying beyond an implicit boundary. Social as well as 'legal' factors may influence where, and where not, players are supposed to go within a game's spatial bounds.

Spatial (and temporal) positions at the start of a sports event are often crucial to participants. In track events which involve confinement to lanes, it is generally regarded as disadvantageous to be allocated to the outside lane. In skiing, pistes become rutted and it is therefore better to be 10th than 40th at the start in downhill ski events.

Sometimes the spatial-temporal aspects of sports can be carried to apparently absurd extremes. For example, 5000 and 10 000 m track races are timed to 0.01 of a second; yet for this to be meaningful in record breaking, every running track would have to be exactly the same distance. If track lengths differ by only a few millimetres it can be argued that 0.01 s is too small an increment of time to be considered as a real

---

* For a review of geography's philosophical positions see Johnston[7].

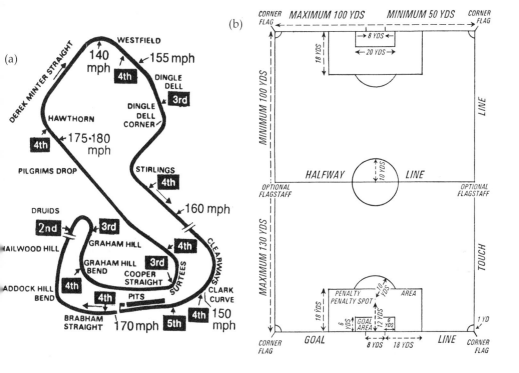

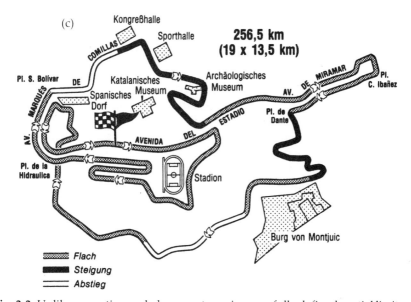

Fig. 2.2 Unlike recreation and play, sport requires carefully defined spatial limits. (a) Brands Hatch Grand Prix motor racing circuit. (b) Spatial regulations for Association Football (soccer). (c) Barcelona Montjuic road race course for 1984 World cycling championships.

improvement in, say, middle distance events. Similarly, space and distance can act as a kind of sporting fetish, as witnessed by the seeming obsession of a large number of people to run exactly 26 miles 385 yards despite the fact that it is often more convenient and easier to run half or a quarter of this arbitrary distance.

Recreation and play are ubiquitous but because of sport's spatial specificity it is relatively localized. In many cases sport involves the dominance of territory or the mastery of distance; spatial infractions are punished and spatial progress is often a major objective[8]. Virtually all sports are essentially struggles over space, but space which has carefully defined limits. For this reason spatial analytic techniques employed by geographers at a macro- or meso-level of geographical scale could also be applied at the micro-level of the field of play. Peter Gould suggests that the geographer can view team sports as dynamic cases of carefully prescribed human behaviour within limited and bounded geographic spaces. He has produced maps showing players in 'interaction space'[9–11]. Using a complex technique called multidimensional scaling Gould and his colleagues have constructed maps in which those players interacting with each other frequently are shown close together, while those passing to each other only a few times are far apart. New views of the conventional space of the playing area are obtained.

The spatial confinement which characterizes – indeed, often defines – sport is also important socially. The compression of 'normal' social intercourse into the artificially created time and space limits of sports permits 'fluid interpersonal experience that would never occur so rapidly or within such permutations in real life'[12]. Such interpersonal relationships include the bringing together of representatives of different cultures, nations, races and classes. But despite the ability to promote an apparent degree of social bonding the micro-spatial patterns of player locations in some team sports serve (literally and metaphorically) to put people in their place. For example, it has been shown in the USA that black baseball players tend to occupy the less glamorous outfield, rather than infield, positions[13]. Likewise, in football it has been suggested that blacks are diverted into positions generally regarded as requiring non-thinking, but athletic, roles. Cashmore[14] has suggested that in British soccer the relative absence of blacks in midfield positions (i.e. those requiring qualities of leadership) is the result of the stereotypical thinking of soccer coaches. Whatever the reasons, societal attitudes seem to manifest themselves in the players' spatial arrangement on the field of 'play'.

In a similar type of study of the micro-geographies enacted on the field of play, it has been suggested that the position of the captain in team sports might be expected to be central or defensive in order both to see and be seen. Some empirical support for this view has been obtained from work on soccer clubs in the English Football League[15].

Sport space compresses normal space in that it brings together people who would normally be unlikely to meet. At the same time, it has been suggested that through sport 'a number of changes in spatial perception are experienced'[16]. Such changes seem to include the perception of more details than usual, and an apparent increase in the size of the field of play occurring at peak moments during the sport experience. These examples serve to illustrate the practical significance of appreciating the spatial dimension at the micro-scale. However, such micro-scale relations may be symbolic of broader landscapes and it is to this theme that we now turn briefly.

BASEBALL		AMERICA
Diamond	Busiest and most sophisticated area; origin of the action.	Urban core
Infield	Active but less crowded	Supporting hinterland
Outfield	Spectacular action; danger.	The frontier

Fig. 2.3 The baseball park can be regarded as a spatial symbol of bygone America.

2.2   SPORT SPACE AS SYMBOL

The space upon which the sporting action is played out sometimes evokes broader regional landscapes and environments. Big-time baseball in the USA has often been viewed as a vestige of the frontier. Ross[17] draws a comparison between the baseball park with its diamond within which most of the action takes place and the outfield which witnesses unpredictability and danger, and urban America, its hinterland and the frontier (Fig. 2.3).

The spatial analogy between baseball and America itself is argued by some to be a major source of attraction of the game. In both baseball and nineteenth century America conditions were the same inasmuch as both players and settlers were necessarily self-reliant; as Oriard[18] puts it 'the baseball space recreates frontier conditions'*. Nostalgic imagery may also be drawn from other sports. For example, cricket in England has been said to serve as a metaphor for the ideal society, carrying with it to the industrial north nostalgic images of a mythical 'Merrie England'[20]. However, although the physical environment of both baseball and cricket can evoke a lost pastoral world, it may be equally true that the attractiveness of such sports lies in the fact that they are similar to, rather than different from, the day-to-day work of the male business worker with their division of labour, specialization of roles and limited independence[21].

Whatever analogies are drawn between the geography of the sports place and the world outside the stadium, it is difficult to deny that space is central to sport. Because it is also central to geography the geographical treatment of sport seems a natural enough field of study. But place as well as space is important to a fuller appreciation of modern sport and a number of significant aspects of place and sport can now be reviewed.

2.3   PLACE ATTACHMENT AND SPORT

Apart from war, sport is one of the few things that binds people to place simply through ascription. Sport has become perhaps the main medium of collective identification in an era when bonding is more frequently a result of achievement. It is in spectator sports that 'the representative teams throw segmental units (i.e. schools, municipalities or nations) into clear-cut confrontations that occur much less frequently in other areas of social life'[22]. Such segmental bonding contrasts with the functional

* See also Crepeau[19].

bonding which characterizes much day-to-day life. Eric Dunning[23] elaborates on this distinction and highlights its significance*:

within the context of domestically pacified nation-states, where the state has established an effective monopoly on the right to use physical force, sport provides one of the few occasions on which large, complex, impersonal and predominantly functionally bonded units such as cities can unite as wholes. Similarly, at an international level, sporting events such as the world cup and the Olympics, apart from providing occasions for limited international contests, are one of the few peacetime occasions when whole nations are able regularly to unite.

If tension exists between cities and nations it is possible that this can spill over into the sporting event, producing conflict between either players or spectators. What is sometimes called 'war without weapons' can erupt into something nearer to the real thing.

At the intra-urban level of scale the catchment areas of supporters of particular clubs may be strongly associated with certain cultural variables, notably religion. In some cases religion influences where people live and as a result sharply demarcated regions of sport support can be identified.

Table 2.2 Religion, location and football team support in West Belfast

Area	Per cent Catholic	Per cent supporting Glasgow Celtic	Per cent supporting Linfield
Clonard	98	73	0
Turf Lodge	99	63	0
Ladybrook	90	11	0
Shankhill	1	0	74
New Barnsley	12	1	63

(*Source:* Boal[27].)

In Belfast in Northern Ireland this is classically illustrated where the Springfield Road traditionally has acted as a divide between the supporters of Linfield (Protestant) and those of Belfast Celtic (Catholic) soccer clubs. With the demise of the latter club, loyalties are now divided between Linfield and Glasgow Celtic (Table 2.2). In such cases sport serves to reinforce other cultural and geographic loyalties. Exactly the same thing happens at a regional scale. In the case of pelota in northern Spain and south-west France, the geographical distribution of the sport serves to reinforce the Basque culture as a visible feature of the landscape.

* See also references [24] and [25].

2.3.1   Place pride

Allied closely to place attachment is place pride. This is often generated by success in sport, be it by a national team or small town high school squad. At the city limits of many small American towns the welcoming billboard often proclaims the place's sporting achievements, however modest (Fig. 2.4(a)). As with expressions of national loyalty (revealed in many countries through the display of national flags), such sport-induced tokens of localism seem frequently to be spontaneous and unforced, though this is not to say that they are totally unattached to, and discouraged by, commercial as well as municipal interests. The fact that such landscape artifacts are highly visible in some countries (USA) but absent in others (e.g. Britain) is one small way in which national ideology acts as a filter through which the global phenomenon of modern sport passes, before appearing in the vernacular landscape. While the sports prowess of small US places is so publicly projected, that of similarly small – and very much larger – British places is not. However, this does not mean that place pride through sport in the UK is not projected visually since it is often advertised as graffiti which acts either as a territorial marker indicating the spatial extent of a club's support, an assertion of power within its territory, or a defiant gesture by 'away' fans who wish to

(a)

assert prestige in another club's territory (Fig. 2.4(b)). Sometimes such place pride can erupt into a kind of ritualized violence by representatives of either city or national teams.

Be it by billboard, bumper sticker or graffiti, the sentiment is essentially the same, namely pride in place through sport. The recent concern in Europe over the problem of football hooliganism has highlighted the presence of a perverse, rabid sense of localism, regionalism and nationalism. Consider, for example, the views of these self-confessed hooligans:

I am fighting for Darlington. Not the team – the town. I feel proud of the town and I want to defend it from people who say it's not very good.*

. . . I won't take verbal when we go away. I won't take it from a northerner. I

(b)

Fig. 2.4 Billboard and graffiti say the same thing in different ways. (a) Perhaps the only thing which could be used to boost the small Oklahoma town of Coyle (not shown in the Rand McNally atlas) is the (former) prowess of its high school basketball team. The photograph was taken in 1986. (b) Graffiti on a wall in Stoke asserts the presence and unlikely superiority over Merseyside clubs, of Stoke City Football Club.

* Quoted in *The Guardian*, 19th December 1986.

followed this club for *years* . . . and I'm not going away with the team for some dirty northern ponse to spit over me. If he spits all over me I'll cut his head with a wine-glass . . . You do it for the reputation of the club.*

Kill the Irish, kill the Irish, kill the Irish . . .†

This final collective quotation, from Coventry fans aimed at an Irish player and chanted at the time of IRA killings in Birmingham, reveals nationalism at its most rabid. According to Williams *et al.*[29],' increasingly to be identifiably *English* at an England game on the continent is, for young fans, to experience the collective cameraderie . . . and the power of an image which has most local fans and passers-by recoiling in terror'. Indeed, at the local level it is the supporters who have become more the representatives of the areas the clubs are named after since few of the players can these days be described as 'home grown'[30].

Fan behaviour such as that described above is basically a masculine celebration of community, displaying strong forms of local identification and an equally strong tendency to denigrate other (opposing) communities by means of songs, chanting, graffiti etc. It has therefore been suggested that solutions to the football hooligan 'problem' might work towards providing in such youths and young men 'forms of local identification, attachment and integration which are of a qualitatively different kind from those generated in the male-dominated public domain of the street'[31]. Such forms would include the experiences and values of all community members and would emphasize knowledge of, and respect for, other cultures and other communities.

A relatively short step away from intense feelings of localism, regionalism and nationalism engendered by sports is the attitude of racism which sport can also encourage. Racial superiority can easily be read into sporting performance (one recalls the infamous Berlin Olympics as a 'laboratory' for the testing of racial 'theories') and in Britain, at least, the football stadium is today the most easily observable forum for racial abuse – black players being regularly insulted from the stands and terraces. Even more sinister is the use of football stadiums as recruiting grounds by the fascist National Front and British Movement‡.

However, success in sport is not necessarily associated with violent outcomes. When Sunderland FC somewhat surprisingly beat the favourites, Leeds United, in the English FA Cup Final in 1973 there followed a period of increased industrial output and a reduction in the crime rate in the Wearside town. Not only had unfashionable Sunderland 'blown a raspberry' at the soccer establishment; place pride had been

* Quoted in reference[28], p. 109.
† Quoted in reference[28], p. 105.
‡ The link between football and the far right is illustrated in references [28] and [32].

generated too. As one local resident put it[33] 'a not particularly glamorous town feels more proud of itself after a win of this sort'. Sport had provided a kind of glue which had bonded the community together. A rather more quantitative assessment of the impact of soccer on the

On the outskirts of dozens of non-descript Texas towns, the resident boosters have erected billboards, usually artless but large, proudly announcing "The Home of the Hutto Hippos" or "Entering Panther Country." Whenever possible these include a list of historical successes – "Class 2A Bidistrict Champions 1964, State Semi-finals 1965" – painted in over the years like entries in an almanac, vintage seasons in the town's career. Positioned strategically in the last open curve of a farm-to-market road, these handmade brags are as often as not the sole claim or welcome encountered on the threshold of a Texas town. Even approaching Gonzales, where the first battle of the Texas Revolution took place, the only notice posted anywhere by the townsfolk reads: "This is Apache Territory, District Champions 1958." It is a truer measure of their values than art or war or politics: the way they choose to declare themselves.

In most small Texas towns there are few enough ways to excite one's passion or ambition, to assert oneself. Life is bounded and determined by the land and the weather and the distant impositions of the government and God – both about equally predictable and final – which means life is physical and seasonal, elemental, stoical. It is commonplace by definition – or as common, that is, as life in a place such as Texas can be. Full of their own rich yearnings, Texans have always seemed to struggle hardest against ordinariness, and for more than half a century now the basic stage and focus for that struggle has been on high school football fields.

High school football is the one thing that can both unify a Texas town and set it apart from the hundreds of other similarly rural and unremarkable Texas towns. Places like Nederland, Junction, or Hull-Daisetta can easily escape the notice of Rand McNally, for instance, but in Texas they are powers to be reckoned with a thousand miles away, denounced by far-flung boosters and politicians, spied on and worried about. Their success at high school football is their one claim to recognition by the larger world, and thus it provides the clearest reflection of their own sense of worth. It is for many Texans the best indication of a town's vitality and pride, its sense of identity, and no one is more conscious of this than the men most concerned with the life of the town.

Vignette I *High school football in Texas.* Writing in the 1920s the Lynds, in their classic book *Middletown*, noted that it was the high school basketball team which united the people of the town better than anything else. Today in rural, small-town Texas, the high school football team serves the same purpose. (Source: Winningham[26].)

Clemson: a visual vignette. Clemson, South Carolina, is a small place of about 8000 people, a university of about 12 000 students and a football stadium accommodating about 85 000 spectators! Clemson means football. The 'Tigers' were national champions in 1981 and the town lets you know this in no uncertain terms. In the 1970s the university, along with its athletic programme, adopted the now ubiquitous Tiger Paw logo. This image adorns the Clemson townscape. Sport's contribution to pride in place can rarely have been so blatant yet it is not entirely untypical of the American scene. The tiger paw logo is a popular icon of a latter day religion.

Main Street contains two of Clemson's three sports shops. Mr Knickerbocker claims to be the 'World's Largest Supplier of Clemson Gifts'!

The Tiger Paw logo adorns . . . the local bank

. . . and the forecourt leading to Long John Silver's (fish restaurant).

community showed that when Sao Paulo's most popular team won production in the city increased by over 12% but when it lost the number of accidents increased by over 15%[34,35]. Place pride is also boosted at the international scale. The success of national teams in say, the World Cup, or of individuals in the Olympic Games can generate 'psychic income' to residents back home. Brazil's first World Cup victory in 1958, for example, possessed great social and national significance, much of which was encapsulated by one of Brazil's finest players, Garrincha:

While anyone could admire his football, Brazilians saw in his play the affirmation of Brazilian values over European and also popular values over those of the elite. For many people in Brazil there was no better sight than a six-foot, blond, superbly-coached and tacitcally-trained European defender on a rigid calorie-controlled diet being made to look like a fool by the devastating artistry of an undernourished, anarchic black winger with two twisted legs who would never have got past the medical exam in European soccer. In class terms, Garrincha was the semi-literate who could get by on his wits and cunning, able to put one over on the rich and the more powerful[36]

Sports undeniably foster localism, regionalism and nationalism. To this we can add an alternative interpretation which seeks to expose the ideological nature of sports when practised at the representative level.

Local, regional and national attachments can be viewed as essentially conservative sentiments which divide the working class on the basis of place attachment, substituting place loyalty and hence reinforcing existing power relations in society. Although some sports like tennis or sailing are relatively class-exclusive, support for 'our team' may blur class differences in many sports. This view is elaborated by Young[37]:

In a conflict-ridden society in which each is the natural enemy of similarly situated competitors for jobs, land and resources, sexual access, and other scarce items, in which there are class antagonists and ethnic opponents, in which ever more people are impoverished, such solidarity activity is important to the masking of these antagonisms. When the home team beats the putative enemy with skill, genius, heroic acts or with deceit or trickery and guile, great delight, joy, and enthusiasm emerge and can be shared with those-present-on-our-side. Class antagonisms and ethnic hatred as well as gender and national hostilities with real conflicting interests can be assimilated to the harmless competition of sports. The structures of privilege, inequality, and oppression are left intact by such use of solidarity moments in sports.

Sport may be more appropriate than other forms of civic display in the fostering of community consensus (from the perspective of society's 'dominant classes') because of its serialized nature[38]. Unlike many modern rituals such as coronations, carnivals and fairs, sport has an element of regular succession. Sport has a season and its contests are more continuous than other rituals. However, the representation of communities by sports teams and clubs may not necessarily have been authorized by the communities concerned. Alan Ingham and his co-workers[38] have suggested that the 'community interest' may have been 'tutored' by big business and real estate speculators and we return to this subject in Chapter 4. Indeed, the view that the sports team and the stadium provide a positive force for community life might be contested by that which sees it as 'a magnet for vice' and for the leading of 'indulgent and unproductive lives'. Negative aspects of sports are discussed further in Chapters 5 and 6.

2.3.2   Place, politics and sport

We have noted how, according to some observers, the (often unaware) ideological nature of sport seeks to defuse revolutionary fervour by welding classes together in support of a place (represented by a sports team) or by promoting a place's political image or ideological integrity. We must stress that it is politically defined places such as cities and nations which most frequently define sports teams and it is rare to find such teams representing physical-geographic or multi-national cultural units (though exceptions such as Ireland in rugby and the West Indies in cricket do exist). Sports teams most often represent either the nation state or the so-called 'local state' (i.e. aspects of government at the sub-national scale such as local authorities). It is therefore difficult to understand the view, often expressed, that sport is in some way independent of politics.

Let us examine briefly the more explicit ways in which sport and politics are related. The impact of politics on sport (and vice versa) may occur as part of either the state's external or internal relationships. If viewed as part of its external relations or activities, i.e. its dealings with other states, sport has an obvious role in international relations. In fact such sport–political relations are not new. The ancient Greek Pan Hellenic festivals which contained sport-like activities, were vehicles for popularity, prestige and power for city states; medieval jousting and tournaments kept national armies in fighting trim; in the early nineteenth century the German turner and Slav sokol movements combined sport and politics in order to encourage Pan-German and Pan-Slavic movements respectively; the late nineteenth century saw the genesis of the modern Olympic movement with de Coubertin seeing the Games as promoting global peace and international co-operation, though paradoxically the Olympics only served to further politicize sports (i.e. through national teams, flags, anthems etc.); and sport as a political tool was also stressed by the early twentieth century workers' sports movement, which sought to develop working class political consciousness through sport. Today nations continue to use success in sport as a means of propaganda, demonstrating the advantages of particular political systems over potential rivals or to achieve diplomatic recognition. We return to this subject in greater detail in Chapter 7.

A second way of viewing sport and politics is in some ways more contentious and refers to the state's internal activities. The state, be it national or local, clearly acts as a provider of sport. Many nation states today have Ministers of Sport and the state often plays a significant role in overall national expenditure on sport. The classic case is perhaps the German Democratic Republic where at least 2% of the Gross National Product is said to be spent on sport. At the local level, public expenditure via local authorities in Britain in 1982–3 on sport-related activities amounted to about 30% of the £836 million spent on all leisure activities[39]. Local authorities may own major facilities such as stadiums and sports halls. In some cases they can also own (or at least be major shareholders in) professional sports teams, as in the case of Peterborough football club in England where the city council is the major shareholder*. Such ownership may derive from the genuine desire to provide the locality with sports facilities but it may also result from desire to curry

---

* Quoted in *The Guardian*, February 11th, 1988.

favour politically, to boost a local political party, or to provide psychic income to potential voters. Acquiring or buying a professional sports team may be as much a political as an economic decision (see Chapter 4).

2.4   PERFORMANCE AND PLACE

So far we have been largely concerned with the way in which perform- ance in sports affects places, principally in the ways people respond to their team's success, or even simply to its presence. We now change the emphasis somewhat and consider ways in which place is important in influencing performance. Two approaches are adopted; first by showing how the physical environment of a place may possess unique character- istics which influence sporting performance and secondly by looking at the apparent differences in performances by sports teams at 'home' and 'away' locations.

2.4.1   Physical effects of place on performance

Although it will be stressed in Chapter 6 that there has been a gradual tendency towards a neutralization of the effects of the physical environ- ment on sports, it cannot be denied that physical factors continue to greatly affect – and in some cases determine – sporting events. Because the various elements of the physical environment – slope, relief, soil, vegetation, weather, etc. – vary geographically, specific places may be more affected (or affected in different ways) by the physical environment than others. This section considers some typical examples.

Regional differences in the physical environment clearly influence sporting performances. Temperature, wind, soil, rainfall and relief (to name a few factors) vary from place to place and affect sporting outcomes in a variety of ways[40–45]. Among the most dramatic influences of place on performance was when the Olympic Games were held at high altitude Mexico City. Spectacular performances were achieved in the sprints and jumps with extremely modest achievements in the longer distance running events. Events held at altitude are affected by a 7% reduction in aerobic power and reduced wind resistance[44].

In events such as long distance running or cycle races hot conditions can progressively produce dehydration, mineral loss and rising body temperatures. In events lasting several hours performance can be seriously impeded in places where such conditions prevail. The London Olympic Marathon of 1908 and the British Empire Games marathon of 1954 are well known examples. In places where the opposite temperature conditions may exist speed and power events are performed poorly since human muscle functions best at 40–41°C.

Some sports require specific weather (and hence locational) conditions before they can even take place. Sailing and skiing are obvious examples. In other cases particular locations are more likely than others to experience weather conditions which will interfere with sport, either causing performances to be affected or influencing the comfort of the spectators (Fig 2.5). Such sports include outdoor tennis, football and field hockey. Some places may be affected by changeable weather conditions which influence some competitors and not others[42]. In golf, for example, players starting on a clear morning would have an obvious advantage over those struggling over a windy, rain-swept course later in the day. Any sport taking place in an area too small to allow all participants to take part at the same time is open to the possibility of a change in the weather affecting the participants unequally. But some places are more likely to experience such conditions than others.

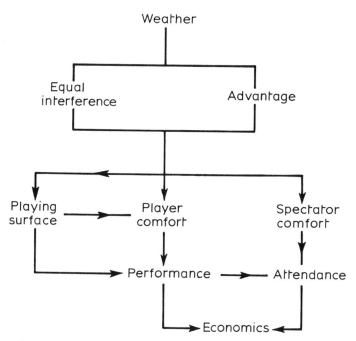

Fig. 2.5 The effect of weather on sport. Ideally, many sports would be best undertaken on 'weatherless' days. The extent to which places approach this ideal varies considerably! Weather may provide an advantage to one team or competitor or interfere equally with all participants. The players, spectators and playing surface can each be affected by the weather which in turn can have economic implications. (After Thornes[42].)

Although wind is a factor to be considered at all outdoor stadia, two parks, Wrigley Field in Chicago, and Atlanta/Fulton Co. Stadium experience conditions of prevailing home run weather. In both cases, home run weather is the result of beneficent breezes which constitute normal conditions for the areas and are associated with diurnal circulation patterns. These patterns are typically discussed at length in introductory physical geography courses. Because the winds involved are diurnal, home run weather is a diurnal phenomenon at both parks.

Atlanta, in addition to being the highest park in major league baseball (1050', 320m), has live air. During the evening hours, air at higher elevations cools more rapidly than does air at lower elevations. Cooler, heavier air begins to flow downslope by gravity during the evening hours (cold air drainage), the evening breeze flowing from the higher elevations of the Appalachians toward the coastal plain. As it moves downslope, it passes through Atlanta, and over Atlanta Stadium, creating a steady breeze which favours hitters. The effects of home run weather at Atlanta can best be appreciated when player performance is considered. Two players, former Braves second baseman, Dave Johnson, and third baseman, Bob Horner, have benefitted profoundly from Atlanta's home run weather.

Johnson hit 43 home runs while playing for the Braves during the 1974 season. This figure is more than double the number he hit while playing for other teams. To point out the effects of Atlanta's home run weather on Johnson's performance, 29 of those 43 home runs were hit in Atlanta, in night games. Horner became an instant celebrity during his rookie season of 1978 when he hit 23 home runs in just 89 games. Closer analysis reveals that 19 of those were hit in Atlanta in 43 night games. This greatly endeared him to the home town fans. If one were to project Horner's performance based upon 81 home dates and all games at night, he would be predicted to average about 38 home runs a year. However, if all games were played at night in Atlanta, he could conceivably produce 76 home runs a year.

Wrigley Field also experiences home run weather as a result of diurnal circulation patterns. Unlike Atlanta, Chicago home run weather prevails in the afternoon. Here winds are produced by a thermally induced pressure gradient. During the morning and early afternoon, land heats more rapidly than does nearby Lake Michigan. As a result, air over the land heats more rapidly than that over the lake. As the warmer air rises, cool air from the lake moves inland, a classic 'sea breeze'. The movement of cool air inland may be inferred from a rapid drop in air temperature typically observed during the mid-afternoon in Chicago. Since all games at Wrigley field are played in the afternoon, and the sea breeze develops in the afternoon, Chicago's Wrigley field experiences prevailing home run weather on a typical summer afternoon. One of the more familiar sights at Wrigley is that of a baseball disappearing over the ivy covered wall as the pennants adorning the stadium are stretched to the limit.

Vignette II *Home run winds.* The wind is one of several physical factors influencing sporting outcomes. This passage describes the effects of two different kinds of winds in two American baseball stadiums. (Extracted from Gilman[45])

It is not only a place's relief, climate and weather characteristics which may affect sporting outcomes. Soil type will influence the degree of bounce of a baseball or cricket ball, for example. It has been shown that the degree of bounce, registered by using a standard test of dropping a cricket ball on to the pitch from a height of five metres, varies directly with the percentage clay content of the soil. 'Thus, the pitches at Adelaide, Melbourne and Sydney, all with over 45 per cent clay, are classed as very fast. Brisbane with 73 per cent clay is exceptionally fast. In contrast, Nottingham and Leeds are moderately fast and Manchester is easy paced'[41].

It has been shown by Shaw[40] that a number of physical geographic factors influenced the games of the 1962 baseball World Series. Not only did each of the factors discussed above contribute to particular results but so did the micro-geographic surface features of individual pitches. For example, shots deflected by pebbles on the pitch can cost a team the game – and the series! Physical geography obviously has great potential in the study of sports.

Of course, place is also important in the effect it has on performance when considered from an economic perspective. Because economic, as well as physical, conditions vary from place to place we would expect levels of economic development to be associated with certain variations in sports performance. Likewise we would expect different places to 'produce' differing quantities of superior sports performers. Chapter 7 is devoted to a consideration of such variations in a review of sports regions.

2.4.2 A home field advantage

It will be obvious to followers of sport that in many team events a 'home field advantage' exists in which the home team is at an advantage over the opposition [46, 47]. Study any set of results involving top level teams and more often than not home wins are found to occur more frequently than away wins[48]. This seems to be common at both national and inter-national levels and, in Britain, seems to have existed since the earliest days of the English Football League[49]. Obviously, not all home teams win but as Table 2.3 clearly shows, away wins are much less frequent than those at home. In soccer in England and Wales, home wins tend to be about two-and-a-half times as common as away wins, though the ratio in Scotland is nearer one-and-a-half.

In addition, point or goal scores tend to be bigger for home winners than away winners. This appears to be widely typical of North American professional and college teams and for British professional soccer and rugby teams (at least), details of which are shown in Table 2.4. These

Table 2.3 Home and away wins in British Soccer, 1982–3

League	Number of wins		Home/away
	Home	Away	
Football League Div. 1	255	96	2.66
Div. 2	220	98	2.24
Div. 3	297	118	2.52
Div. 4	283	127	2.23
Alliance Premier	247	102	2.42
Scottish Premier	83	51	1.63
Scottish Div. 1	116	92	1.26
Div. 2	121	85	1.42

(Source: Rothman's Football Yearbook 1983–4, Queen Anne Press, London, 1983.)

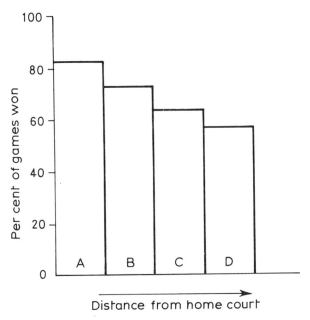

Fig. 2.6 Percentage of games won and distance from home court; Big Five Basketball 1952–66 (out-of-town opponents only). (Source of data: Schwartz and Barsky[47].)

kinds of findings are likely to be present in a number of other top-class events. For example, for over 6000 European soccer games involving four nations and three European Cup competitions, it was established that, on average, playing at home created an advantage of 0.47 goals per game, or

Table 2.4 Goals and points scored and conceded in American and British football

		Points/goals scored	
		Home winners	*Away winners*
349 professional football	For	27.03	25.45
games, USA	Against	12.29	13.97
577 college football games,	For	30.25	26.84
USA	Against	11.13	12.95
600 Football League soccer	For	2.63	1.92
games, UK	Against	0.55	0.59
310 Southern League soccer	For	2.78	2.27
games, UK	Against	0.55	0.65
501 Rugby League games,	For	22.70	18.50
UK	Against	8.70	9.20

(*Source:* references [46] and [50].)

about one goal in six. In US gridiron football, on the other hand, the home advantage is thought to be about one point in twelve.[51]

Some evidence also exists to show that 'the probability of winning forms a clear gradient according to distance from the home team fieldhouse' in the case of five university basketball teams in Philadelphia. This relationship is shown in Figure 2.6 and reveals that the proportion of home wins declines progressively with distance away from the home campus (A), taking in a neutral arena within Philadelphia (B), neutral courts outside the city (C) and finally in opponents home courts (D).

An analogous situation has been found to exist in British soccer in which 'local derby' games are less likely to produce a home advantage than in the matches played against teams who have travelled a greater distance to compete[49].

How are we to explain the undoubted presence of a home field advantage? In part it might be thought to derive from certain aspects of territoriality, i.e. the identification with a specific place. After all, the home team will be more familiar than the opposition with the micro-geography of the field, the various locational cues like the billboards and architecture surrounding it, and even the actual size of the pitch which can vary in sports like soccer and baseball. These are not the only kinds of possible explanations, however. Others might include the tiring effects of travelling to an away game for the visiting team, the bias of the referee in favour of the home team, and the social effect of a home audience, constantly reminding them that the team is representing a particular place.

An interesting American study by Barry Schwartz and Stephen Barsky[47] tried to identify the key variables 'explaining' the home field advantage. They examined a number of sports, namely baseball, ice hockey, football and basketball, and found (contrary to some people's expectations) that the home advantage was least visible in the very sport which was most likely to have the least uniform playing areas and conditions, i.e. baseball. It was in ice hockey rinks and on basketball courts – where conditions are almost the same everywhere – that the home field advantage was most marked. This led Schwartz and Barsky to conclude that the home advantage was socially determined and was at its most pronounced when the social congregation before which a team performs is at its most intimate. They argued that sports events provide a forum for the local community to celebrate its existence. Subsequent studies have suggested that the home advantage will be greatest for well-established teams in small cities and in arenas located within the central city, since these will generate most intense local identification and pride[52].

Some final caveats need to be made at this stage in this review of home advantage studies. First, it may be that while the home advantage is present for most of the time, in *decisive*, end of season games, a paradoxical home field *disadvantage* exists. This hypothesis is based on the view that a supportive audience may have excessive expectations in key games which actually interfere with the execution of sufficiently skilful responses from players[53]. The evidence for this hypothesis is mixed at the present time[54] and further research will be needed to test its validity.

A second caveat is that it remains unclear as to the extent of a home advantage in non-team sports such as boxing, tennis or golf. At the international level, national support may replace the local support found in most of the events which have been scrutinized by scholars involved in home-advantage studies. National identification with a particular competitor may be as potent as that at the local level.

Finally, all studies of the home advantage have focused on top-class sports. It remains to be seen whether the same patterns exist as we move 'down' the sports hierarchy into amateur and recreational sports activities.

The kinds of findings described above strongly suggest that *place* is of importance in team sports. Whether such a fundamental geographical attribute as territoriality* explains this in total is, of course, debatable, but

---

* Among geographers who touch on this phenomenon, Malmberg[55] probably over-stresses the significance of territoriality *per se*.

it does seem to go part of the way towards explaining a common occurrence at sporting events.

2.5 CROSS CULTURAL VOYEURISM

International sport remains one of the few live forms in which large numbers of people actually encounter and witness the feats of those of other lands. It seems that people have an almost innate fascination with the opposing team – especially if it comes from a foreign territory. In the late nineteenth-century this curiosity about people from 'strange' places was satisfied to some extent by the emergence of international sports. For the cultural elites of the 1850s onward the same need was satisfied by upper class cultural societies and organizations based on ethnography, anthropology and geography. The Royal Geographical Society was the place at which travellers' tales exposed the mysteries of far away places with strange sounding names and where social elites vicariously encountered the exotica of Africa, Asia, North America and the European periphery. Popular and mass culture formalized its means to this and through the international exhibition (or exposition) and the Olympic Games[56]*. At the 1904 Games in St. Louis, 'anthropology days' were held at which 'representatives from various peoples considered primitive and worthy of observation'[57] were put into competition with one another. This may have represented the apogee of the association of special sports with particular racial groups (an association for which a residual affection lingers on among some sports fans). Arguably, the early and continuing appeal of the Olympics is based in part, at least, on the continuing tradition of popular ethnography. At the 1984 Olympics in Los Angeles American television producers subconsciously recognized this by superimposing 'educational' captions describing, in an albeit ethnocentric way, individual countries as their teams marched into the Olympic Stadium. For example, Finland was described as being 'in Northern Europe, as long, but not as wide, as Idaho'.

2.6 A DATA RICH SUBJECT

In reviewing the virtues of sport for sociological study the late Donald Ball [58] noted that there were a few activities which were as assiduously and publicly recorded as modern sport. Such a comment applies equally to the geographical study of sport. Much of the publicly available information

---

* Note the reference in MacAloon's scholarly work[56] to the influence of Frederic Le Play on de Coubertin. Le Play was also a major influence on the growth of social geography.

about sport is not only expressed precisely and quantitatively but also frequently involves geographical information on the place at which a game was played, the birthplaces of players, the fixture lists of teams and so on. In Britain, books such as *Rothman's Football Yearbook* or *Wisden's Cricketers' Almanac* are veritable mines of geographical data. Such commercially produced publications are complemented by sources such as those produced by the large number of governing bodies of sport. National and international sports associations often list the locations of the affiliated members. In addition, annual ranking lists in sports like swimming or track and field athletics show the geographic affiliation of each athlete, be they regional or national, while in the US, college athletic department rosters reveal birthplaces and high school locations of student athletes.

A particular virtue of such data is their low cost and ready availability. As they are usually published annually, they also provide a basis for historical-geographic studies as well as examinations of present day regional geographies of sport.

FURTHER READING

Readers approaching this book from a background in Sport Studies may be unfamiliar with the current character of geography. They may therefore find it helpful to consult the eminently readable *The Geographer at Work* by Peter Gould, Routledge, London, 1985, or Ron Johnston's *Geography and Geographers: Anglo-American Human Geography since 1945*, Arnold, London, 1987. Readers whose background is in Geography might likewise wish to familiarize themselves with an academic approach to the study of sport. Good introductions are Allen Guttmann's *From Ritual to Record: the Nature of Modern Sports*, Columbia UP, New York, 1978 and Jay Coakley's *Sport in Society: Issues and Controversies*, Mosby, St. Louis, 1982.

The geographical bases of sport can be pursued further by reading Phillip Wagner's Sport: Culture and Geography, in *Space and Time in Geography: Essays Dedicated to Torsten Hägerstrand*, (ed. A. Pred), Lund Studies in Geography, Series B, **48**, pages 85–108. Explorations of sport and place-pride can be followed up in a number of works dealing with geographical units of various sizes. For example, at the village level see the seminal social study of the role of football in a north Wales village in Ronald Frankenberg's *Village on the Border: a Social Study of Religion, Politics and Football in a North Wales Community*, Cohen and West, London, 1957. The role of high school football in small town Texas is marvellously described with the aid of superb photographs in Geoff Winningham and Al

Reinert's evocative *Rites of Fall; High School Football in Texas,* University of Texas Press, Austin, 1979, while at the national scale Janet Lever's *Soccer Madness,* University of Chicago Press, Chicago, 1983, undertakes a detailed examination of the place of soccer in Brazil. Place attachment, and its perversion into sports hooliganism, is stressed in Eric Dunning's Social bonding and violence in sport, in *Quest for Excitement: Sport and Leisure in the Civilising Process* (edited by Dunning and Norbert Elias), Blackwell, Oxford, 1986, pages 224–44. This theme is taken further in Eric Dunning, Patrick Murphy and John Williams', *The Roots of Football Hooliganism: An Historical and Sociological Study,* Routledge, London, 1988.

Further information on the home field advantage, from a North American perspective is provided by John Edwards's The home field advantage, in *Sports, Games and Play: Social and Psychological Perspectives,* edited by Jeffrey Goldstein, Erlbaum, Hillside, NJ, 1979, pages 409–38. A British view of the same subject is found in Richard Pollard's Home advantage in Soccer: a retrospective analysis, *Journal of Sport Sciences,* **4**, 3, 1987, pages 237–48. There are many books on sport and politics. One which looks at the way sports act as expressions of explicit political doctrines is John Hoberman's *Sport and Political Ideology,* University of Texas Press, Austin, 1984.

REFERENCES

1. Meier, K. (1982) On the inadequacy of sociological definitions of sport. *International Review of Sport Sociology,* **16**, 103–14.
2. Rigauer, B. (1981) *Sport and Work,* Columbia UP, New York.
3. Allison, L. (1975) Association football and the urban ethos. *Stanford Journal of International Studies,* **13**, 203–28.
4. Lipsyte, R. (1976) *Sportsworld; an American Dreamland,* Quadrangle Books, New York.
5. Shaw, T. (1979) Towards a political economy of international sport; interstate, transnational and neo-Marxist approaches. *Arena Newsletter,* **3**, 2–9.
6. Haywood, L. (1986) Hegemony; another blind alley for the study of sport, in *Sport, Culture and Society; International Historical and Sociological Perspectives* (eds A. Mangan and R. Small), E. and F. N. Spon, London.
7. Johnston, R. (1983) *Philosophy and Human Geography,* Arnold, London.
8. Wagner, P. (1981) Sport: culture and geography, in *Space and Time in Geography* (ed. A. Pred), Gleerup, Lund.
9. Gould, P. and Gattrell, A. (1979) A structural analysis of a game; the Liverpool v. Manchester Utd. Cup Final. *Social Networks,* **2**, 253–78.
10. Gould, P. and Greenwalt, N. (1981) Some methodological perspectives on the analysis of team games. *Journal of Sports Psychology,* **4**, 283–304.
11. Gattrell, A. and Gould, P. (1979) A micro-geography of team games: graphical explanations of social relationships. *Area,* **11**, 275–8.
12. Denney, R. (1957) *The Astonished Muse,* University of Chicago Press, Chicago.
13. Loy, J. and McElvogue, J. (1970) Racial segregation in American sport. *International Review of Sport Sociology,* **5**, 5–23.

14. Cashmore, E. (1982) *Black Sportsmen*, Routledge, London.
15. Murphy, W. and Parker, S. (1986) Some relationships between leadership, captaincy, management and playing position in the English Football League, in *Sport, Culture and Society; International Historical and Sociological Perspectives*, E. and F. N. Spon, London.
16. Murphy, M. and White, R. (1978) *The Psychic Side of Sports*, Addison-Wesley, Reading, Mass.
17. Ross, M. (1973) Football and baseball in America, in *Sport and Society* (eds J. Talimini and C. Page), Little, Brown and Co., Boston.
18. Oriard, M. (1976) Sport and space. *Landscape*, **21**, 32–40.
19. Crepeau, R. (1978) Urban and rural images in baseball. *Journal of Popular Culture*, **9**, 315–24.
20. Bailey, P. (1978) *Leisure and Class in Victorian England*, Routledge, London.
21. Gelber, S. (1983) Working at playing: the culture of the workplace and the rise of baseball. *Journal of Social History*, **16**, 3–22.
22. Henricks, T. (1974) Professional wrestling as moral order. *Sociological Enquiry*, **44**, 177–88.
23. Dunning, E. (1981) Social bonding and the socio-genesis of violence, in *The Sociological Study of Sport; Configurational and Interpretive Studies*, (ed. A. Tomlinson), Brighton Polytechnic, London, p. 26.
24. Hardy, S. (1981) The city and the rise of American sport, 1900–1920. *Exercise and Sport Sciences Review*, **9**, 183–219.
25. Dunning, E. (1983) Social bonding and violence in sport; a theoretical-empirical analysis, in *Sports Violence* (ed. J. Goldstein), Springer-Verlag, New York, pp. 129–46.
26. Winningham, G. (1979) *Rites of Fall; High School Football in Texas*, University of Texas Press, Austin.
27. Boal, F. (1970) Social space in the Belfast urban area, in *Irish Geographical Essays in Honour of E. Estyn Evans* (eds N. Stephens and R. Glasscock), Queens University, Belfast.
28. Robins, D. (1984) *We Hate Humans*, Penguin, Harmondsworth.
29. Williams, J., Dunning, E. and Murphy, P. (1984) Come on you whites. *New Society*, **68**, 310–11.
30. Pratt, J. and Salter, M. (1984) A fresh look at football hooliganism. *Leisure Studies*, **3**, 201–30.
31. Williams, J., Dunning, E. and Murphy, P. (1986) *Professional football and crowd violence in England: the case for a community approach*, Dept. of Sociology, University of Leicester.
32. Williams, J., Dunning, E. and Murphy, P. (1985) *Hooligans Abroad*, Routledge, London.
33. Derrick, E. and McRory, J. (1973) Cup in hand; Sunderland's self image after the Cup. *Working Paper 8*, Centre for Urban and Regional Studies, University of Birmingham.
34. Lever, J. (1973) Soccer in Brazil, in *Sport and Society* (eds J. Talimini and C. Page), Little, Brown and Co., Boston.
35. Lever, J. (1981) *Soccer Madness*, Chicago University Press, Chicago.
36. Humphrey, J. (1986) No holding Brazil; football, nationalism and politics, in *Off the Ball* (eds A. Tomlinson and G. Whannell), Pluto, London.
37. Young, T. (1986) The sociology of sport; structural marxist and cultural marxist approaches. *Sociological Perspectives*, **29**, 3–28.

38. Ingham, A., Howell, J. and Schilperoort, T. (1987) Professional Sports and Community: a review and exegesis, *Exercise and Sport Sciences Reviews*, **15**, 427–65.
39. Kirby, A. (1985) Leisure as commodity: the role of the state in leisure provision, *Progress in Human Geography*, **9**, 1, 64–84.
40. Shaw, E. (1963) Geography and baseball. *Journal of Geography*, **62**, 74–6.
41. Morgan, R. (1976) Rain starts play. *Area*, **8**, 257–8.
42. Thornes, J. (1977) The effect of weather on sport. *Weather*, **32**, 258–67.
43. Elsom, D. (1984) The Olympics under a cloud. *The Geographical Magazine*, July, 338–40.
44. Mackay, D. (1976) Environment, in *Sports Medicine* (eds J. Williams and P. Sperryn), Arnold, London.
45. Gilman, H. (1982) Home run weather. Unpublished paper presented to the Annual Meeting of the Association of American Geographers, San Antonio.
46. Edwards, J. (1979) The home field advantage, in *Sports, Games and Play: Social and Psychological Viewpoints* (ed. J. Goldstein), Erlbaum, Hillside, NJ, pp. 409–38.
47. Schwartz, B. and Barsky, S. (1977) The home advantage. *Social Forces*, **55**, 641–661.
48. Dowie, J. (1982) Why Spain should win the World Cup. *New Scientist*, 10 June, 693–5.
49. Pollard, R. (1986) Home advantage in soccer: a retrospective analysis. *Journal of Sports Science*, **4**, 237–48.
50. Webb, R. (1982) *The Concept of Territoriality; the Home Ground Advantage in Selected British Sports*, undergraduate dissertation (unpublished), University of Keele.
51. Stefani, M. (1985) Observed betting tendencies and suggested betting strategies for European football pools. *The Statistician*, **32**, 319–29.
52. Mizruchi, M. (1985) Local sports teams and celebration of community: a comparative analysis of the home advantage. *The Sociological Quarterly*, 506–18.
53. Baumeister, R. and Steinhilber, A. (1984) Paradoxical effects of supportive audiences on performance under pressure: the home field disadvantage in sports championships. *Journal of Personality and Social Psychology*, **47**, 85–93.
54. Gayton, W., Matthews, G. and Nickless, C. (1987) The home field disadvantage; does it exist in hockey? *Journal of Sports Psychology*, **9**, 183–5.
55. Malmberg, T. (1980) *Human Territoriality*, Mouton, The Hague.
56. MacAloon, J. (1981) *This Great Symbol: Pierre de Coubertin and the Origins of the Modern Olympic Games*, University of Chicago Press, Chicago.
57. Mrozek, D. (1983) *Sport and the American Mentality 1880–1910*, University of Tennessee Press, Knoxville.
58. Ball, D. (1975) A note on method in the sociological study of sport, in *Sport and Social Order*, (eds D. Ball and J. Loy), Addison-Wesley, Reading, Mass., pp. 35–47.

Chapter 3

ORIGINS AND DIFFUSION OF MODERN SPORT

The purpose of this chapter is to trace the geographical development of sport from its folk-game prototypes to its modern, international form. We first show how the antecedents of sport were regionally differentiated; we proceed to suggest that rather than growing at independent origins, many sport-like activities developed as a result of a geographical diffusion process. The decline of folk-games was paralleled by the emergence of modern sports and local activities were replaced by national and later international organizations whose function was to control and administer them.

In other words, the spatial margins of modern sports have been progressively extended away from the core areas at which they originated. Just as the early folk-games appeared to spread in a sequential way, so too the modern sports empires have appeared to grow via predictable patterns of penetration. In order to evaluate the extent to which the growth of sport *per se* (and the growth of individual sports) can be said to have grown in a relatively orderly way, we apply to the historical development of sport the geographical concept of spatial innovation diffusion. A crucial result of two centuries of such diffusion is that today the world of sport is, like the economy (of which it is increasingly part), a global system.

3.1 FOLK ORIGINS

The indigenous activities which we have described as folk games took place throughout the world on unstandardized terrain with vague and imprecise spatial limits. Organization of such games was often spontaneous and often lacked time, as well as space, limits. Dunning and Sheard[1] have identified a number of characteristics of folk games which

Table 3.1 The structural properties of folk games and modern sports

Folk games	*Modern sports*
1. Diffuse, informal organization implicit in the local social structure	Highly specific, formal organization, institutionally differentiated at the local, regional, national and international levels
2. Simple and unwritten customary rules, legitimated by tradition	Formal and elaborate written rules, worked out pragmatically and legitimated by rational-bureaucratic means
3. Fluctuating game pattern; tendency to change through long-term and, from the viewpoint of the participants, imperceptible 'drift'	Change institutionalized through rational-bureaucratic channels
4. Regional variation of rules, size and shape of balls, etc	National and international standardization of rules, size and shape of balls, etc
5. No fixed limits on territory, duration or numbers of participants	Played on a spatially limited pitch with clearly defined boundaries, within fixed time limits, and with a fixed number of participants, equalized between the contending sides
6. Strong influence of natural and social differences on the game pattern	Minimization, principally by means of formal rules, of the influence of natural and social differences on the game pattern: norms of equality and 'fairness'
7. Low role differentiation (division of labour) among the players	High role differentiation (division of labour) among the players
8. Loose distinction between playing and 'spectating' roles	Strict distinction between playing and 'spectating' roles
9. Low structural differentiation; several 'game elements' rolled into one	High structural differentiation; specialization around kicking, carrying and throwing, the use of sticks, etc
10. Informal social control by the players themselves within the context of the ongoing game	Formal social control by officials who stand, as it were, 'outside' the game and who are appointed and certificated by central legislative bodies and empowered, when a breach of the rules occurs, to stop play and impose penalties graded according to the seriousness of the offence
11. High level of socially tolerated physical violence; emotional spontaneity; low restraint	Low level of socially tolerated physical violence; high emotional control; high restraint
12. Generation in a relatively open and spontaneous form of pleasurable 'battle excitement'	Generation in a more controlled and 'sublimated' form of pleasurable 'battle excitement'
13. Emphasis on physical force as opposed to skill	Emphasis on skill as opposed to physical force
14. Strong communal pressure to participate; individual identity subordinate to group identity; test of identity in general	Individually chosen as a recreation; individual identity of greater importance relative to group identity; test of identity in relation to a specific skill or set of skills
15. Locally meaningful contests only; relative equality of playing skills among sides; no chances for national reputations or money payment	National and international superimposed on local contests; emergence of élite players and teams; chance to establish national and international reputations, tendency to 'monetization' of sports

(*Source:* reference [1].)

readily distinguish them from modern sports*. These properties are shown in Table 3.1 and apply mainly to European pre-industrial games. The extent to which they all apply to non-Western games in tribal societies is debatable[3]. For example, fixed limits clearly existed for sport-like activities in the stadiums of the Roman Empire and for the ball games (played on stone courts) during the Mayan civilization.

Folk games certainly seem to have originated in certain 'culture hearths', diffused away from these cultural cores, and in so doing modified their form. Smith[4], for example, basing his conclusions on anthropological evidence, suggests that the ball-play concept among indigenous North Americans spread from meso-America and at the same time assumed a variety of different forms. Table 3.2 indicates the variety of ball-playing sticks and rackets, as well as footballs which have been found. It is clear that there were a number of gaming implements on the west coast but these were lacking in the northeastern and southeastern woodlands. Salter[5] has described how many of the indigenous American folk games had various meteorological associations, according to their location. Lacrosse in the Huron and Iroquois nations, for example, invoked spirits to avert harsh weather, produce rains, or provide favourable winds.

Another example of the diffusion of pre-industrial sport can be provided from Europe where an antecedent of modern tennis called *cache* existed in Picardy at the end of the thirteenth century. It is suggested by

Table 3.2 Regional differences in indigenous American folk games

	West coast	Southwest	Great Plains	North-eastern woodlands	South-eastern woodlands
Shinny	X	X	X		
Racket (single)	X		X	X	
Racket (double)					X
Double-ball	X	X	X	X	
Football	X		X		X
Ball-race	X	X			
Foot-cast-ball	X				
Hand-foot-ball			X	X	
Tossed ball	X	X	X	X	X
Hot ball	X	X			
Ball juggling	X	X	X		

(After Smith[4].)

* For a geographic analysis of folk games at the present time see Smulders[2].

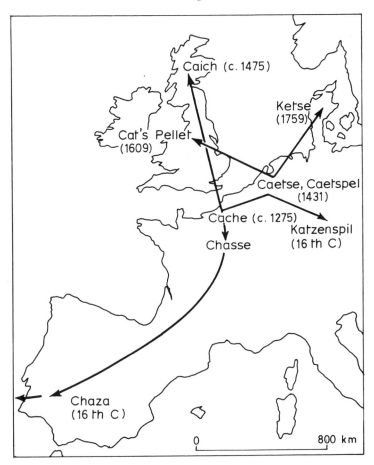

Caich (c. 1475)

Ketse (1759)

Cat's Pellet (1609)

Caetse, Caetspel (1431)

Cache (c. 1275)

Katzenspil (16 th C)

Chasse

Chaza (16 th C)

0   800 km

Fig. 3.1 The migration of the Picardian game of cache. Evidence of trans-Atlantic diffusion to South America is inferred from the Colombian 'juego de la chaza'. (Source: Gillmeister[6].)

Gillmeister[6] that the game spread to Holland where it was translated as Kaetspel while the English 'cat's pellet' was a popular version of the Dutch name. The similarity of the names, first recorded in Picardy, and subsequently used in Scotland, Germany, Denmark, Spain and Colombia in South America led Gillmeister to conclude that the early French game of *cache* had diffused – and in doing so changed its form – between countries and continents (Fig. 3.1). Tylor[7], regarded by many as the 'father of modern anthropology' noted that while some simple games such as wrestling or throwing a ball had grown up independently in a number of separate geographic locations, others seemed so distinct and artificial that it was unlikely that their distinctiveness could be hit upon more than once. Such sport-like activities, he argued, could be traced from a common geographical centre and therefore be used to provide evidence of cultural diffusion. It was suggested, for example, that games of Polynesia and New Zealand diffused from Asia; likewise 'various forms of arrow throwing or shooting games show remarkably similar terminology, from Egypt, through Polynesia and much of the New World'.[8] Variations in types of folk games which were broadly similar but lacked any standardized rules, any organizing bureaucracy and any formalized records meant that even if widespread and efficient international travel had existed, international competition would have been meaningless.

At a local scale, geographical differences existed in pre-industrial sports. In England, for example, a wide variety of types of football could be found[9]. It is clear, therefore, that before 1700 prototype forms of modern international sports such as football, hockey, cricket, lacrosse and tennis existed. In some cases what are sports today were in earlier times essential skills – riding, skating, archery, skiing, etc. In other cases modern sports have grown out of war-like activities like fencing and kendo.

Folk games were still being played widely in Britain in the seventeenth century and in North America in the nineteenth. But between 1700 and 1900 their geographic specificity declined and they began to die out. Sport, bound by rules, precision, quantifiable, record-seeking and under bureaucratic control, increasingly came to mirror society at large. The transition from folk game to sport typically followed five stages, in total spanning less than a century and in some cases as little as fifty years. These phases were:

(1) The folk game stage.
(2) The formation of clubs.
(3) The establishment of a rule-making national bureaucracy.
(4) The diffusion and adoption of the sport in other countries.
(5) The formation of an international bureaucracy.

Some would suggest that sport developed as a result of the reduction in working hours, and possibly also the emergence of the 'weekend'. However, as Theodore Zeldin[10] points out, sports developed before working hours were reduced by law and, anyway, the working class was usually the last to participate in modern sports. Zeldin regards the emergence of sport as a reaction against the lack of free time rather than a cult associated with modern mass leisure. In similar vein Lewis Mumford[11] suggested that perhaps sport began originally as 'a spontaneous reaction against the machine', though as we will see in Chapter 6, it has

At Llanwennog, an extensive parish below Lampeter, the inhabitants for football purposes were divided into the Bros and Blaenaus . . . The Bros . . . occupied the high ground of the parish. They were nick-named 'Paddy Bros' from a tradition that they were descendants from Irish people. . . . The Blaenaus occupied the lowlands and, it may be presumed, were pure-bred Brythons . . . the match did not begin until about midday. . . . Then the whole of the Bros and Blaenaus, rich and poor, male and female, assembled on the turnpike road which divided the highlands from the lowlands. The ball . . . was thrown high in the air by a strong man, and when it fell Bros and Blaenaus scrambled for its possession, and a quarter of an hour frequently elapsed before the ball was got out from the struggling heap. . . . Then if the Bros . . . could succeed in taking the ball up the mountain to . . . Rhyddlan they won the day; while the Blaenaus were successful if they got the ball to their end of the parish. . . . The whole parish was the field of operations, and sometimes it would be dark before either party secured a victory. In the meantime, many kicks would be given and taken, so that on the following day the competitors would be unable to walk, and sometimes a kick on the shins would lead the two men concerned to abandon the game until they had decided which was the better pugilist. There do not appear to have been any rules . . . ; and the art of football playing in the olden time seems to have been to reach the goal. When once the goal was reached, the victory was celebrated by loud hurrahs and the firing of guns, and was not disturbed until the following Christmas Day.

Vignette III *A description of folk football in south-west Wales in the early 1880s. Although the rules for the Association (soccer) game had been drawn up in 1863 this account is reminiscent of the kind of game being played centuries earlier. (Quoted in reference [1], pp. 29–30.)*

become increasingly machine-like. However, in a very general way, sport and industrialization seem to be related. They both grew out of the changed outlook derived from the Newtonian revolution which stressed qualities which both sport and society were to embrace. As the eighteenth and nineteenth centuries progressed bureaucracy, quantification, record breaking, and the achievement principle became increasingly evident. In addition, time and space confinement increased in all walks of life. A time consciousness became imposed; there was a time for work and a time for leisure. In sport the growing regulation of day-to-day life was reflected in the standardization of sports places and the imposition of specified time limits on various events. All this has been interpreted by some scholars* as part of the hegemony of capitalism.

* For example, Thrift[12].

3.2 FROM LOCAL TO NATIONAL

According to Stovkis[13], sailing and horse racing were strictly organized in seventeenth century Holland and a specialized personnel served to check the violation of rules. Other regulatory bodies existed elsewhere in sport prior to the widespread formation of clubs in team sports in the late nineteenth century. But such organizations were initially set up to ensure a satisfactory basis for gambling; it was only later that the more amateur-oriented ethic of 'fair play' became the dominant reason for standardization and hence the need for governing bodies. Prior to the nineteenth century there also existed a surprising degree of inter-regional, as opposed to merely intra-regional, organization and movement in sports. Horse racing was a case in point, the sports historian Dennis Brailsford[14] establishing, for example, that in 1797 a horse based in the county of Somerset (in south-west England) competed at meetings in Dorset, Wiltshire, Worcestershire, Warwickshire, Northants and Leicestershire, all within the space of three months. Similar pre-nineteenth century national sporting activity also occurred in boxing and to a somewhat more limited degree in cricket. Of course, with the growth of the national transport network such inter-regional movement became commonplace.

Table 3.3 Early sports governing bodies in three countries

British* national sports associations founded before 1870

1750	Horse racing	1866	Athletics
1754	Golf	1866	Canoeing
1788	Cricket	1869	Swimming
1863	Football		

American† national sports associations formed before 1880

1868	Skating	1878	Swimming
1870	Horse racing	1879	Lacrosse
1871	Rowing	1879	Athletics
1875	Bowling	1879	Cricket
1876	Professional baseball		

German** national sports associations formed before 1900

1860	Gymnastics	1888	Skating
1883	Bowling	1891	Athletics
1884	Cycling	1897	Fencing
1887	Swimming		

* *Source:* various.
† *Source:* Lewis[15].
** *Source:* Woeltz[16] and others.

Much eighteenth-century sport had been organized by private entrepreneurs who promoted contests between regional (and national) champions for what were often high financial rewards. By the mid-nineteenth century, however, their activities were being overtaken by those of the national governing bodies. A principal function of these organizations was not only to administer and arbitrate but also to uphold the amateur sports ethic which had its roots in the English universities and private schools. In Britain and North America national governing bodies grew most rapidly in number during the last quarter of the nineteenth century (Table 3.3). Associated with their growth was the emergence of national consciousness which replaced the local consciousness which had been associated with folk games.

Switzerland possessed a national shooting federation as early as 1824 but this was as untypical of events on mainland Europe as was the formation of the pre-nineteenth century English organizations. The first Russian national association was the Russian Gymnastics Society, founded in 1883[17] and by the end of the century many European states possessed a number of such bodies. Extremely rapid growth occurred in the development of British governing bodies into the 1900s, and at the present time shows little sign of slowing down (Fig. 3.2).

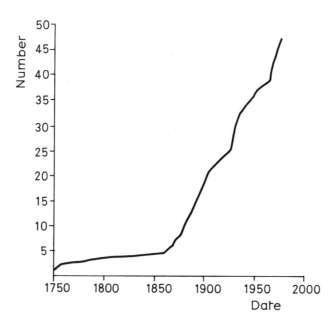

Fig. 3.2 Cumulative frequency curve of dates of formation of forty-seven national sports associations in Great Britain. (Based on data from the Sports Council.)

The transition from folk game to sport was perhaps most dramatic when European cultural groups adopted and adapted a game which had been played by a native minority. Consider, for example, the game of lacrosse[18]. Until around the 1830s this was a game played by the indigenous nations of North America. The first white lacrosse club was set up in Montreal in 1839 or 1840. Rules, the vital requirement before inter-regional competition could commence, were formulated in Canada in 1867 and in the same year the National Lacrosse Association of Canada was formed. In 1868 the game took on an international aspect when the Mohawk Club of New York was formed. The US Amateur Lacrosse Association was formed in 1879 and the sport became formally internationalized with the establishment of the International Lacrosse Association in 1928. In less than 90 years an indigenous American folk game had become an international sport.

The case of football in England is similar. Here it was a case of one class rather than one race transforming a widespread native pastime. The folk games of football where village played village in a rough and tumble kind of way gradually became replaced by games between representatives of schools and universities and, in the 1850s, clubs. However, the game needed greater control and organization and in 1863 the 'Cambridge rules' were formulated[9, 19]. In the same year the Football Association (so novel was such an organization that the use of the adjective 'English' was not felt necessary) was formed and the game grew rapidly in popularity. Scottish and Welsh associations were set up in the 1870s and Irish, French, Dutch and Danish associations in the 1880s. In 1902 the International Football Federation was established to govern the sport at a global scale. A period of less than sixty years had elapsed between the folk-game stage and the formal internationalization of what has become the world's most popular sport.

An ethnocentric overemphasis on events in Europe and North America obscures the fact that the codification and 'export' of sport was going on elsewhere in the world where a 'scientific world view' was being adopted. In Japan widespread indigenous martial and warlike pursuits were becoming sports following the Meiji restoration in 1868, of which classic examples are kendo and judo. The former had been a kind of swordsmanship which trained participants for war. The transformation of a weapon of war to a weapon for sport was encouraged by the Japanese government until the All Japan Kendo Federation was formed in 1928[20]. The case of judo is perhaps more dramatic. Having studied the traditional Japanese martial arts and self-defence Jigoru Kano integrated the best of these techniques into modern judo in 1882[21], at about the same time as the Europeans and North Americans were formalizing many of their own folk games. In Japan Kano was establishing a ranking system (i.e. quanti-

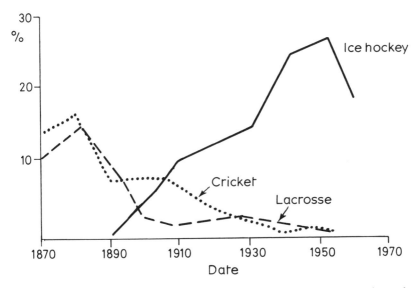

Fig. 3.3 The rise and fall of various sports in Canada. The graphs show the changing percentages of the sports page of the *Toronto Globe* devoted to lacrosse, cricket and ice hockey between 1870 and 1960. (Source: Metcalfe[25].)

fying) in order to identify different exponents in judo[22]. Twenty years after its formalization, the sport was introduced to the USA and within fifty years possessed an international federation.

The growth of modern sport has meant a growth in the number of individual sports. As we have seen, many possessed folk game antecedents. But others were invented from scratch. The origin of basketball, for example, can be pinpointed precisely, having been invented by J. Naismith in Springfield, Massachusetts in 1892[23]. Likewise, volleyball was invented by W. J. Morgan in Holyoake, Massachusetts, in 1895. For these and more modern 'technosports' no folk game stage existed.

As new sports continue to grow, their acceptance as international phenomena seems to take much less time than their nineteenth century equivalents. Trampolining is a case in point. Originally a circus act, American PE teachers and YMCA directors adapted the 'bouncing bed' for use with their gymnastics classes. After some years of research and development the 'Nissen trampoline' was patented in 1939 and subsequently produced *en masse*[24]. By 1948 trampolining was an official event at NCAA and AAU gymnastics meetings and by 1965 an international federation had been formed – a mere twenty-six years after the sport had been invented.

As sports grew and developed, their relative significance changed. New sports overtook others in popularity. In the 1870s and 1880s, for example, imported cricket was still a relatively popular sport in Canada, attracting as much media interest as indigenous lacrosse (Fig. 3.3). After about 1900, however, interest in the 'home grown' sport of ice hockey rapidly eclipsed both cricket and lacrosse and subsequently became Canada's national sport.

3.3   A GLOBAL SYSTEM

Although national associations had developed apace, the absence of any international bureaucracies before 1875 meant that international competition as we now know it could not take place because of different interpretations of rules and of amateur status. What did exist was the international sports entrepreneur who, like his national counterpart, engaged the skills of one champion against another. International sport of a private character involved considerable cash prizes. One entrepreneur, Jack Macdonald, brought the American, Deerfoot, to run for cash prizes against the best runners England had to offer. Professional scullers organized races for very high stakes. In speed skating Axel Paulsen won cash prizes in Britain, Holland, Norway, Sweden, Germany and Russia[13].

In the last quarter of the nineteenth century the private ventures of the entrepreneurs were overtaken by those of the international organizations. The need to improve the regulation of international events was a prime reason for their growth. The first sports to establish international governing bodies were the upper class activities of yachting (1875) and horse racing (1878). Sports which were attracting mass participation were also controlled by people from the upper echelons of society. After all, considerable travel and international contact were required to set up such organizations which revolved around the international social networks of the leisured classes. Dates of formation of fifty-one international sports federations, for which data are available, are shown in Table. 3.4.

The significance of international sports bureaucracies was that the sports system, like the economic system, had become a world system. Standardization of rules permitted movement internationally, the transfer of sports personnel across national boundaries and meaningful international competition. What differences did exist in sport increasingly came to result, not from local idiosyncracies in the nature of sport-like activities, but from national differences in sports ideology. Sport in Poland, Ohio, was played according to the same rules as in Poland, Europe, but the experience of sport in each place differed according to the national ideological filters through which sports, their

Table 3.4 Dates of formation of 51 international sports federations

1875	Yachting	1928	Handball
1878	Horse racing	1928	Lacrosse
1881	Gymnastics	1929	Pelota
1886	Rugby Union	1931	Archery
1892	Rowing	1932	Basketball
1892	Ice skating	1933	Softball
1892	Cycling	1934	Badminton
1904	Association Football	1939	Ice yachting
1907	Shooting	1946	Boxing
1908	Swimming	1946	Water skiing
1908	Ice hockey	1947	Volleyball
1909	Cricket	1948	Rugby League
1911	Wrestling	1948	Modern pentathlon/biathlon
1912	Athletics	1951	Judo
1913	Tennis	1955	Bandy
1913	Fencing	1957	Luge
1920	Weightlifting	1959	Sub-aqua
1921	Equestrianism	1960	Netball
1922	Motor sport	1961	Ski bob
1923	Bobsleigh and tobogganing	1961	Orienteering
1923	Korfball	1962	Surfing
1924	Hockey	1965	Trampolining
1924	Canoeing	1967	Squash
1924	Roller skating	1968	Cycle polo
1924	Skiing	1970	Karate
1926	Table tennis		

(*Source:* various, but mainly Arlott[26].)

aims and their objectives, were interpreted. For example, in the USA the high school and college became a focus for top-level sport to a much greater extent than in much of Europe where the club system evolved as the principal set-up for sport. In Britain the single-sport club contrasts with the multi-sport form of organization more common in Europe.

During the course of the twentieth century the spatial margins of sporting activity have been pushed further and further away from the points at which sports originated. A good index of the spatio-temporal growth of sport is the number of countries taking part in the Olympic Games. Whereas only thirteen nations were represented at the first modern Olympics at Athens in 1896 by the time the Antwerp games of 1920 were held the figure had risen to twenty-nine and by the notorious Berlin games of 1936 the figure had grown to forty-nine. In 1960 eighty-four nations participated in Rome and in Munich in 1972 a total of 125 countries sent Olympic teams. This figure was not surpassed (because of boycotts) until the Los Angeles games of 1984, though the 140 nations at these games represented a smaller proportion of the world's population than had previously been the case (Fig. 3.4).

The Winter Olympics have likewise increased in size and sophistication. Only sixteen nations competed in the first winter games in Chamonix in 1924, in the 1964 games at Innsbruck there were thirty-five and at Calgary in 1988 fifty-seven nations were represented. Even in a sport like skiing, where strong physical and economic constraints limit participation in many countries, the number of countries contesting Olympic skiing events had increased from twelve in 1924 to thirty-seven in 1968.

3.4   THE GROWTH OF SPORT AS INNOVATION DIFFUSION

It is now appropriate to turn to a much more explicitly geographical treatment of the growth of sport. It is widely asserted that Great Britain (and more specifically England, and most specifically southern England) was the place which gave sport to the world. This view raises the question of whether it is possible actually to demonstrate that sport *per se* diffused away from England in a relatively ordered way, much as the old folk games had done from their various cores (Fig. 3.1). Do generalizations which apply to the growth of sport also apply to the development of individual sports? The section which follows tries to answer this and other questions by using the conceptual framework of geographical innovation diffusion*.

Geographical innovation diffusion theory comprises three broad ideas. First, it is assumed that innovations display a temporal and spatial pattern of adoption, rather than instantaneous transmission over space and that initially only a small number of potential adopters actually adopt the innovation. At a second stage a 'band wagon' effect is observed when the majority of adoptions occur, followed by a final period when the 'laggard' adopters finally succumb to the innovation. When plotted as a cumulative frequency curve (or adoption curve) this approximates to an S-shaped or logistic curve. A second characteristic of the theory is that the size of the adopting unit (i.e. town or country) is of importance. Large places adopt innovations before smaller places, the innovation 'trickling down' an economic hierarchy. A third theme is that distance from an existing adopter of the innovation acts as a basic barrier to adoption, implying some kind of imitative, contagious or 'neighbourhood' effect. Treating

---

* The basic ideas are outlined in references [27] and [28].

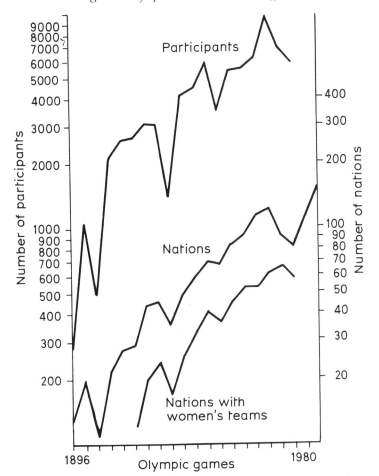

Fig. 3.4 Increases in the number of participants and nations taking part in the Olympic Games.

sport as an innovation (sport was something new in both time and space) means that we might expect its diffusion to exhibit evidence of both hierarchical and neighbourhood spread. Let us seek evidence, at both continental and national scales, of such patterns.

3.4.1 The hierarchical diffusion of sport*

How can we actually 'operationalize' the notion of sport in order to compare its growth and development between different countries? One

* Most of the remainder of this, and the following section is based on Bale[28]. More detailed references can be found therein.

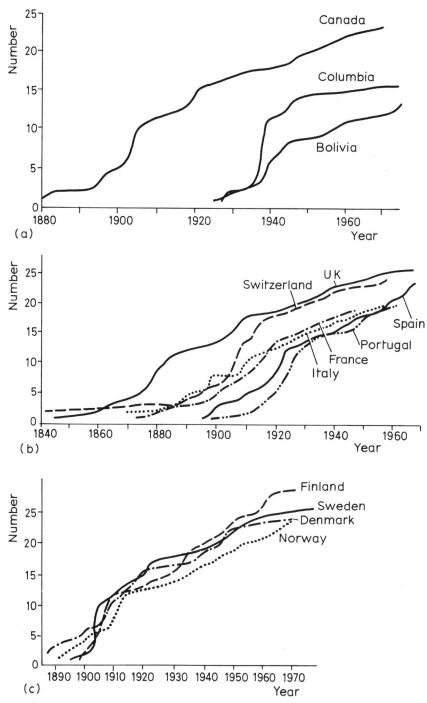

Fig. 3.5 Adoption curves for Olympic sports; (a) in Canada, Colombia and Bolivia; (b) in six European countries; (c) in Scandinavia.

way of doing this is to take all Olympic sports (using this collection as a surrogate for sport *per se*) and construct adoption curves for different counties over time. This is done by plotting the cumulative growth curve for the dates of formation of national associations for each Olympic sport in individual countries. An example is shown in Fig. 3.5(a), where we can see that the growth curve for sport (i.e. the total number of Olympic sports) for Canada lies well above that for the South American countries of Colombia and Bolivia. Canada was an early adopter of modern sport compared with the two South American countries. Initially a slow period of sports development took place in Canada, the national equestrian and rowing federations being formed in 1873 and 1881 respectively. Such 'upper class' sports were often among the earliest for which national federations were formed – the social diffusion of sport going on alongside its geographical spread. In the early 1900s the Canadian curve is seen to steepen – sports like canoeing (1900), fencing (1905), soccer (1912), gymnastics (1905), wrestling (1905), and shooting (1905) all being institutionalized during a rapid period of adoption. By 1920 over half of the present day Canadian Olympic sports had been adopted – the long 'tail' to the adoption curve indicating the way in which the country has completed the overall adoption of Olympic sport, and, of the course, the way in which new sports have continually been added to the Olympic syllabus. The cases of Colombia and Bolivia also display this historical trend. In these countries sport was adopted later than in Canada, the adoption curves lying below that of their northern neighbour. In both nations rapid growth of sports took place in the 1930s, two decades later than in Canada, and continued to be adopted in Bolivia during the period 1940–5. In neither case has the number of sports federations grown in number to match that of Canada.

Figure 3.5(b) likewise compares adoption curves for Olympic sports for a number of European nations. Switzerland and the UK stand out as adopters of Olympic sports. Of course, in England certain non-Olympic sports had been adopted in the late eighteenth century and the dependence on Olympic sports therefore reduces somewhat the true relationship between sports development in the two countries. The fact remains, however, that Britain and Switzerland were the major industrial powers in Europe in the early nineteenth century. After 1860 the UK forged ahead in sport development and within twenty years had twice as many federations for Olympic sports as its nearest rival. France experienced the industrial revolution much later than Britain, some economic historians placing it as late as 1860. The development of its national sports federations was correspondingly slower (Fig. 3.6(b)). Although some sports such as football and athletics were adopted soon after the British precedent, sport *per se* was adopted much later in France. Likewise, Italy,

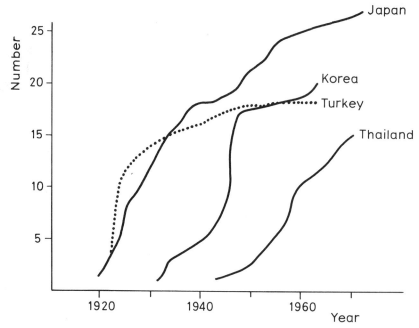

Fig. 3.6 Adoption curves for sport in four Asian countries. (Source: reference[28].)

Spain and Portugal exemplify European nations for whom industrialization occurred at later dates, although Italy's economy advanced more rapidly than that of the other two after the mid-1890s. It is notable that a sharp upward turn in the growth curve for Italy's sports associations occurs at this time. For the European countries in Fig. 3.6(b), therefore, an S-shaped model summarizes graphically the fact that the rate of sports growth was, in general, associated with levels of economic or industrial development.

This belief is confirmed when countries with similar levels of economic development are compared. The countries of Scandinavia are a case in point. They all experienced economic development in the late nineteenth and early twentieth centuries and Fig. 3.5(c) shows that in each case Olympic sports developed at the same time. Interestingly, Finland, the last of the Scandinavian states to adopt modern sports, also possesses least evidence of a slow period of initial growth in the number of sports associations. Finland is somewhat different from the other Scandinavian countries in this respect. However, as Seppänen[29] implies, the initial growth of sport in Finland was almost a case of active propagation, sport being used in the early twentieth century to serve purposes of national integration of society in a country which suffered problems of internal political disorder. What, perhaps, is more interesting in the case of the Scandinavian nations, however, is the remarkable similarity in the temporal pattern of growth of sport in a group of nations whose economic development has also run a parallel course.

Examples of sports growth in countries outside Europe also seem to demonstrate broad relationships with levels of economic development. Western notions of sport were adopted in Asia and Africa following the First World War. Figure 3.6 shows adoption curves for Olympic sports for four countries in Asia. A characteristic of each curve is its initial steepness, especially in the cases of Japan and Turkey. The rapid growth of Olympic sports in Japan in the 1920s and 1930s coincided with the rapid industrialization and modernization of that country. The case of Turkey is even more dramatic in this respect; the very rapid increase in the number of Olympic sports associations in the 1920s was concurrent with the westernization of Turkey by Kemal Ataturk. Thailand and Korea were later adopters of Western development and their sports adoption curves are positioned accordingly.

The notion of modern sport, interpreted here as the sum total of Olympic sports, seems undeniably to be associated with levels of economic development, interpreted in a Western sense. In American, European and Asian examples, the adoption curves for sport in the more economically advanced nations lie above those for the less economically advanced.

We can now turn to the question of individual sports diffusing down an economic hierarchy. It seems that for some sports there is a marked correlation between the date of adoption (i.e. the date at which a national federation was set up) and the level of economic development. Consider, for example, the case of soccer in Europe. The first nation to adopt was England in 1883. Figure 3.7(a) shows that subsequently the sport showed a tendency to 'trickle down' the European economic hierarchy – countries with large proportions of their male workforce in manufacturing at the turn of the century tending to adopt soccer earlier than those with smaller proportions. There were exceptions, Ireland being the most obvious, but the relationship between rank date of adoption and the rank level of economic development (as interpreted here) is clearly positive. In fact the rank correlation coefficient is 0.68 (a one-to-one positive relationship would produce a coefficient of 1.00; no relationship would produce one of 0.0).

A second example, that of track and field athletics (Fig. 3.7(b)), also shows a 'trickling down' pattern but not as clearly as in the former case. Again, England was the first to adopt in 1860 but the relationship between adoption and economic development is weaker – in this case a rank

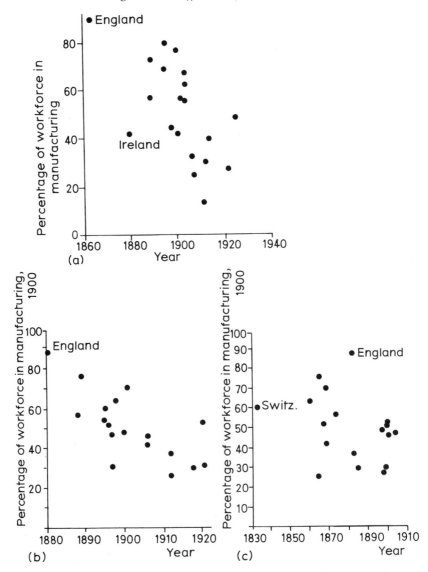

Fig. 3.7 The correlation between the date of formation of a national sports association and the level of economic development varies in strength between sports. It is far from perfect, as the examples of (a) soccer, (b) track and field athletics and (c) gymnastics in Europe show. (Sources: (a) *FIFA Handbook*, 1982; (b) *IAAF Handbook*, 1931; (c) Huguenin[30].)

correlation coefficient of 0.55. The case of gymnastics illustrates further the danger of over-generalizing about the diffusion of sports from advanced levels of economic development to those of less advanced status. It is true that the first country to adopt gymnastics was Switzerland in 1832. Given the significance of the 'turner'* movement it is not surprising that Germany (1860) was another early adopter, followed by Belgium (1865) and the Netherlands (1868), showing a relationship between early adoption and major industrial nations. However, the overall European pattern is less convincing of hierarchical diffusion in the case of gymnastics (Fig. 3.7(c)) than was the case for track and field and soccer. For gymnastics the rank correlation coefficient is 0.38 – a positive but much weaker relationship. Britain, the continental industrial leader, was only ninth among the nations of Europe to adopt gymnastics.

The conclusion to be drawn from this section is that while the development of sport seems to be related to the level of economic development, the development of individual sports need not be so. We should therefore be cautious of crudely Marxist interpretations which might indiscriminately relate sports growth to industrial growth. Some sports are so related; in other cases the relationship is weak. Indeed, some relatively unindustrialized nations adopted some modern sports first – judo and Japan being the obvious example.

3.4.2   Neighbourhood diffusion and modern sports

This chapter started with some examples of pre-industrial games spreading geographically from their source areas or 'culture hearths' to embrace continents and, indeed, move intercontinentally. We now return to this theme but in the context of modern sport. We noted in the previous section that a characteristic of the temporal growth of sport was the S-shaped adoption curve. The fact that all countries did not adopt sports at the same time infers that some kind of barrier exists in the diffusion process. With pre-industrial games it seems reasonable to suggest that distance did present a fundamental barrier to the rapid spread of games, but evidence of a neighbourhood effect in modern sport is more problematic. This is because by the late nineteenth century news about innovations such as sports could be spread rapidly – virtually instantaneously – from place to place. Yet evidence from maps showing the geographic growth of sport may be suggestive of a neighbourhood effect.

Before countries adopted sports (in the sense that they established national bureaucracies to administer them) they needed to have been

---

* The 'Turners' were a romantic, nationalistic gymnastic movement, inspired by the German physical educationalist Jahn, in the nineteenth century.

made aware of them. It is the setting up of national sports federations, not the introduction of the sport as such, that we mean by adoption in the present context. Before looking at adoption and the way in which some kind of geographical order seems to exist, let us first provide some evidence for the importance of geographical proximity in the actual spread of knowledge of modern sports.

For football in France, Holt[31] argues that 'proximity to Britain was clearly important in the early years', and in its diffusion to France the sport pursued 'predictable lines of penetration'. The sport entered France via the Channel port of Le Havre in 1872, adoption taking place in 1888 with the formation of a national association. Other examples can be readily cited of sports entering a country from their nearest neighbour: lacrosse from Canada to the USA, rugby from England to Northern France, gymnastics from Czechoslovakia to Poland (the 'Sokol' idea quickly spread through all Slavic countries after 1862), bullfighting from Spain to south-west France and gymnastics from Germany to Alsace in eastern France. In all these examples geographical proximity was of obvious importance in the diffusion of knowledge about particular sports. The role of proximity in subsequent diffusion to further neighbouring states remains unexplored, however.

Let us take three sports as they spread across Europe and look for evidence of neighbourhood diffusion. For football (soccer) the only countries to adopt the sport before 1890 were geographically adjacent to England where initial adoption had occurred in 1863. The last countries to adopt the sport were at the geographic periphery of Europe. A Spearman rank correlation coefficient for the relationship between date of adoption and the distance of the capital city of the adopting nation from London is strongly positive ($r_s = 0.83$).

For athletics (Fig. 3.8(a)) the pattern is very similar. Track and field was another English sport, the Amateur Athletic Association (AAA) being formed in 1880 and the Scottish AAA three years later. Two cross-channel nations, France and Belgium, had adopted before 1890. Apart from Greece, where the first modern Olympics no doubt stimulated the uncharacteristically (for that part of Europe) early growth of modern sport, no country in eastern Europe had adopted track and field before 1900. The Spearman rank correlation coefficient for the association between distance of national capital from London and the national date of adoption is again positive (i.e. 0.53) but not as strong as in the case of soccer.

By 1931 data collected by the international federation (the IAAF) suggested that one person in about 234 000 was a practising track and field athlete. Even though it was originally a British sport, by 1930 a well defined 'athletics region' had emerged in Scandinavia and Germany.

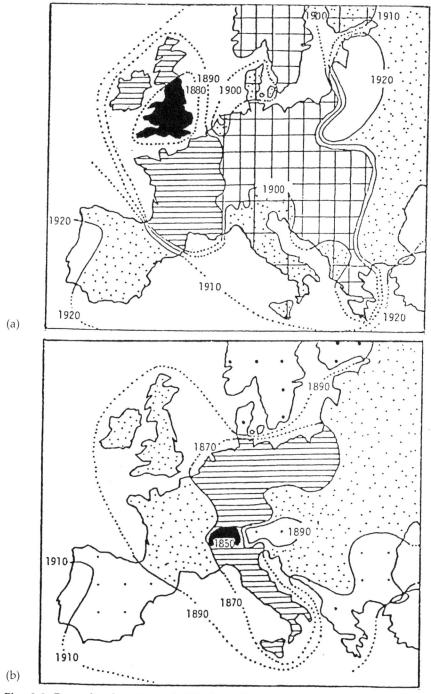

Fig. 3.8 Generalized pattern of diffusion of two sports in Europe. Isopleths enclose areas where adoption had taken place by the date shown. (a) Athletics (isopleths at ten-year intervals); (b) gymnastics (isopleths at twenty-year intervals). (Source: Bale[27].)

Sweden had over four times the continental average number of track and field athletes per head of the population. Despite the fact that the early adoption of athletics in Germany may have been retarded by the 'turner' view that racing was fit only for animals[32], by 1930 Germany, along with Finland and Estonia, had more than twice the continental per capita average number of athletes.*

The third example, gymnastics (Fig. 3.8(b)), again shows a superficial impression of a neighbourhood effect, its growth throughout the continent 'spreading' from its heartland in Switzerland and Germany. Neighbouring states of Poland, Belgium, the Netherlands and Italy had all adopted before 1870. Again, peripheral Europe was last to adopt the sport, Portugal not establishing a federation until after World War II. In this case the rank correlation coefficient is 0.52 – again a positive relationship and similar to that for athletics, but again weaker than that for soccer. The impression is once more given that the sport spread outwards in a way not dissimilar from the ancient folk games. By the end of the first decade of the present century Switzerland had over 3½ times more practising gymnasts than the continental per capita figure. The sport had been adopted at a reasonable level in France (1½ times the norm), Zeldin[10] suggesting that gymnastics was attractive to the French because they 'would be trained to beat the Germans with their own methods'. The German model of gymnastics would teach discipline and movement in unison rather than the individual agility of the Swedish model. Indeed, as Gerber [33] noted, 'Swedish gymnastics never really became popular, even in Sweden'. While the association of gymnastics with liberal nationalism may have made the sport popular in much of central Europe and northern Italy, the elements of 'völkisch' within the early gymnastic movement may have had to be eliminated before the activity became palatable to the British†.

The patterns provided by these three examples are suggestive of a neighbourhood effect. Further support is provided at the national level, but before turning to examine this it is worth recording that in some cases sports changed their forms soon after crossing national boundaries – rather than being adopted they were adapted to new cultural or political ideologies. Such a phenomenon is well illustrated by the transformation of rugby into the 'gridiron' game in America[34], to 'Aussie' rules in Australia[35] and to Gaelic football in Ireland where the rules were modified for explicitly political reasons[36]. Once any new sport became established in a particular country, the diffusion process began to operate at the national level.

* Calculated from data in the IAAF *Handbook*, 1929–31.
† I am grateful to Allen Guttmann for this point.

3.4.3   The national scale

A pattern similar to that shown above at the international scale can be discerned at the national level. In pre-Victorian England, for example, cricket was still strongly concentrated in south-east England. The counties of Kent, Surrey, Hampshire and Essex had a quite disproportionate number of cricket clubs per head of the population, compared with the country as a whole. The south-east corner of the country tended to have at least four times as many clubs as the national per capita norm while many of the counties to the north appeared to have less than half the national average[37]. The innovation (i.e. modern cricket) remained relatively localized until geographical interaction improved with the coming of the railway. This reduced the friction imposed by distance and the sport could grow by leapfrogging over geographic space to such an extent that in Yorkshire cricket clubs became so numerous as to outshadow the southern counties in which the modern game originated.

In the USA the modern rodeo had its origins, like English cricket, in folk culture. Early competitions grew out of work activities such as roping and riding. Not surprisingly the sport's 'culture hearth' lay in beef country and today the major area of rodeo activity lies west of the Mississippi[38]. The Canadian boundary did not prevent the northward diffusion of the sport, the famous 'Calgary stampede' being established some forty years after the first 'cowboy contests' in Nebraska. The Mexican border did, however, act as an impermeable barrier and here bullfighting established itself as a rival sport.

In 1945 the minority sport of American college soccer was still concentrated in the New England states, New York, Pennsylvania and Maryland. In the immediate post-war period college soccer diffused into the Ohio Valley area and began to penetrate the urban industrial centres of Ohio, Illinois and Indiana. By 1950 it had reached the South. Although still regionally concentrated, contagious or neighbourhood diffusion appears to have been the dominant process at work within, and from, the region in which it is most played (Fig. 3.9). It is noteworthy that a major barrier to the adoption of soccer is found in Texas where, by 1970 the sport had barely taken root. The reason for this seems most likely to be the tremendous emphasis placed on gridiron football in the Lone Star State (a subject we return to in Chapter 7), against which soccer has to wage an almost insurmountable battle in order to gain a footing.

A similar example of a pattern of diffusion in which distance from the initial adopter and the date of adoption are clearly related is that of lacrosse in Canada. The first provincial lacrosse association was formed in 1856 in Montreal. Subsequently, adoption of the sport took place in Ottawa in 1862 before spreading to the provinces of Ontario (1863),

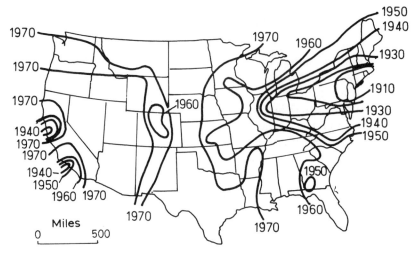

Fig. 3.9 Spatial diffusion of intercollegiate soccer participation, 1910–70. (Isolines show extent of adoption at date shown) (Based on maps in reference[39].)

Manitoba (1871), Alberta (1883) and British Columbia (1886). Adoption of the first clubs in New Brunswick and Nova Scotia came in 1889 and 1890 respectively and the sparsely populated province of Saskatchewan succumbed to lacrosse in the 1890s[18] (Fig. 3.10).

Lacrosse was not the only sport in Canada which was first established in Montreal. Thirteen other clubs, which were the first of their kind in British North America were set up there between the early nineteenth century and the late 1880s. This pattern of major city dominance in early adoption is certainly typical for other countries. In England most modern sports were formalized in London, the capital being a centre of innovation, leadership and fashion in many facets of life besides sports. Here we have an element of hierarchical diffusion of sport at the national scale.

3.4.4 Innovations in sports

Innovations in sports, as well as sports as innovations, often saw the first light of day in the national capital. In Britain the first cinder running track, the first synthetic running track, the first public squash courts, the first artificial ice rink and many more sports innovations were first seen in London. Sports innovations, often also being economic innovations, are usually launched first in the largest market. Metcalfe[40] has shown how in early twentieth century Ontario the largest city, Toronto, not only possessed a greater diversity of sports facilities than other centres but was also first in the field with the majority (Table. 3.5). Likewise, in Sweden,

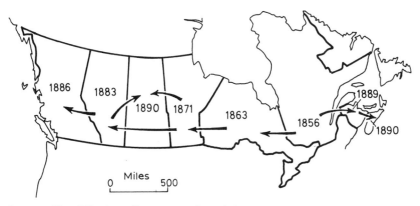

Fig. 3.10 The diffusion of lacrosse in Canada based on the date of formation of the first club in each province. (Source: Metcalfe[18].)

Torsten Hägerstrand[41], the doyen of geographical diffusionists, has shown how Stockholm and Göteborg, the two largest cities, were the first to introduce such facilities as sports halls and swimming baths. Their diffusion over time and space was similar to that pattern already observed to occur at the continental scale (Fig. 3.11).

We can also see the hierarchical diffusion of sports innovations at the national scale by applying the idea of the adoption curve shown earlier (Fig. 3.5). For example, Fig. 3.12 shows how in Finland cities were first to adopt a national sports policy (i.e. the provision of facilities such as playing fields, ski centres, ice halls etc.) before boroughs and rural communes. By 1940 80% of the cities had adopted the sports policy whereas the respective figure for rural communes was only 5%.

This is not to say that all innovations in sport were metropolitan in origin. Professionalism in British football is a good example. The sporting amateur with time to spare in which to train and hence defeat teams made up of those who worked for a living was mainly found in southern England. The winners of the Football Association Cup (the only yardstick of success in the sport prior to the formation of the Football League) regularly came from the south of England in the first decades of the competition's existence. The hegemony of the southerners was broken in 1883 when Blackburn Olympic defeated the Old Etonians. For more than a decade and a half, clubs from the north and midlands continued to win the cup (Fig. 3.13), their success being generally attributed to the fact that they had adopted professionalism. It is widely accepted that the first professional football club was Darwen in Lancashire who decided that it was necessary to pay their players in 1879. Yet by 1885 professionalism had not spread beyond the north-west and the midlands (Fig. 3.14). It

Table 3.5 Town size and facilities provided in ten Ontario urban areas, 1919–39. (X indicates that the facility was provided before 1919, the date indicates the date of provision.)

Town	Population in 1941	Team sports fields	Hockey rinks	Skating rinks	Toboggan slides	Swimming pools	Lawn bowling greens	Tennis courts	Golf courses	Quoits pitches
Toronto	667 457	X	X	X	X	X	X	X	X	
Hamilton	166 337	X	X	X		X	X	X	1924	X
London	78 134	X	X	X		1923		X	1924	
Kitchener	35 657	X			X	1931		X	1935	
Brantford	31 948	X	X	X						
St Catherines	30 275	X	X	X						
Sault Ste Marie	25 794	X	X	X						
North Bay	15 599	X	X	X						
Waterloo	9 025	X	X		X			X		
Exeter	1 589	X								

(Based on Metcalfe[40].)

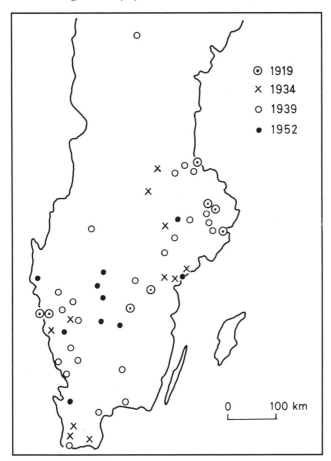

Fig. 3.11 The spatial diffusion of sports halls in Sweden. (Dates indicate the years the sports halls were made available.) (Based on Hägerstrand[41].)

took a decade to reach the south-east and the geographical peripheries, especially the south-west and East Anglia, did not succumb to professionalism until after the turn of the century. A very similar pattern is true for cricket in England, the counties in the north traditionally being forced to employ large numbers of professionals in order to compete on an equal footing with clubs from the south[43].

While on the subject of professionalism in British soccer, it is worth using this innovation to comment on the problem of geographical scale when exploring the diffusion of innovations. We have implied in our comments on the diffusion of professionalism in football that it was more of a neighbourhood than hierarchical form of spread – that it was in the small town of Darwen in Lancashire, not in London, that the innovation

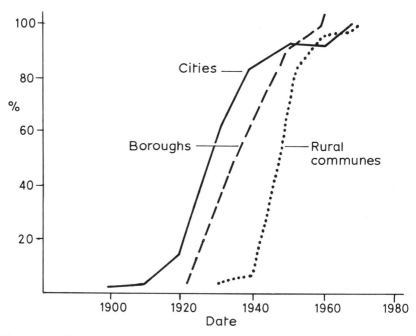

Fig. 3.12 Diffusion of sports policy in Finland. (Source: Harisalo[42].)

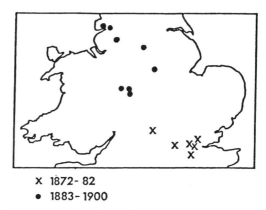

X 1872- 82
● 1883- 1900

Fig. 3.13 The locations of the Football Association Cup winners, 1872–1900. (Source: Bale[27].)

started diffusing. Indeed, at a national scale there is at first sight little evidence to support the hierarchical model. However, at the regional scale several areas exemplify hierarchical diffusion 'down' a local urban hierarchy. In the south-west, for example, Bristol was the first city to adopt, smaller places like Exeter and Plymouth adopting the innovation in an order related to their size[27]. This example illustrates the danger of assuming that one model only applies to the spread of sport from place to place; what might not appear to be present at one level of scale may be so at another.

The growth of modern sport and of innovations in sport, can be summarized as a twin hierarchical and neighbourhood diffusion model. This appears to apply at both national and international levels of scale. However, such diffusion models are essentially heuristic devices; they are suggestive but in no way describe processes. They obscure the fact that it was people who carried sport from place to place and that it was people who adopted sport. This means that at a given point in time, some people had access (geographical as well as social) to sports, while others were deprived of such access by the nature of their location in geographic space *vis à vis* an advancing innovation wave.

Despite the apparent evidence of neighbourhood and hierarchical effects we should be cautious in using map evidence alone in support of such a model. It is possible that the development of national and regional sports associations and sports innovations may have been influenced partly by the activities of neighbouring places, but the presence of pattern in no way infers a process. Until more research is undertaken which provides us with evidence of how sports actually crossed boundaries and what motivated or stimulated the adoption of formal sports associations, we should use the term 'pseudo-neighbourhood' diffusion to describe what we see on our maps.

The examples we have seen in this section confirm at least three things. First, sport, interpreted as the sum total of Olympic sports, does appear to have spread from economically advanced nations to those of an advancing (in the Western sense) status. Adoption curves for the former lie above those for the latter. Secondly, for individual sports, the correlation between date of adoption and level of economic development is positive but even when a small number of sports are examined it is clear that it is far from a one-to-one relationship. What appears true for sport *per se*, may not be true for individual sports. The third point brought out so far is that ideas derived from geographical innovation diffusion appear appropriate for analysing the growth of sport as it meshes together both time and space at both international and national scales.

3.4.5   Paracme in sport

The diffusion of certain sports has been followed by what Barker[44] has termed 'paracme', that is, the disinnovation of something no longer

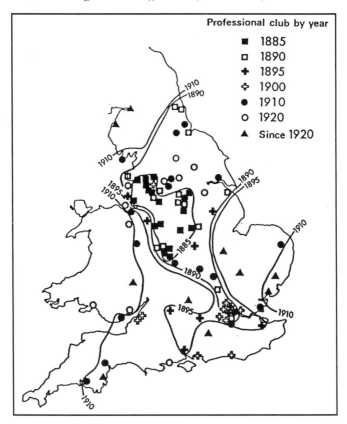

Fig. 3.14 The spatial diffusion of professionalism in football in England and Wales. (Isopleths indicate the maximum extent of professionalism at the date shown.) (Source: Bale[27].)

thought worthwhile. One example of disinnovation is in the winter sport of bandy. The game of bandy (like ice hockey but played on an ice-covered field, usually the size of a football pitch) was born in England at the start of the nineteenth century. A National Bandy Association was formed in 1891 – the first in the world. Subsequently associations were formed in Austria, Denmark, Germany, Switzerland, Norway, Sweden, Finland, USSR, Netherlands and the USA. Following the bifurcation of bandy and the resultant development of ice hockey, the number of countries playing bandy steadily declined so that today only six national federations remain. It would be interesting to see how many other international sports contract their geographic margins in this way, and whether the pattern of decline of interest in each sport represents a mirror image of its adoption curve.

At the national scale paracme has occurred in several cases, notably speedway racing and rugby league in Britain. Likewise the 'sport' of skateboarding experienced a rapid burst of innovation diffusion in the 1970s but has all but disappeared today. Some examples of the spatial contractions of sport are discussed in Chapter 4. There has been little research into the paracme of sports in the manner of the diffusion studies described earlier.

3.5 SPORT AS SOCIAL CONTROL

The geographical diffusion model emphasizes general patterns and stresses distance and economic potential ('size' of country or city) as barriers to the adoption of an innovation. The barriers tend to be emphasized at the expense of the carriers – and their motives. Sports historians have, in fact, documented the deeds of many of the prose-lytzers who took sports to many parts of the world. Scholars such as Tony Mangan[45] have shown in illuminating detail the ways in which 'muscular Christians' took sport, along with school and bible, to parts of Africa and Asia. The personalities and charisma of such people must frequently have been crucial in their success in planting many of the English private school sports in alien soil.

In some cases it seems likely that cultural conversion was unimportant in the carrying of a sport from one country to another. Hockey was introduced into the USA by Miss Constance Applebee, a member of the British School of Physical Education, who demonstrated it at a Harvard Summer School in 1911[46]. In the case of basketball, the sport was introduced to Britain by Madame Osterberg who, having seen the game played while visiting America, introduced it to her teachers' college in London. Similarly, it could hardly be argued that the Scottish coffee planters who introduced golf to Malaya at the end of the nineteenth century[47] were intent on using their sport as a form of social control. More likely it created cultural exclusion rather than assimilation.

However, the notion that sport was introduced to places, both outside and inside their countries of origin, in order to divert revolutionary fervour or covertly to control potentially hostile elements in the host society is widely-held. Indeed, there is explicit evidence that in some cases sport was introduced in order to teach discipline, reduce crime and encourage teamwork. This appears to have been the case with the introduction of soccer by English factory owners to Russia in the late nineteenth century[17]. A particularly detailed study[48] of the introduction of sport as a means of social control indicates that, in the inter-war years, soccer was introduced on the Witwatersrand of South Africa with the aim of 'defusing Native passions', winning over 'the raw native' and

Today association football is the most popular game in the world, played in every quarter of the globe and for the most part disseminated in the recent past by British imperialist soldiers, teachers, traders and missionaries. Srinagar furnishes a delightful illustration of the introduction of soccer to a distant outpost of Empire through the medium of a self-righteous autocratic muscular missionary. The effort comprises a vignette of imperial self-confidence incorporating ethnocentricity, arrogance and determination in the face of indigenous religious customs and social habits. In 1891 Tyndale-Biscoe took a wife and a football to Kashmir. The football aroused no interest. Its reception by the assembled school was scarcely heartening as Tyndale-Biscoe recorded in his *Kashmir in Light and Shade*:

TB	'This is a football
Boys	What is the use of it?
TB	For playing a game.
Boys	Shall we receive any money if we play that game?
TB	No!
Boys	Then we shall not play that game.
Boys	What is it made of?
TB	Leather.
Boys	Take it away! Take it away!
TB	Why should I take it away?
Boys	Because it is jutha (unholy) we may not touch it, it is leather.
TB	I do not wish you to handle it. I want you to kick it . . . and today you are going to learn how to kick it, boys.
Boys	We will not play that jutha game.'

Despite his pupils' obduracy instruction about the pitch, positions and rules followed. The response was less than enthusiastic. As Tyndale-Biscoe has recorded: 'Before the end of school I perceived that there would be trouble, so I called the teachers together and explained to them my plans for the afternoon. They were to arm themselves with single-sticks, picket the streets leading from the school to the playground, and prevent any of the boys escaping en route. Everything was ready, so at 3 o'clock the porter had orders to open the school gate. The boys poured forth, and I brought up the rear with a hunting-crop. Then came the trouble; for once outside the school compound they thought they were going to escape; but they were mistaken. We shooed them down the streets like sheep on their way to the butchers. Such a dirty, smelling, cowardly crew you never saw. All were clothed in the long nightgown sort of garment I have described before, each boy carrying a fire-pot under his garment and so next to his body. This heating apparatus has from time immemorial taken the place of healthy exercise. We dared not drive them too fast for fear of their tripping (as several of them were wearing clogs) and falling with their fire-pots, which would have prevented their playing football for many days to come.'

The ground was reached, the sides were picked, the ball put in position, the whistle blown, and blown again. The boys were adamant. They had absolutely no intention of kicking 'an unholy ball'. Tyndale-Biscoe for his part, had every intention that they should. The teachers were lined up with their sticks menacingly along each goal line, the boys were given five minutes to reflect on their decision. Five minutes past. The master charged, sticks and voices raised, the game began.

Vignette IV The introduction of soccer to Srinagar, Kashmir. Sport as an innovation was frequently resisted by indigenous peoples but the energies of the proselytizers invariably prevailed. (Source: Mangan[45]) 'channelling superfluous energies along proper lines'. White liberals and missionaries viewed sport as 'an agent for ameliorating the dilemmas associated with Black unemployment, crime and political radicalism'.

Such motives were undoubtedly true of many parts of the world and are a continuing element of government spending at the national scale. Stephen Jones[49] suggests that in the inter-war period in Britain, the substantial government spending on sports facilities throughout the country served to act as an agent of social control. However, it should be pointed out that not all people, be they blacks on the Witwatersrand or alienated inner city youth in the 1980s, take part in sport; indeed, the proportion of the national population which is interested in sports from the viewpoint of serious participation may be surprisingly small (see Fig. 7.16, for example). For this reason the social control function of sport should not be overestimated. It can also be argued that participation in sport and political activism are not necessarily mutually exclusive. Finally it might be reiterated that sports introduced to foreign countries may, in the first instance, have deliberately excluded the native population and when indigenous elements did participate they tended to be local social elites anyway. As with many other questions in both sport and geography, it is difficult to generalize, in this case about the role of sport *per se* as an agent of social control.

3.6 CONCLUSIONS

Modern sport had its roots in the folk game prototypes of pre-industrial times. Both industrialization and sport probably grew out of the changed outlook following the Newtonian revolution of the seventeenth century; sport was no exception to the many aspects of culture affected by the desire for precision, quantification and the quest for records.

As a generalization, sport as a modern phenomenon had its roots in Britain and tended to diffuse from more advanced to advancing (in a Western economic sense) nations. The adoption of sport in general may be equated with Western notions of economic development, although this may not apply so well to individual sports. Indeed, some of the richest countries in the world have yet to adopt to any degree sports pioneered in England in the late eighteenth century.

Sports and sports innovations continue to diffuse over the face of the Earth. The numbers of clubs, federations and sports are all growing and it is difficult to know if such a trend will stop. Given the increasing treatment of sport as a commodity and integration of sports into the global economic system, it is likely that sports entrepreneurs, as well as those who promote sport for its own sake, will continue actively to diffuse

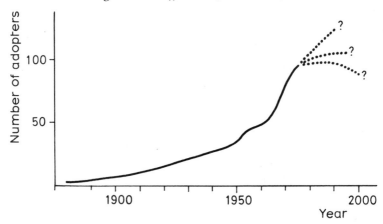

Fig. 3.15 Adoption curve for intercollegiate lacrosse in the USA. After a slow period of growth over the first half of the present century the sport 'took off' in the 1950s and 1960s, but it is impossible to predict what shape the curve will continue to take. (Source: Harper[51].)

sport from place to place. However, it does seem that 'trade' in sport has tended to be rather unbalanced. As Richard Gruneau[50] points out, the Olympic Games, for example, contain no tribal or 'Third World' games. They do, however, contain many sports which are beyond the financial reach of the overwhelming majority of the nations of the world – sports like yachting, skiing and even swimming, for example.

Many diffusion curves are similar in shape to that shown in Fig. 3.15, which shows no clear sign of whether it is starting to reach the 'laggard' stage or whether it will continue rising at its present rate. In many countries new sports continue to be adopted at a staggering rate. Few could have forseen, for example, the surprising success of gridiron football in Britain – a classic example of cultural colonialism if ever there was one – but we really do not know at the present time whether it will go the same way as skateboarding, a victim of paracme (see Section 3.4.5).

One innovation which is likely to continue is the growth of participation by women in sports thought previously only suited to men. Culture rather than biology has retarded the participation by women in many sports and the growth curve for participation by women in many formerly male-dominated activities is rising steeply, as in Fig. 3.15. However, the regional pattern of the diffusion of women's sports is likely to differ from that for the same sport for men. It is possible that the barriers to the adoption of sports by women are more the result of differing regional attitudes to women *per se* and some evidence exists to suggest that geographic variations in women's status are related to their participation rates in sports. In Africa, for example, the boom in men's distance running in Kenya and Ethiopia has hardly been matched by a similar response from women. In Britain the places which have adopted women's soccer tend to be in the more progressive south than in the north where sex roles are more traditionally delineated[52].

In one of the most global of sports, track and field athletics, post-1945 innovations such as synthetic running tracks and fibre-glass vaulting poles have been developed with great success. Because such investment-intensive innovations are associated with the more developed regions and nations of the world their adoption tends to be a function of Western notions of economic 'development'. In track and field athletics, relatively low standards of achievement by athletes from Africa and Asia are evident in those events in which the 'West' has pioneered major technological innovations. An African 'running revolution' can occur because long distance running does not require the capital investment needed for success in say, the sprints or jumping events. Sports innovations have had, and will continue to have, significant impacts upon the landscape, a subject we explore in some depth in Chapter 6.

Geographical innovation diffusion reminds us that space must be taken into account when describing the growth of sport. Sports are still diffusing over geographic space, although, at the same time, sports which have become well established are undertaking other kinds of locational changes and adjustments. It is to these that we turn in the next chapter.

FURTHER READING

A vast number of books deal with the historical development of sport and much of this material possesses implicitly geographical dimensions. For example, see Richard Mandell's excellent *Sport; a Cultural History*, Columbia UP, New York, 1982, for a thorough overview. Emphasis is placed on the 'carriers' of sport – the innovation change agents – who took many British sports to the (former) colonies in Tony Mangan's colourful *The Games Ethic and Imperialism: Aspects of the Diffusion of an Ideal*, Viking, London, 1986. Although Britain is widely regarded as having given sport to the world, the role of the USA in the international growth of sports is well exemplified in William J. Miller's The American sports empire, in *Sports in Modern America* (eds W. J. Baker and J. M. Carroll), River City Publishers, St. Louis, 1983. Books on the growth of specific sports also allude to their geographic spread frequently, albeit in a somewhat naive geographical way. Much sports geography can be teased out of Eric Dunning and Kenneth Sheard's excellent social history of British rugby, *Barbarians, Gentlemen and Players*, Robertson, Oxford, 1979. Likewise, studies of sports growth at the city level provide many spatial insights. See, for example, Stephen Hardy's *How Boston Played: Sport, Recreation and Community, 1865–1915*, Northwestern University Press, 1982. For a more explicitly geographical treatment of the spatial diffusion of sports see John Bale's Sports history as innovation diffusion, *Canadian Journal of History of Sport*, **15**, 1, 1982, pages 38–63.

The only 'geographical' paper to explore the growth of sport as a form of social control, and hence look at diffusion in a more problematic way, is Cecille Badenhorst and Chris Rogerson's 'Teach the native to play'; social control and organized sport on the Witwatersrand, 1920–1939, *GeoJournal*, **12**, 2, pages 197–202. Three journals of sports history frequently carry papers of a historical-geographic nature; these are *Journal of Sports History* (USA), *The Canadian Journal of the History of Sport* and *The International Journal of Sports History*, (UK).

REFERENCES

1. Dunning, E. and Sheard, K. (1979) *Barbarians, Gentlemen and Players*, Martin Robertson, Oxford.
2. Smulders, H. (1983) Demarcation of the spatial distribution of folk games in Flanders, in *Geographical Perspectives on Sport* (eds J. Bale and C. Jenkins), Department of PE, Birmingham University, pp. 169–72.
3. Dunning, E. (1979) *Soccer: the social origins of the sport and its development as a spectacle and profession*, Sports Council/SSRC, London.
4. Smith, J. (1972) The native American ball games, in *Sport in the Socio-Cultural Process* (ed. M. Hart), Brown, Dubuque, Iowa, pp. 346–60.
5. Salter, M. (1975/6) Meteorological play-forms of the eastern woodlands. *History of Physical Education and Sport Research and Studies*, **3**, 11–25.
6. Gillmeister, H. (1981) The origin of European ball games, a re-evaluation and linguistic analysis. *Stadion*, **7**, 19–51.
7. Tylor, E. (1880) Remarks on the geographical distribution of games. *Journal of the Anthropological Society of Great Britain and Ireland*, **9**, 23–30.
8. Jett, S. (1971) Diffusion versus independent development; the bases of controversy, in *Man Across the Sea; Problems of Pre-Columbian Contacts* (eds C. Riley, J. Kelley, C. Pennington and R. Rands), University of Texas Press, Austin.
9. Dunning, E. (1971) The development of modern football, in *The Sociology of Sport* (ed. E. Dunning), Cass, London.
10. Zeldin, T. (1977) *France 1848–1945*, Vol. 2, Oxford University Press, Oxford.
11. Mumford, L. (1973) Sport and the "bitch goddess", in *Sport and Society* (eds J. Talimini and C. Page), Little, Brown and Co., Boston, pp. 60–65.
12. Thrift, N. (1981) Owners' time and own time; the making of a capitalist time consciousness, in *Space and Time in Geography* (ed. A. Pred), Gleerup, Lund.
13. Stovkis, R. (1982) Conservative and progressive alternatives in the organisation of sport. *International Social Science Journal*, **92**, 197–220.
14. Brailsford, D. (1987) The geography of eighteenth century English spectator sports. *Sport Place*, **1**, 1, 41–56.

15. Lewis, G. (1968) On the beginnings of an era of American sport. *Proceedings,* 72nd Annual Meeting of the National College PE Association for Men.
16. Woeltz, R. (1977) Sport, culture and society in late imperial Weimer Germany; some suggestions for future research. *Journal of Sport History,* **4**, 295–315.
17. Riordan, J. (1977) *Sport in Soviet Society,* Cambridge University Press, Cambridge.
18. Metcalfe, A. (1976) Sport and athletics: a case study of lacrosse in Canada. *Journal of Sports History,* **3**, 1–19.
19. Walvin, J. (1975) *The People's Game,* Allen Lane, London.
20. Schmidt, A. (1979) Nippon-To(The Japanese Sword); transition from war to sport. *Abstracts* of *Research Papers,* AAHPER convention, 11.
21. Hayashi, N. (1972) Judo, in *The Little Known Olympic Sports* (ed. H. Jessup), AAHPER, Washington, D.C.
22. Harrison, E. (1913) *The Fighting Spirit of Japan,* Fisher Unwin, London.
23. Betts, J. (1974) *America's Sporting Heritage,* Addison Wesley, Reading, Mass.
24. Loken, N. (1949) *Trampolining,* Overbeck, Ann Arbor.
25. Metcalf, A. (1979) The use of the newspaper in sports history research. *Proceedings,* VII International HISPA Conference, Paris.
26. Arlott, J. (1976) *The Oxford Companion to Sports and Games,* Oxford University Press, Oxford.
27. Bale, J. (1978) Geographical diffusion and the adoption of professionalism in football in England and Wales. *Geography,* **63**, 188–97.
28. Bale, J. (1982) Sports history as innovation diffusion. *Canadian Journal of History of Sport,* **15**, 38–63.
29. Seppänen, P. (1981) Olympic success; a cross national perspective, in *Handbook of Social Sciences in Sport* (eds G. Lüschen and G. Sage), Stipes, Champaign, Ill.
30. Huguenin, A. (1981) *100 Years of the International Gymnastics Federation,* International Gymnastics Federation.
31. Holt, R. (1981) *Sport and Society in Modern France,* Cambridge University Press, Cambridge.
32. Mandell, R. (1984) *Sport; a Cultural History,* Columbia University Press, New York.
33. Gerber, E. (1971) *Innovators and Institutions in Physical Education,* Lea and Febiger, Philadelphia.
34. Reisman, D. and Denny, R. (1969) Football in America; a study in culture diffusion, in *Sport, Culture and Society* (eds J. Loy and G. Kenyon), Macmillan, London.
35. Turner, I. (1979) The emergence of "Aussie Rules", in *Sport in History* (eds R. Cashman and M. McKernan), University of Queensland Press, St Lucia, pp. 258–71.
36. Mandle, W. (1979) Sport as politics; the Gaelic athletic association, 1884–1916, in *Sport in History* (eds R. Cashman and M. McKernan), University of Queensland Press, St. Lucia, pp. 99–123.
37. Bale, J. (1981) Cricket in pre-Victorian England. *Area,* **13**, 119–22.
38. Jordan, T. and Rowntree, L. (1982) *The Human Mosaic,* Harper and Row, New York.
39. Rooney, J. and Johnson, M. (1983) Soccer in the United States, in *Geographical Perspectives on Sport* (eds J. Bale and C. Jenkins), Department of PE, Birmingham University, pp. 85–123.

40. Metcalfe, A. (1983) The urban response to the demand for sporting facilities; a study of ten Ontario towns/cities, 1919–1939. *Urban History Review*, **12**, 31–46.
41. Hägerstrand, T. (1966) Quantitative techniques in the analysis and spread of information and technology, in *Education and Economic Development* (eds C. Anderson and M. Baverman), Cass, London, pp. 244–80.
42. Harisalo, R. (1982) Diffusion of innovations in Finnish municipal administration, *Scandinavian Political Studies*, **5**, 169–86.
43. Bale, J. (1982) *Sport and Place*, Hurst, London.
44. Barker, D. (1977) The paracme of innovations. *Area*, **9**, 259–64.
45. Mangan, A. (1986) *The Games Ethic and Imperialism*, Viking Penguin, Harmondsworth.
46. Tennyson, C. (1959) They taught the world to play. *Victorian Studies*, **2**, 214.
47. Butcher, J. (1979) *The British in Malaya, 1880–1941*, Oxford University Press, Kuala Lumpur.
48. Badenhorst, C. and Rogerson, C. (1985) 'Teach the native to play'; social control and organized black sport on the Witwatersrand, 1920–1939. *GeoJournal*, **12**, 197–202.
49. Jones, S. (1987) State intervention in sport and leisure in Britain between the wars. *Journal of Contemporary History*, **22**, 163–82.
50. Gruneau, R. (1983) *Class, Sport and Social Development*, University of Massachusetts Press, Amherst.
51. Harper, G. (1975) *Intercollegiate Lacrosse in the United States, 1879–1975*, masters dissertation (unpublished), Oklahoma State University.
52. Bale, J. (1980) Women's football in England and Wales. *Physical Education Review*, **3**, 137–45.

Chapter 4

SOME MODERN LOCATIONAL TENDENCIES

Modern sport continues to adjust geographically, not only in the hierarchical and neighbourhood ways described in the last chapter but also through processes of relocation and through the growth and decline in importance of different sport locations. Additional changes have occurred in the size of sport catchment areas, both in terms of spectators and of players. These adjustments are in part related to the continuing economic imperatives of modern sports and to the broader regional and national economic conditions within which sports find themselves. The present chapter illustrates a number of such locational adjustments but first describes some general location patterns in modern sports, drawing on geography's famous central place theory as a conceptual base. We observe that the location of sports outlets is arranged on a reasonably predictable basis. There are, of course, exceptions to such geographical rules, some sports outlets appearing to be in rather aberrant locations. However, the chapter proceeds to stress that sports are becoming increasingly rational in terms of their locational patterns resulting from the increasingly rational behaviour of sports entrepreneurs on the one hand, and the stresses and strains of the economic system within which the sports industries are embedded, on the other. Such developments seem to have produced four geographical outcomes, namely (a) sports club relocation at both the national and urban scales, (b) changing national centres of success as a small number of sports clubs come to dominate regional markets for team sports and newly successful clubs emerge in economic growth areas with only tenuous sporting traditions, (c) shifting geographic margins of viability with sports clubs going out of business as part of a downward economic spiral in declining economic regions, and (d) widening spatial margins of recruitment of the raw materials of the sports industries, the athletes themselves.

4.1 SPORTS HIERARCHIES

Central place theory is one of geography's most well known contributions* and we can apply it to an introduction to the location of sports. It can be conceived of as a normative model (i.e. what ought to be, according to certain built-in assumptions) to assist in the sensible location of a range of sports activities, ranging from, say, a First Division soccer club to a couple of recreational tennis courts. For our purposes we will call our model a sports place theory and describe it as follows.

(1) The main function of a sports place is to provide sports outlets for a surrounding hinterland. Sports places are therefore centrally located within their market areas.
(2) The greater the number of sports provided, the higher the order of the sports place.
(3) Low-order sports places provide sporting facilities that are used by small catchment areas; the threshold population needed for the viability of a low-order place is small.
(4) Higher order places are fewer in number and are more widely spaced. They have large population thresholds.
(5) A hierarchy of sports places exists in order to make as efficient as possible the arrangement of sports opportunities for (a) consumers who wish to minimize their travel to obtain the sport they want and (b) producers of sport who must maintain a minimum threshold to survive.

An ideal spatial pattern for a sports system is shown in Fig. 4.1. Here, sports teams or sports facilities able to draw on a regional catchment are located further apart than those catering for a district catchment which, in turn are sited at more distant intervals than those only able to draw on a local sphere of influence. Each order of outlet has its own demand curve (or demand cone – the result of rotating a demand curve through 360°) which creates its trade area, represented ideally as a hexagon so that no areas will be left unserved (as they would be in the case of less easily 'packed' circular trade areas).

In practice such a classification is often used in the planning of recreational sports facilities, especially at the intra-urban scale. In urban areas recreational sports sites are chosen and provided with facilities to serve a surrounding hinterland of given size. Such facilities can be arranged as a hierarchy, each level serving a different sized catchment. At the lowest level, for example, would be the playground possessing a sphere of influence of say, 800 m in radius, and providing informal

---

* Reviews of central place theory are found in virtually every urban or economic geography text. This summary is based on Berry *et al.*[1].

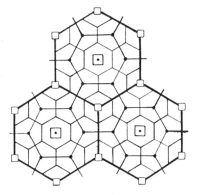

☐ Centre of regional catchment
☐ Centre of district catchment
• Centre of local catchment

Fig. 4.1 Theoretical organization of a sports system, using the principles of central place theory.

facilities for pre-sporting activities of 6 to 14 year olds. The second level of the hierarchy would be the playing field with a variety of sites for field and indoor sports. This might serve an area of about 2 km radius while a third level might be made up of a top-level sports complex with athletic stadium and swimming pool included and designed to serve an entire community. Such a hierarchy would approximate to the tenets of central place theory.

Proximity to population is another major criterion frequently used in planning publicly funded sports facilities. For example, in Britain it is suggested that the threshold size for a nine-hole golf course should be 18 000, while six acres of playing fields should be provided for every 1000 people. In the USA, baseball diamonds and tennis courts have respective thresholds of 6000 and 2000 respectively[2].

Public sports facilities should be as close to the potential users as possible in order to maximize pleasure from the sport experience and to minimize travel, and hence cost. The concentration of public sports outlets in areas of high density population is therefore desireable on equity grounds. Of course, different criteria apply for private funded developments where profit, rather than population access is crucial. In reality the spacing of sports outlets is far from uniform and the hexagonal pattern rarely observable. This is because of a variety of factors, not least the legacy of history and inertia, but also the physical nature of the landscape and the variability of the funding available for such developments. Several studies of professional sports have identified threshold

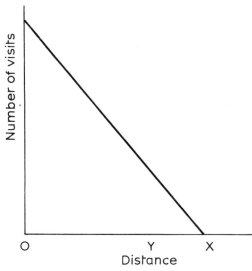

Fig. 4.2 Spatial demand curve for sport.

populations above which a sports team will be regarded as a viable economic proposition. In the USA it has been suggested that a figure of one million fan visits per season is a critical threshold for a professional baseball franchise[3–5]. Clearly, this figure is unlikely to be reached by many metropolitan areas.

Let us now return to the idea of a sports team's sphere of influence. This can be interpreted as a spatial demand curve which will decline with distance from a given sports outlet (this applies to both top-level and recreational sports) as potential 'consumers' are necessarily confronted with the increasing costs of overcoming the friction of distance. The slope of the curve will depend on a variety of factors but beyond the point where it intersects the distance axis (at X in Fig. 4.2) people will not find it worthwhile travelling to consume sport (either as spectators or as participants) at O. This provides the potential for another facility to be located somewhere near X in order to serve those for whom travel to O is prohibitive. In planning for such provision there is always the danger, however, that the new facility, if located at Y, for example, would divert demand from O[6]. Such a situation could create problems in professional team sports where the slope of the spatial demand curve can change dramatically as the fortunes of the team change. In such a situation, spatial competition would exist and this is avoided in the United States sports industries (football, baseball, etc.) for which each team in the league is assigned an exclusive franchise to conduct league contests within some specific geographic area[3]. This displays a degree of economic rationality absent in the major British team sports where a considerable degree of spatial competition for support exists.

In Britain it has been suggested by Sloane[7] that those who run both football and cricket are motivated more by the maximization of utility than profit. As Wiseman has put it, 'club directors are often fanatical supporters who find their involvement a rewarding hobby in itself'[8]. As directors they are able to get the best seats at games and wine and dine their (often business) colleagues. A directorship is also good for prestige, image and business.

The central place approach to sports geography stresses what ought to exist given certain underlying assumptions and ideal circumstances. These include things like an even population distribution, a homogeneous plane surface, and economic rationality. We have already indicated that in reality a number of irregularities exist which will make the real world different from that predicted by normative models A vast number of physical, economic and social barriers will contribute to a distortion of the central place model. For example, in the British football and cricket industries, the spatial pattern is a virtual fossil of what existed at the start of the present century when conditions in Britain were totally different. In addition, sporting tastes vary from place to place, 9% of the population supporting football in Carlisle in the north of England and only 1.5% in Bournemouth in the south[9]. In the case of ice hockey in North America in a Canadian city of 3.5 million, attendance will average, all other things being equal, over 4000 fans per game higher than in the United States[4].

Much of the supply of sport, particularly at the recreational level, is made by the public sector whose resources vary dramatically over space. In such situations, what ought to exist is likely to be dramatically different from the pattern of sports facilities in the real world. Despite these 'aberrant' characteristics, however, a good deal of spatial order does appear to exist in the location pattern of sports. Let us consider initially the evidence for sports hierarchies, both in the form of provision by population size and in terms of the spatial arrangement of facilities or outlets. Despite the historical basis of the British football industry and the absence of profit maximization among those who run it, there does appear to be a reasonably well-defined relationship between size of metropolitan area and number of outlets, shown in Fig. 4.3. Although the relationship is apparently curvilinear, there are a number of anomalies. Some standard metropolitan labour areas (SMLAs) (travel to work areas and hence better indications of market area populations than city populations) seem to have fewer clubs than might be expected, Newcastle-upon-Tyne being an obvious example. Figure 4.3 shows that on the other hand, Stoke-on-Trent and, more dramatically, Chester have more

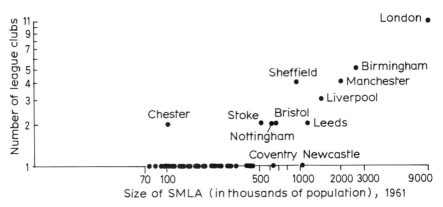

Fig. 4.3 The relationship between the number of football league clubs and the size of the standard metropolitan labour area (SMLA) (log scales).

clubs than might be expected (though the Chester case is readily explained by the Welsh border dissecting that particular SMLA and hence creating a cultural 'need' for two clubs, Chester and Wrexham).

The number of games played would also be expected to correlate with town size. Big places can support more events than small places and in many countries national championships in particular sports are always held in the national capital or largest city. Figure 4.4 shows the number of county cricket matches played during the 1973 English season. Note, however, that there is an imbalance in the supply of games, many large centres being given very few matches while some smaller places were given more than might seem appropriate.

Examples such as this demonstrates that human and cultural factors can upset the rationally economic world predicted by central place models. Tradition, variations in interest, and sheer inertia all have to be taken into account in understanding some of the apparent anomalies in the world of sport.

We should also expect to find a relationship between the number of sports represented in a given area and that area's population size. This is clearly illustrated in Table. 4.1 which shows the 1988 distribution of major sports franchises in the USA and the sizes of the top 37 metropolitan areas. New York, with a population of over 17 million had nine franchises; lower down the hierarchy Pittsburgh with nearly 2.4 million had three; further down still, Salt Lake City, with a population of just over 1 million, had one franchise. While hierarchical order clearly does exist in the real world of sports, Fig. 4.3 and Table 4.1 also indicate that certain places with populations apparently big enough to support a professional sports team do not, in fact, have one. This provides the potential for relocation, a subject we return to in subsequent sections of this chapter.

Table 4.1 Distribution of major league professional sports franchises by Metro-politan Statistical Areas, 1988, United States

1984 population rank	Metropolitan area	1984 population (in thousands)	Franchises 1988				
			Baseball	Hockey	Basket-ball	Football	Total
1	New York	17 807	2	3	2	2	9
2	Los Angeles	12 373	2	1	2	2	7
3	Chicago	8 035	2	1	1	1	5
4	Philadelphia	5 755	1	1	1	1	4
5	San Francisco	5 688	2	–	1	1	4
6	Detroit	4 577	1	1	1	1	4
7	Boston	4 027	1	1	1	–	3
8	Houston	3 566	1	–	1	1	3
9	Washington	3 427	–	1	1	1	3
10	Dallas–Ft. Worth	3 348	1	–	1	1	3
11	Miami	2 799	–	–	–	1	1
12	Cleveland	2 788	1	–	1	1	3
13	St Louis	2 398	1	1	–	1*	3
14	Atlanta	2 380	1	–	1	1	3
15	Pittsburgh	2 372	1	1	–	1	3
16	Baltimore	2 245	1	–	–	1	2
17	Minneapolis	2 231	1	1	–	1	3
18	Seattle	2 208	1	–	1	1	3
19	San Diego	2 064	1	–	1	1	3
20	Tampa	1 811	–	–	–	1	1
21	Denver	1 791	–	–	1	1	2
22	Phoenix	1 715	–	–	1	–*	1
23	Cincinnati	1 674	1	–	–	1	2
24	Milwaukee	1 568	1	–	1	–	2
25	Kansas City	1 477	1	–	–	1	2
26	Portland	1 341	–	–	1	–	1
27	New Orleans	1 319	–	–	–	1	1
28	Columbus	1 279	–	–	–	–	–
29	Norfolk	1 261	–	–	–	–	–
30	Sacramento	1 220	–	–	1	–	1
31	Buffalo	1 205	–	1	–	1	2
32	Indianapolis	1 195	–	–	1	1	2
33	San Antonio	1 187	–	–	1	–	1
34	Providence	1 095	–	–	–	–	–
35	Charlotte	1 031	–	–	–	–	–
36	Hartford	1 030	–	1	–	–	1
37	Salt Lake City	1 025	–	–	1	–	1
	Totals		24	14	23	27†	

* In 1988 the Cardinals moved from St. Louis to Phoenix.
† The football total does not include Green Bay (Packers).

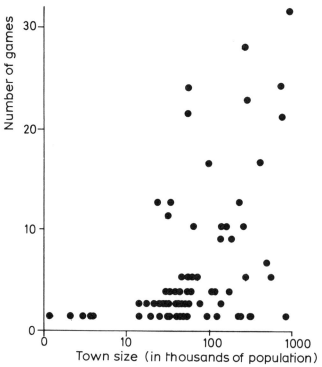

Fig. 4.4 Correlation between the number of cricket matches played in the 1973 English season and the size of the settlements within which the grounds are located. (Source: Toyne[10].)

Generally speaking, large cities not only contain more clubs, they also contain the most successful clubs. Large cities possess the potential to attract larger crowds; larger crowds bring in higher revenues, higher revenues purchase better players. Although it is not always as simple as this, there is, in the increasingly cut-throat world of professional sport, the tendency for clubs in the largest places to buy success. This is another topic which is dealt with later.

Where sports are arranged on a league basis, we find that minor leagues 'nest' with larger league areas, according to the pattern predicted in Fig. 4.1. One of the few empirical attempts to map the spatial pattern of sports team support is shown in Fig. 4.5, which illustrates the spatial organization of Australian Rules football in Victoria. It is clearly seen how the minor leagues nest within the more spatially extensive major leagues.

Although irregularities will obviously exist to distort the idealized model of sport locations, it is nevertheless useful to think in terms of the functional and spatial hierarchy when planning for sport or when considering the spatial reorganization of existing provisions.

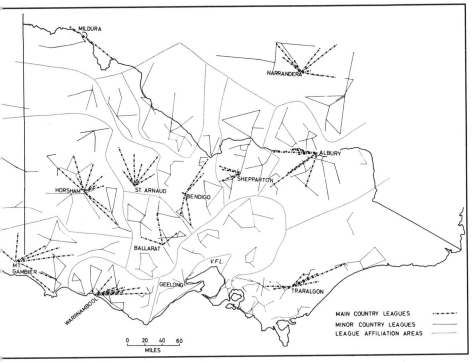

Fig. 4.5 The territorial organization of Australian Rules football under the auspices of the VFL league affiliation areas encloses the minor country leagues according to the centre of a main country league through which they are administered. Spheres of influence are constructed by joining each team to others playing in the same competition. (Source: Rimmer and Johnston[11].)

4.2 PERIODIC MARKETING OF SPORT

Where a sports club operates from a 'home turf', spectators will travel to it. An alternative form of spatial organization is for the sport to travel to the people in order to attract sufficient business to meet its threshold population. At the same time periodic marketing can be regarded as improving the welfare of sports consumers if it allows them access to sports they would otherwise be denied. Sport in its varied forms provides evidence of increased levels of periodic marketing in some cases and of decline in others.

The traditional way of marketing cricket in many English counties has been for the county clubs to engage in a tour of various grounds within their counties during the course of a season. A typical and traditional example is provided by the games of the county of Essex for the 1952 season (Fig. 4.6). Their games were played at eight venues throughout the season. Although this did incur considerable transport costs it did

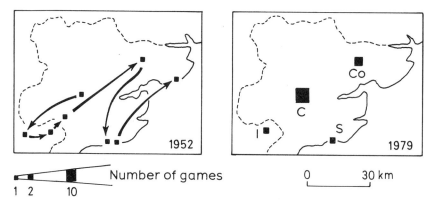

Fig. 4.6 Essex cricket, 1952 and 1979. The decline of periodic marketing and the concentration of cricket at Chelmsford. I, Ilford; S, Southend; Co, Colchester; C, Chelmsford. (Source: Bale[12].)

ensure that people in various parts of the county had the chance of seeing their team play. However, such a form of organization may be best suited to sports in which it is less easy to capitalize on a 'home field advantage' (see Section 2.4.2).

The 1970s and 1980s witnessed a reduction in the number of locations at which many English county teams played. The Essex case is exemplary (Fig. 4.6) with only half the number of grounds used in 1952 being frequented in 1979. However, in the cases of other clubs, an increase in the number of venues has taken place over the same period; indeed nationally the number of venues has increased and this could be interpreted as providing improved welfare for cricket lovers nationwide*. In this particular sport the increase in the number of venues has been a result of the growing number of one-day games.

Periodic marketing is popular in other sports at the international level. The quadrennial marketing of the Olympics at geographically diverse venues might be regarded as an example, but international golf and tennis circuits are perhaps the most well known cases. For the 'European' golf tour, the 1983 pattern is typical. The year started in Tunisia in mid-April, moving on to Madrid and Sardinia before the end of the month. The spatial organization of professional golf is strongly motivated by the hope of good weather at the tournament location and for this reason the tour did not reach Britain until mid-May, via Paris earlier that month. Throughout May and June the focus of attention is in Britain, in 1983 major tournaments being held at places such as Leeds, Southport, Jersey, Chepstow and Porthcawl, with a brief interruption in Sweden

---

* For a detailed treatment see Walford[13].

before returning to England and Scotland in July. A number of continental locations were included on the tour in August, including Utrecht, Dublin, York, Switzerland and Sunningdale (England). By late September the location of European golf activity is switching back to Iberia and apart from one early October tournament in southern England, all October/November events are in Madrid, Paris, Barcelona or on the Algarve†. Similar forms of spatial organization are found in activities like Grand Prix motor sports and other events lacking a 'home turf'.

In some sports it is the actual event, rather than a sequence of different events, which moves from place to place. Car rallies are an example but perhaps the most famous is the Tour de France cycle race, a mobile spectacle for a widely scattered rural population unable to support other forms of professional spectator sport[15].

The locational principles based on central place theory and periodic marketing are found in many sports. However, the geographical organization of sport is in a state of flux as locations of teams change, as successful locations change, as clubs go out of business altogether, and as they scour the world for the most suitable 'labour'. In the remainder of this chapter, examples are given of each of these locational tendencies.

4.3   RELOCATION

The movement of sports clubs from one location to another represents one of the most evident tendencies in late twentieth century sports. Such movement might be expected in situations where profit maximization was the norm, sports club relocation occurring at two levels of geographic scale. Movements at the intra-regional and inter-regional scales form the subject of this section. The former type of move invariably involves the suburbanization of sports stadia but the latter might involve a transcontinental move. Both forms of relocation reflect the growing rationalization and economic imperatives associated with modern sports.

In north American sport, in particular, suburbanization has been a frequent occurrence in recent decades. Such relocations are relatively easy in a USA context since the move often involves staying within the league's (or cartel's) specified geographic area (see page 80). Such moves illustrate stadium relocation which is obviously not synonymous with franchise relocation.

Before 1960 none of the twenty-eight teams playing in the major baseball leagues or the National Football League played their home games anywhere but in a central city. By 1977 ten of the fifty-three professional baseball and football teams played in suburban locations,

† A similar pattern is found in the USA, see Rooney[14].

including eight who moved from a central city to a suburban community[16]. Luxurious new stadium complexes often characterize these suburban locales. In the 1970s the Dallas Cowboys, Detroit Lions, New York Giants, Capital Bullets and Anaheim's California Angels (formerly Los Angeles) and Rams were in the vanguard of the sports suburbanization process[17]. Sports teams see the suburbs as newly accessible locations in times of freeways, by-passes and high levels of car ownership. The suburbs also possess a different image from the inner city; the Los Angeles Rams moved to Anaheim in 1980 – in response to Orange County's more glamorous image, higher income population, and locational convenience for fans[17]. For the owners of the Rams, Anaheim was a much better investment risk than rennovating the Coliseum Stadium in the Watts area of Los Angeles. As the Rams moved within the NFL's 75 mile territorial limit, it was not treated officially as a relocation at all but just a switch of stadium within a defined market area. The new location was also in a prosperous white neighbourhood – good for the sport's image. At the time of writing the San Francisco Giants were seriously considering leaving their windswept home stadium at Candlestick Park and moving 20 km south to a freeway interchange location at San Mateo. From the viewpoint of the suburban municipalities the presence of a professional sports team is seen to provide both economic and 'psychic' benefits. However, hard evidence of economic gains seems difficult to find since the benefits from newly located clubs tend to be spread over regions, rather than restricted to individual suburbs[18].

In Britain the intra-urban movement of professional football clubs was commonplace at the end of the nineteenth century. Among the most spectacular was the 15 km trek of Arsenal from south-east London (Woolwich) to Islington, then at the northern limit of the metropolis. More recently, in 1986, Bristol Rovers left their historic Eastville ground (occupied since the 1880s) and relocated 20 km away at Bath. Other clubs, notably Leicester City, Southampton, Luton and Oxford United have toyed with the idea of relocating in greenfield, suburban locations. In the case of Oxford United, no fewer than 19 peripheral sites have been considered since 1965. In such cases, opposition to the occupancy of 'green belt' land may be extremely vociferous.

While the clubs perceive the benefits of such relocations as the occupation of less congested sites and more comfortable stadiums, the problem is whether existing fans would continue to identify with, and hence support, them some distance (again by British standards) from their historic origins. In Britain, local identification with a team can be stretched to the maximum even if relatively short distance moves are mooted. For example, a study of whether Chelsea Football Club in London would remain 'Chelsea' and continue to be perceived as such if it

Charlton's vale of tears

Things that make sense don't always make sense. Economically, and in all practicality, Charlton Athletic are right to leave their amphitheatre of a Valley ground and plough seven miles around the South Circular to share with Crystal Palace. They don't own the Valley anyway, so there's not much choice: but even if there was a choice, the vast bills for making the currently-closed East Terrace safe again can't easily be met from gates which, this season, are a twelfth of the throngs that once came to Charlton. Sharing makes sense.

And yet, we shall have to wait and see, for football is more than balance sheet inevitabilities. Selhurst Park, one end consumed by a new supermarket, so that visiting strikers must seemingly queue at the check-out before shooting, is an efficiently soulless ground, a concrete monument of the Clockwork Orange era. There is a slightly rootless, commuter feel to the people on its terraces. Turn right and right again and you're in Croydon. The Valley for good or ill, is utterly different. A great natural bowl. Stand on the top of the East Terrace and, even if the football gladiators far below are having a bad day, the panorama across dockland is one of the great sights of London. There's a sense of history in the higgledy-piggledy mix

of spare acres, 50-year-old stands and the goals that Sam Bartram once defended. When the sun shines, it's one of the most endearing grounds in the land; when a storm crackles over the Thames, you watch the Twilight of the Gods from a natural balcony.

Can these two be made to go into one? Seven miles of driving may seem a trifle, but that could be an hour's struggle through the chaos of South London on a shopping Saturday. And when the men from Greenwich and Kidbrook and Plumstead, the men from the other side of Millwall, arrive at the Palace, will they recognise the experience, will they come to call it home? If this bit of desperate sharing works, then many more clubs will follow the same route: and that, in straitened times, will be desperately sensible. But if it doesn't work, if transplanted Charlton withers in a Catford traffic jam, then the whole concept of sharing may, in turn, slip down the agenda. That would be bitter, for this is actually one of the trickiest mergers in the League. With the Valley's closure, football loses one of its most remarkable venues. No offence to the Palace, but things at Selhurst Park can never be the same.

Fig. 4.7 This leader article from *The Guardian* (9 September 1985) highlights some of the problems of ground sharing in the case of English football. The 1985–6 season saw Charlton sharing Crystal Palace's ground at Selhurst Park. Note from the leader how the writer adopts a rather 'humanistic' approach to the landscape of the two grounds, an approach which is returned to in Chapter 6.

moved a few miles to Wormwood Scrubs revealed that the answer was a 'fairly emphatic "no" '[19].

Although the rugby league club Liverpool City moved suburbanward to Huyton and in 1985 to Runcorn, the suburbanization of British soccer has been more discussed than implemented in the last decade. In the mid-1980s the proposal to relocate the Luton club in the new city of Milton Keynes, 30 km away, was rejected as a result of the strength of feeling of the local supporters' club. A more dramatic example from 1984 is provided by the proposal by entrepreneur and newspaper magnate Robert Maxwell to merge his football club at Oxford with that at Reading and locate the new club (tentatively called 'Thames Valley Royals') at an intermediate site at the town of Didcot. Like the Luton proposal, this floundered, Maxwell having failed to anticipate the strength of local support for the survival, *in situ*, of both clubs. Oxford United is an example of a club which, given director Maxwell's finances and a location in a growth area of southern England, has improved its status dramatically in recent years. At the present time it is an example of a First Division club in a non-league location and given the failure of the merger proposal, pressures exist to move to a suburban, green belt site on the northern outskirts of the city. Given the growing desire of clubs to relocate it would seem essential to test the strength of the ties which bind clubs to their locale.

The same applies to sports teams contemplating another form of relocation, ground sharing with a not too distant neighbour. Ground sharing is common in many cities on mainland Europe but in Britain is relatively rare, a few soccer clubs sharing with rugby league. Yet it makes economic sense at a time when the finances of many British soccer clubs are precarious, to say the least. With grounds unused for the larger part of the week, they are a luxury which many clubs can ill afford. While recommended by a number of observers, ground sharing has only been entered into as a serious proposition by one club. This occurred in 1985 when the south London club, Charlton Athletic, commenced sharing the Selhurst Park ground of the Crystal Palace club. As Fig. 4.7 so graphically describes, a number of problems were anticipated. Yet within a year of sharing the ground Charlton had climbed out of Division Two of the Football League, having met with somewhat unexpected success in their adopted home. However, considerable pressure continues to exist to persuade Charlton to move back to their former locality.

In some cases it may be that it is not the relocation of the club that is important in improving attendances but the rearrangement of the league in which it plays so that it can benefit from the well-known 'local Derby' effect, i.e. the more local the opposition, the greater the attendance. Paradoxically, clubs in the lower divisions of the English Football League incur greater transport costs in order to fulfil their league commitments than the wealthier clubs in the higher divisions. This is because the clubs in the lower divisions tend to be more peripherally located. It has been shown that the lower the division, the more sensitive attendances are to the distances between the teams competing[20] and several commentators have therefore strongly recommended a return to the regionalization of the lower divisions of the league.

THE TAMPA TRIBUNE, Thursday, March 27, 1986

Game of musical franchises adds to league's instability

Here it is playoff time and the game goes on in the CBA.

The game of musical franchises, that is.

Already there are numerous reports of franchise shifts for 1986–87.

Detroit is supposedly headed for Savannah, Ga., Baltimore, which was bounced from its Towson (Md.) State University facility because of non-payment of rent, is headed for someplace called Pittsfield, Mass., after moving from Lancaster, Pa., this season.

Maine, which moved from Puerto Rico for 1985–86, is in deep financial trouble in Bangor and Evansville's recent problems were well-chronicled.

Wyoming, unless its gets new financing, is in jeopardy and so is Wisconsin.

Kansas City, a first-year franchise, toyed with moving to Topeka but has since changed its mind.

Only Toronto, which made an early-season move to Pensacola, and LaCrosse (Wisx.), which moved from Louisville before the season began, have found greener pastures at the turnstiles. Albany remains the only stable franchise in the league.

And the league is talking expansion to as many as three or four new sites.

You'd think the CBA would have learned its lesson from the defunct North American Soccer League, which expanded too quickly and died within six years of such a move. Prior to the Rowdies joining the league in 1974, there were 15 NASL teams. In 1975 when the Rowdies entered the NASL, there were 20 teams. Four years later there were 24 teams and by 1984, the league was gone.

The only difference is the NASL paid over-inflated salaries to most foreign players who were generally at the end of their careers. The CBA has a $500 weekly salary cap to prevent that insanity.

You get the idea that the 14-team CBA needs stability badly, though.

Not that the league hasn't survived all these years, sometimes in spite of its owners.

Richard Mudry

Fig. 4.8 The Continental Basketball Association (CBA) in the USA has been typical of American sport franchise relocation in recent years. But expansion and relocation have their dangers, as this newspaper article shows.

The relocation of sports clubs assumes a rationality on the part of club owners (and consumers) which appears to be present in some countries but not in others, a reflection of differing national sporting ideologies. In the USA it is widely accepted that the owners of professional sports teams are in the business to maximize profits. As a result, dramatic transcontinental movements of sports clubs are not uncommon (Fig. 4.8), professional sports franchises making relocation decisions with a degree of regularity which would surprise the average British sports fan. We have seen how in Britain community solidarity and fan support have successfully countered the apparent plans of some clubs to relocate. In the USA, however, fans rarely if ever oppose such moves with any degree of success and Ingham and Hardy[21] are probably correct when they argue that 'when capital confronts community it is capital which wins the day'. Such a tendency is undeniably emerging in Britain at the present time with moves towards merging football teams being mooted in cases where two existing clubs are sited relatively close to one another.

Because spectator sports are, by definition, market oriented, their owners might be expected to seek locations which have the largest market potential. Although we have seen that regional variations in demand do exist as a result of different tastes, the greatest returns are generally found in large cities. For example, in the early 1970s the after-tax profit of the most successful US baseball team was $1 075 000. That of the least successful was −$500 000. A major source of such disparities was estimated by economist Roger Noll[22] to be the exclusivity of the geographical space afforded to each team – the regional franchise in the most lucrative markets (New York, Los Angeles and Chicago, for example) being immune from spatial competition, irrespective of the level of demand for the sport. Such a situation invites the possibility of the establishment of rival leagues but the American experience suggests that established clubs tend to win such economic competitions and that new leagues can only succeed in new territory.

In the twentieth century in the USA there has been a broad economic and population shift to the west and south. The locational dynamics of US sports teams reflect this shift in no uncertain terms (see Fig. 4.9). Some people date the decline of New York City to the mid-1950s when the Giants and the Dodgers left for the west coast and the affluence of California. We have already noted that in team sports the magic figure of one million fan visits is crucial for a team to break even. Hence, small city teams rarely succeed in terms of profit even if grass roots interest is greatest in a relative sense. However, as Quirk[3] has shown for US baseball relocations, though fan visits and profits may be high in the 'honeymoon' period immediately following a move, this can decline rapidly after a few years and induce further relocation. Such behaviour clearly demonstrates the significance of profit maximizing behaviour in US sports. Indeed, it has been suggested that a logical extension of existing franchise movement would be to internationalize sports leagues into Japan, Mexico and Canada – something which could yet happen[5].

In the case of ice hockey it is not just large city dominance and the importance of profits, but also the presence of American control and ownership of the National Hockey league which helps explain the location pattern. In 1917 all North American professional ice hockey teams were in Canada. By the mid-1970s only three of the eighteen National Hockey League teams were in Canada and only five of the World

Hockey Association's fourteen teams were so located. Kidd[23] views such developments as part of the Americanization of Canada and observes that 'not surprisingly this non-Canadian organisation (i.e. The National Hockey League) has rarely acted in the best interest of the Canadian community . . . Given the commercialisation of the game its Americanization is inevitable'. It is not grass roots interest but the television revenues which accrue from the more densely populated USA which are of greater locational significance.

Even in some sports which have been geographically organized according to the tenets of periodic marketing (Section 4.2), commercial pressures have had the effect of increasing big-city dominance. In the case of the Tour de France, for example, recent years have witnessed places outside France bidding successfully to be stages in it. The mobile spectacle is no longer literally a tour of France but has taken in parts of Belgium and Germany. In 1987 West Berlin paid £1 million to stage the start, the riders not actually reaching France until the sixth stage.

4.4   SHIFTING CENTRES OF SUCCESS

The locational changes such as those described so far might be most obviously associated with sports in which profit maximization is the norm. This appears to be the case in American team sports* but in Britain the activities of those who run professional soccer and cricket appear to be more related to the maximization of utility. Even so, certain geographical changes can be readily observed which suggest that even when the broad location pattern may be relatively static or fossilized, clubs in large cities and market areas tend to benefit from certain economic changes taking place both in the sport and in society at large. Success in sport is being increasingly associated with large cities and regional economic growth points. Let us illustrate these general tendencies with specific examples.

In Britain the removal of the maximum wage in soccer in the early 1960s meant that clubs in large population centres who could, all other things being equal, generate larger crowds, stood to gain from their in-built market potential. A bigger population meant bigger gates, which in turn produced the revenue to pay the newly spiralling wages of the best players. At the same time the general public was becoming more geographically mobile, car ownership and the motorway and by-pass networks increasing at the same time. Consumers could by-pass smaller clubs and head for the newly emerging super clubs which became locked

---

* However, it has been suggested that owning a sports team is not an especially profitable form of investment – though this is not to say that owners do not act in a profit-maximizing way[24].

The 1950 s

The 1960 s

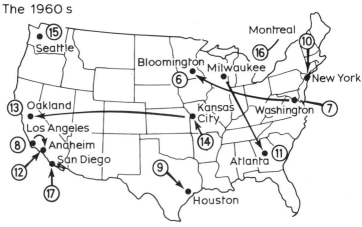

The 1970 s

The 1950s

1. 1953 – Boston Braves (NL) move to Milwaukee
2. 1954 – St. Louis Browns (AL) move to Baltimore as the Orioles
3. 1955 – Philadelphia Athletics (AL) move to Kansas City
4. 1958 – New York Giants (NL) move to San Francisco
5. 1958 – Brooklyn Dodgers (NL) move to Los Angeles

The 1960s

6. 1961 – Washington Senators (AL) move to Bloomington, Minn., as the Minnesota Twins
7. 1961 – Washington awarded AL expansion franchise, the Senators
8. 1961 – Los Angeles awarded AL expansion franchise, the Angels
9. 1962 – Houston awarded NL expansion franchise, the Colt .45s
10. 1962 – New York awarded NL expansion franchise, the Mets
11. 1966 – Milwaukee Braves (NL) move to Atlanta
12. 1966 – Los Angeles Angels (AL) move to Anaheim, become the California Angels
13. 1968 – Kansas City A's (AL) move to Oakland
14. 1969 – Kansas City awarded AL franchise, the Royals
15. 1969 – Seattle awarded AL franchise, the Pilots
16. 1969 – Montreal awarded NL franchise, the Expos
17. 1969 – San Diego awarded NL franchise, the Padres

The 1970s

18. 1970 – Seattle Pilots (AL) move to Milwaukee, become the Brewers
19. 1972 – Washington Senators (AL) move to Arlington, Texas, become the Texas Rangers
20. 1977 – Seattle awarded AL franchise, the Mariners
21. 1977 – Toronto awarded AL franchise, the Blue Jays

Fig. 4.9 The locational dynamics of American baseball, 1953–77. (Source: *The Miami Herald*, 24 March 1985.)

into an upward spiral of success, being marketed to a more 'rational', discriminating consumer, and old, local allegiances were dying. The overall result of these tendencies was that clubs in large cities obtained a greater share of their region's spectators. During the 1950s the share of the Football League's receipts going to the fifteen wealthiest clubs increased from 34% in 1950 to 45% in 1964[25]. Table 4.2 shows dramatically how in the county of Lancashire the four giant clubs, Manchester United and City, Liverpool and Everton, received an increasing share of regional support during the period 1951–71.

At the national level, Walker[20] has shown that a significant statistical relationship exists between the league standings of clubs and the ranks of the SMLAs in which they are located. What is more important to the present discussion, however, is that between 1968 and 1973 the relationship became progressively stronger – and has almost certainly continued to do so into the 1980s.

Growing 'primacy' in British sport is also exemplified by horse racing. As a result of decisions made by the Jockey Club and Horserace Betting Levy Board in 1980 certain courses, most of which are located in a ring around London, will receive help for capital projects such as the building of new stands. Others will obtain money for the course, stables and rooms while a lower tier of courses will be left to fend for themselves. In essence, the larger courses are subsidized and some of the smaller ones may have to close[26].

In some cases shifts in sports success may be associated with regional change in the economy. In Britain it would be tempting to link the growth of the East Anglian football clubs of Norwich and Ipswich with the growing affluence of that part of England. Likewise, the recent success of Aberdeen FC is associated with the oil boom off the east coast of Scotland. Most graphically, perhaps, has been the broad southward shift of success in the English football scene. As Brian Goodey and his associates

Table 4.2 Shifting shares of support in Lancashire, 1951–71

Year	Total number of supporters watching games in Lancashire	Approximate percentage of supporters watching Everton, Liverpool, Man. Utd and Man. City
1951	7 million	40
1961	6 million	50
1971	5.5 million	66

(*Source:* Rivett[9].)

Table 4.3 The southward shift of the First Division of the English Football League, 1910–87

Year	Percentage of clubs in			Index of southernness*
	North	Midlands	South	
1910	70	15	15	22.5
1930	64	18	18	27
1950	50	23	27	36.5
1970	41	27	32	45.5
1987	27	18	54	63

* The index of southernness ranges from 0 (all clubs in the north) to 100 (all in the south). It is calculated by applying the simple formula: $((N \times 0) + (M \times 1) + (S \times 2))/2$, where N, M and S are the percentages of clubs in the north, midlands and south respectively. (Source of data: *Rothman's Football Yearbook*.)

conclude*, there is 'an increasing coincidence between First Division football and the affluent south-east' (Table 4.3).

As areas of traditional industry decline and the tertiary sectors of the economy expand, so the location of sports clubs seems to adjust accordingly. In Portugal, for example, geographer Jorge Gaspar and his colleagues have charted the changing geography of the Portugese Football League[28, 29]. The proportion of league clubs within 50 km of Lisbon declined from 30% in 1970 to 24% in 1983. Clubs in the 'interior' on the other hand, increased in number, growing from 12% of the total in 1970 to 17% a decade later. Spectacular growth had especially taken place in Madeira and the Azores. Whereas at the start of the decade they had no league clubs, by 1980 they together had five (Fig. 4.10).

4.5   CHANGING SPATIAL MARGINS OF VIABILITY

The spatial dynamics of modern sports do not only involve the question of relocation. In some cases clubs disappear from the map altogether, the result of going out of business. This section looks at some of the geographical manifestations of such decline. The death of sports clubs may be caused by the supply of clubs exceeding the demand, as occurred in the early days of professional sports in the USA in the late nineteenth century. Of the 850 professional baseball clubs formed between 1869 and 1900, for example, only 50 lasted 6 years or more[30]. We have seen that this problem of over supply can be solved by the practice of collusion

* The quote is taken from an, as yet, unpublished English version of the paper by Goodey *et al.*[27].

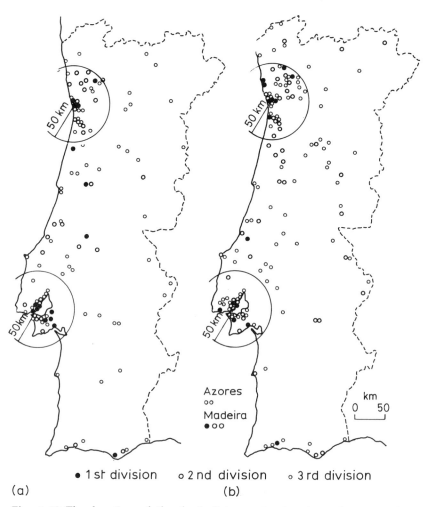

• 1st division   o 2nd division   o 3rd division
(a)   (b)

Fig. 4.10 The location of the football teams in the three divisions of the Portuguese Football League, 1972–3 (a) and 1980–1 (b). (Source: Gaspar *et al.*[29].)

between league members (or cartelization). But the fact that places which at one time have accommodated professional sports teams no longer do so may also be related to changes in the economic structures of the nations or regions in which they are found. It is to this theme that we now turn.

Like any other industry which faces a decline in demand for its product, adjustments are made by firms going out of business. But there is a regional dimension. Of the league clubs in the British football industry which have been forced to leave the Football League since 1920 only one was located south of one of Britain's most famous geographical divisions,

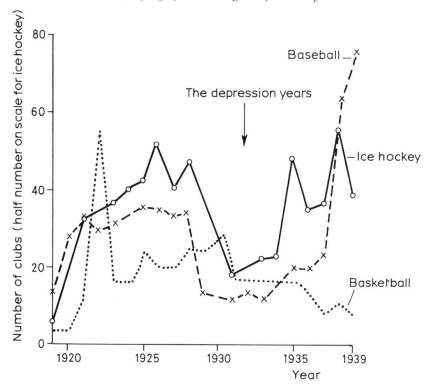

Fig. 4.11 Numbers of amateur clubs in three sports in Windsor, Ontario, 1919–39. (After Short[33].)

the Tees–Exe line, separating older, industrial Britain from the more twentieth century growth region of the south-east. The clubs which have left the league sound like a roll-call of the towns of the industrial revolution – for example Aberdare, Merthyr Tydfil, Gateshead, Barrow, Accrington and New Brighton. The newcomers, on the other hand, include Wimbledon, Hereford, Shrewsbury, Bournemouth, Oxford, Cambridge, Peterborough and Ipswich. The Welsh historian, Gareth Williams[31], has shown how in the years of the Great Depression in South Wales, it was principally those rugby clubs in the most severely depressed areas of the coalfield which suffered and went out of business while those in the somewhat more buoyant coastal areas remained viable. It should be noted that these were amateur, not professional, clubs and decline and demise associated with economic conditions should not be thought of solely as affecting sports as business enterprises. Recession and depression will affect the ability of participants to take part in amateur as well as professional sports (Fig. 4.11).

In professional sport, clubs at the economic margin and geographic periphery are often forced to sell their best young players in order to survive. Having paid something into the bank to reduce their overdrafts they buy a replacement player and are back to square one, hoping that more youngsters will make the grade. Stepney[32] commented that 'this kind of asset stripping invariably angers supporters because it highlights the commercial imperatives of the game'. Those who stand to gain from the 'embourgeoisment' of football are the large, successful clubs in the larger cities.

As already noted, clubs can go out of business because there has been too rapid an increase in the number of clubs and the demand for the sport has been more than satisfied. The case of now defunct North American Soccer League is a case in point (Fig. 4.8). Two British examples illustrate how in such cases the spatial margins at which the sport is viable contract and hence reduce the distribution of the sport over geographic space. Speedway racing in the 1950s is our first example. In the immediate post-war years speedway experienced a rapid rise in popularity. Towns throughout the UK adopted speedway racing teams; clubs were found from Cornwall to Scotland. By the 1950s speedway was becoming increasingly dominated by the Wimbledon team and results got rather predictable. Because uncertainty of outcome is regarded (by some economists) as essential in maintaining attendances at professional sports, interest in speedway began to decline in the mid-1950s. By 1957 the number of clubs had more than halved and the craze for speedway had passed its peak. But the clubs which closed down were not randomly located; they tended to be geographically peripheral and in small towns. As Fig. 4.12 shows, the spatial margins to viability had contracted and what speedway remained was concentrated in the areas of greatest economic potential in the national space economy.

A not dissimilar picture is found in the case of rugby league in Britain, although in this case the spatial margins have ebbed and flowed somewhat. Until about 1980 the spatial margins to viability had been contracting since the 1930s. The sport, introduced unsuccessfully to South Wales, Birmingham, Greater London and the north-east, seemed incapable of survival outside its cultural heartland in the north of England. Economic constraints to the inter-war expansion of the sport included long distance travelling south for the majority of the clubs and intervening sporting opportunities in the areas in which it was being promoted. During the 1980s there has been another attempt to expand the geographical margins of the sport into London (the Fulham club closed down in 1986), South Wales, the East Midlands and the *terra incognita* of north Kent (the former Maidstone club quickly relocated at Southend in Essex).

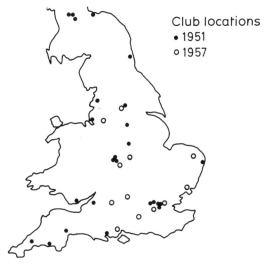

Club locations
- 1951
o 1957

Fig. 4.12 Changing spatial margins to profitability in the British speedway industry during the 1950s. (Source: Bale[12].)

Decline and demise can be brought about also by the desire of club owners to switch their investment from sport to alternative, more profitable, land uses. If a new location is not found the club either merges with another or goes out of business. This form of asset stripping involves not the sale of players but the rejection of the sport altogether. The situation is most likely to arise when sports clubs are located at prestigious inner city sites from which alternative land uses are vastly more profitable. In London a crisis currently exists for the survival of several clubs which are faced by merger, which, in effect, means closure. The single borough of Fulham and Hammersmith possesses three professional soccer clubs, Chelsea, Fulham and Queens Park Rangers, whose sites are basically all owned by one property company. The commercial logic is to develop the sites and merge, or relocate the clubs. However, when the merger of Fulham and Queens Park Rangers was seriously proposed in early 1987, with a view to developing expensive residential accommodation on Fulham's riverside site (valued at over £20 million) an alliance of local supporters' groups, the Football Association, Members of Parliament and other lobbyists succeeded in preventing (temporarily?) such a move. However, the signs are clear; just as we have seen the decline of clubs in the north of England we may be witnessing pressure for decline and closure of clubs in the metropolis – but for different reasons.

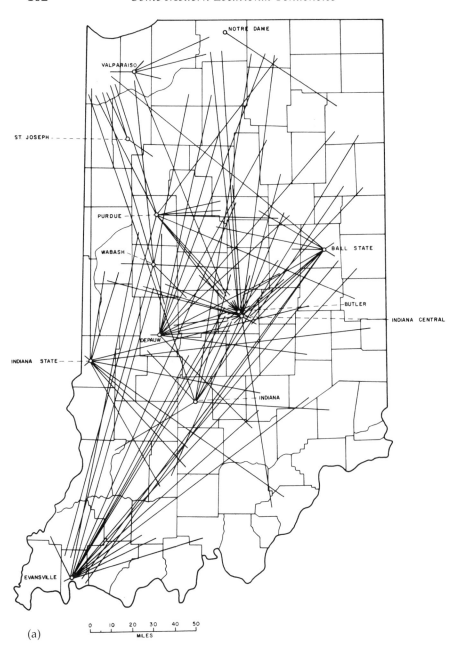

(a)

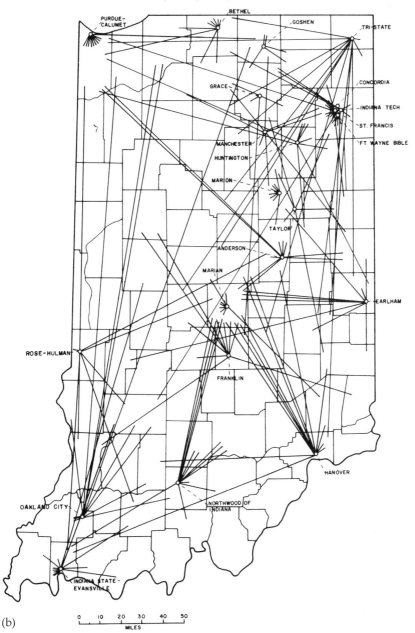

(b)

Fig. 4.13 Basketball recruiting in Indiana. (a) In-state recruiting of collegiate basketball player by NCAA institutions in Indiana, 1971–2. (b) In-state recruiting of collegiate basketball players by NAIA institutions in Indiana, 1971–2. (One line indicates the migratory route of one player from his home county.) (Source: reference[14], pp. 239–40.)

4.6 WIDENING MARGINS OF RECRUITMENT

The final manifestation of growing rationality in the spatial organization of sport is the more systematized methods used by sporting organizations (clubs and colleges) to recruit superior talent. A basic characteristic of folk games and early sport was their localness. Teams were mainly made of players from the neighbourhood of the club. Indeed, in folk games ascription (i.e. being a member of a village or town) was more important in qualifying for membership than was the achievement criterion, now a universal characteristic of modern sport. As seriousness, increased competitiveness and professionalism spread into sport, the catchment areas from which clubs drew their players increased.

Within individual countries the spatial margins of recruitment vary according to the resources of the various clubs or, in the USA, colleges. For example, in Britain the giant soccer clubs have the world as their recruiting oyster; clubs languishing in the lower reaches of the Fourth Division, on the other hand, tend to rely on local talent*. The same is true in the USA where big-time sports colleges out-recruit in a spatial sense, the smaller colleges. This is illustrated in Fig. 4.13, where the in-state recruiting of college basketball players by NCAA institutions in Indiana is compared with the pattern of recruiting by the generally smaller NAIA institutions.

Clubs in areas which produce an insufficient number of players to meet their own needs make do by recruiting from elsewhere. This tendency has existed for many years. For example, the English south coast football team, Brighton and Hove Albion, imported what amounted to an entire team from Dundee in Scotland when they were formed in 1900[34]. Indeed, Scotland has long been a source of soccer talent for English clubs, over 1600 Scottish born players having been lured south between 1946 and 1981[35].

In Europe and North America the importation of players from outside the local area has in no way appeared to alienate support. As Korr[36] has put it, in the context of the early days of the London soccer club, West Ham United, 'what the community wanted was not local representation on the field, but the chance to participate in a vicarious battle that would end in victory for their "gladiator" '[35]. Yet there is always a danger in assuming that such perspectives transcend all national boundaries. In Australian Rules football, for example, players have traditionally tended to be 'local representatives' and recent importation of non-local players to some clubs has resulted in objections being raised by supporters.

The intensification of professionalism (either implicit or explicit) and commercialism in sport, along with improved national and international

* See, for example, reference [12], p. 39.

modes of communication and a relaxation in restrictions on the international movement of sportsmen and women, has meant that in several sports the spatial margins of recruitment embrace almost the entire world. This tendency can be illustrated with several examples.

The number of foreign players in British soccer increased during the 1970s and 1980s following the lifting of restrictions on the international movement of labour within the EEC. At the same time the American soccer industry attracted many Europeans. In 1986 about 4% of English league professionals had, at some time in their careers, played for foreign clubs. Those who went to North America to play in the erstwhile North American Soccer League often obtained inflated salaries despite being near the end of their careers. Younger players have been lured by the lire to Italy. Players from countries such as Denmark, where the professional game is relatively poorly developed, have been attracted to Germany, Italy, France and England and South American players have also been recruited by the European clubs. The extent of global recruiting in soccer can be clearly illustrated by the composition of some of the national squads playing in the finals of the 1986 World Cup. In the cases of Denmark, Uraguay, Canada and Algeria, over 40% of their players were engaged with foreign clubs at the time of the competition.

In the USA a substantial number of foreign recruits have been drafted to both professional and college sports, the numbers increasing dramatically since the 1950s. In the case of baseball, for example, 10% of the

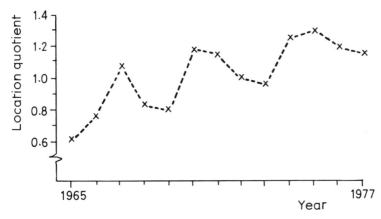

Fig. 4.14 Production trend for Latin American recruits to US baseball, 1965–77. Whereas the tendency was for recruits from Latin America to increase, that for Canada remained stable over the same period. The Canadian location quotient was always less than 0.3, (The location quotient shows the extent to which the area departs from the norm. Quotients of more than 1.0 would indicate 'over-representation' by the group concerned.) (Source: Rupert[37].)

14 000 first-year signings (1967–77) came from overseas, the major source nations being the Dominican Republic and Puerto Rico. Figure 4.14 shows the gradual increase in the supply of Latin American players to the US baseball scene. Of the 1200 or more major league players, 7.5% were foreigners[37].

Intercollegiate sports have also witnessed the increase in overseas recruiting[38]. In track and field, for example, virtually no foreign recruits featured in the USA track scene in the early 1950s. At the present time, however, over 5% of recruits in major colleges are foreign while over 12% of athletes in the USA 'top 50' are foreign collegians. The widening margin of recruitment in this sport is graphically illustrated by the fact that in the mid 1960s Africa provided only 4% of elite foreign track recruits; two decades later the respective figure was 30%, with Kenya alone supplying over 10%. As college sports in the USA become increasingly part of the entertainment business and the emphasis on winning becomes greater, so talent scouts have increased the spatial range over which they are prepared to recruit. Indeed, it may be actually cheaper to recruit overseas than to do so in the USA, given the right contacts or just good luck. A telephone call to Britain, for example, may be cheaper than scouring the whole of North America; in addition, out-of-state college fees are sometimes waived for foreigners, thus making their scholarships cheaper than those of in-state students. Although track and field is probably the most well-known of the college sports in which international recruiting takes place, similar trends have

Table 4.4 Estimated numbers of foreign student-athletes in NCAA Division I universities; six sports (men), 1987. Figures refer to numbers of all student-athletes who are foreign

Sport	*Foreign recruits*	
	Number	*Percent*
Basketball	156	3.5
Track and field	484	5.3
Swimming	260	6.2
Golf	222	6.7
Soccer	569	10.6
Tennis	537	16.0
	2228	7.1

(*Source:* Bale[39].)

occurred in a number of other sports, notably in tennis and soccer (Table 4.4). Even gridiron football has not been totally immune.

The growing internationalization of recruiting has not been without reaction from the host countries. For example, in US baseball, rules were imposed in the mid 1970s to restrict major league clubs from increasing their signings from the Caribbean by assigning a quota to each club based on its previous usage of foreign athletes[37]. In the case of English cricket, where in 1987 7.7% of the registered county players were not qualified to play for England, a limit of two foreign players per county is imposed, with only one being allowed to play in any one game. A similar situation may develop in France where a substantial number of foreigners have been playing with rugby clubs (Fig. 4.15) while in British ice hockey, long stocked with Canadians, each club is presently restricted to three foreign players.

In the USA colleges there have been frequent demands for a reduction, or even a ban on the recruiting of foreign student-athletes who have been perceived as competing at an unfair advantage over often younger American athletes and also taking away athletic scholarships from native Americans. The view that more mature recruits are at a competitive advantage over recently graduated high school students has frequently been aired. Attempts to reduce the amount of 'athletic eligibility' for athletes recruited over the age of twenty have been partially successful in reducing the flow of such migrants but at the 1986 NCAA track and field championships the contribution of foreigners had never had never been

Table 4.5 The foreign contribution to NCAA track and field championships (men) 1977–86

Year	Percentage of total points gained by foreigners	Number of foreign winners
1977	29.9	7
1978	26.3	5
1979	29.2	7
1980	27.9	6
1981	33.3	9
1982	34.6	8
1983	36.0	10
1984	27.5	5
1985	29.7	4
1986	38.7	6

(*Source: Track and Field News* (1986) **39**, 8, p. 58.)

French ration their imports

There are now 33 South Africans, 18 New Zealanders, and a total of 83 foreigners playing for the 80 teams in the top division of the French club championship. This is causing a stir across the Channel not just because of fears that some of the overseas players may be mercenaries but also because the presence of so many outsiders may discourage French clubs from nurturing their own local talent. Moves are now afoot to limit clubs to one foreign player each.

What is causing particular concern to the French authorities is that many of these foreign players are arriving in France in time to take part in only the second half of the club championship. The club championship is run on the basis of each of the ten clubs in a league playing each of the others home and away.

At the half-way stage, the fixtures of the first half of the championship season are reversed. There must be a temptation for clubs which have not done well in the first half of the event to import overseas players to reinforce their sides for the second half.

The president of the French Rugby Federation, Albert Ferrasse, is fully aware of the problems. "Last year we had a number of overseas players, but this year it has become an avalanche," he said. "To start with I am going to propose to my committee that clubs should be restricted to one foreign player each. If that does not work, we may have to say that no foreign player may play in the championship until he has been resident in France for a year."

David Frost

Fig. 4.15 The international movement of sports talent is not restricted to soccer, baseball and track and field, as this item from *The Guardian* (16 December 1986) clearly shows.

higher (Table 4.5). In England the Professional Footballers' Association has always had an ambivalent attitude towards foreign players, for the same kinds of reasons as some college coaches and athletes in the USA, i.e. that it takes work away from, and inhibits the development of, native talent. In such a situation there is clearly a conflict between players' freedom to move internationally and the survival of an increasingly scarce number of jobs[40].

A somewhat more sinister phenomenon has been the attempts by South African athletes to assume the nationality of foreign countries in order to be able to compete at the highest levels, given South Africa's exclusion from the world stage in many sports. The infamous Zola Budd case is the most well known but similar tactics have been adopted, successfully, by several other South African athletes, notably in tennis, golf and track and field, who have gained access to high level competition by obtaining athletic scholarships to the campuses of sports-oriented universities in the United States. Such is the pressure to succeed by individuals, academic institutions and nations.

4.7 CONCLUSIONS

In large part, modern sport is part of the entertainment industry. As profit and commercialization have become increasingly prevalent in Western sports, so sports clubs have engaged in a number of geographical readjustments. Clubs relocate at more profitable locations; success in sports shifts to the growth points in the national space economy; spatial margins of viability of sports clubs reflect growth and decline in regional economies and the desire for success induces clubs to widen their geographical areas of recruitment. It seems likely that sport will continue to adjust geographically in response to the increasing seriousness with which it is taken. This chapter has dealt with the locational implications of such a trend but given the increased significance of sport it would be unsurprising if it has not also had significant economic-geographical and landscape impacts. It is to these subjects that we turn in the next two chapters.

FURTHER READING

A detailed spatial analysis of modern sports has yet to be written but much of the economic geography of sports can be teased out of Roger Noll's edited work on *Government and the Sports Business*, Brookings Institute, Washington, DC, 1970. The spatial implications of *Baseball Economics and Public Policy* are well stated in the book of that title by Jesse W. Markham and Paul W. Teplitz, Lexington Books, Lexington, 1981. A detailed study of team movements in American baseball is found in James Quirk's An economic analysis of team movements in professional sports, *Law and Contemporary Problems*, **38**, 1973, pages 42–46.

The effects of city size and sports success is explored in Bruce Walker's The demand for professional league football and the success of football league teams; some city size effects, *Urban Studies*, **23**, 3, 1986, pages 209–219. A conceptual framework for studying international recruiting, with a case study of American college recruitment of foreign track and field athletes, is found in John Bale's international recruiting game; foreign student-athletes in American universities, in *Educational Society* (eds E. Bondi and H. Matthews), Croom Helm, London, 1988. Foreign recruitment in soccer and cricket is explored in different ways by Steve Redhead, You've really got a hold on me; footballers in the market, in *Off the Ball* (eds A. Tomlinson and G. Whannell), Pluto, London, 1986, pages 54–66 and David Lemmon, *Cricket Mercenaries*, Pavilion, London, 1986, respectively.

REFERENCES

1. Berry, B., Conkling, E. and Ray, M. (1976) *The Geography of Economic Systems*, Prentice Hall, Englewood Cliffs, NJ.
2. Ashworth, G. (1984) *Recreation and Tourism*, Bell and Hyman, London.
3. Quirk, J. (1973) An economic analysis of team movements in professional sports. *Law and Contemporary Problems*, **38**, 42–66.
4. Noll, R. (1974) Attendance and price setting, in *Government and the Sports Business*, Brookings Institute, Washington DC, pp. 115–57.
5. Aldini, C. (1978) A regression model for baseball franchise location forecasting; paper read at the annual meeting of the Association of American Geographers.
6. Gratton, C. and Taylor, P. (1985) *Sport and Recreation; An Economic Analysis*, E. and F. N. Spon, London.
7. Sloane, P. (1980) Sport in the market? The economic causes and consequences of the Parker revolution. *Hobart Paper*, **85**, Institute of Economic Affairs, London.
8. Wiseman, N. (1977) The economics of football. *Lloyds Bank Review*, **123**, 29–43.
9. Rivett, P. (1975) The structure of league football. *Operational Research Quarterly*, **26**, 801–12.
10. Toyne, P. (1974) *Recreation and Environment*, Macmillan, London.
11. Rimmer, P. and Johnston, R. (1967) Areas of community interest in Victoria as indicated by competitive sport. *Australian Geographer*, **10**, 311–13.
12. Bale, J. (1982) *Sport and Place*, Hurst, London.
13. Walford, R. (1983) The spread of first class cricket venues since 1945; a study in "colonial expansion", in *Geographical Perspectives on Sport* (eds J. Bale and C. Jenkins), Department of PE, Birmingham University, pp. 127–46.
14. Rooney, J. (1974) *A Geography of American Sport; from Cabin Creek to Anaheim*, Addison-Wesley, Reading, Mass.
15. Holt, R. (1981) *Sport and Society in Modern France*, Cambridge University Press, Cambridge, p. 101.
16. Rosentraub, M. and Nunn, S. (1978) Suburban city investment in professional sport. *American Behavioral Scientist*, **21**, 393–414.
17. Muller, P. (1981) *Contemporary Suburban America*, Prentice-Hall, Englewood Cliffs, NJ, p. 165.
18. Rosentraub, M. (1977) Financial incentives, locational decision making and professional sports; the case of the Texas Ranger baseball network and the city of Arlington, Texas, in *Financing Local Government; New Approaches to Old Problems* (ed. M. Rosentraub), Western Social Sciences Association, Fort Collins, Col.
19. Bishop, J. and Booth, R. (1974) People's images of Chelsea Football Club, *Working Paper*, **10**, Architectural Psychology Research Unit.
20. Walker, B. (1986) The demand for professional football and the success of football league teams; some city size effects. *Urban Studies*, **23**, 209–20.
21. Ingham, A. and Hardy S. (1984) Sport; structuration, subjugation and hegemony. *Theory, Culture and Society*, **2**, 85–103.
22. Noll, R. (ed.) (1974) *Government and the Sports Business*, Brookings Institute, Washington DC.
23. Kidd, B. (1970) Canada's national sport, in *The Americanization of Canada* (ed. I. Lumsden), University of Toronto Press, Toronto, pp. 257–74.

24. Davis, L. and Quirk, J. (1975) Tax write offs and the value of sports teams, in *Government and the Sports Business* (ed. R. Noll), Brookings Institute, Washington, DC, pp. 263–75.
25. Political and Economic Planning (PEP) (1966) The football industry. *Planning,* **32**, 496.
26. Tomlinson, R. (1986) A geography of flat racing in Great Britain. *Geography,* **71**, 228–39.
27. Goodey, B., Guttridge, I. and Smales, L. (1986) Indicado da tensao espacial. *Arquitetuia Urbanismo,* **2**, 78–83.
28. Gaspar, J., Honario, F., Honario, J. and Simoes, J. (1981) O futebol; mobiliade geografica e social, in *Proceedings,* HISPA Conference, Lisbon, pp 143–57
29. Gaspar, J., Honario, F., Honario, J. and Simoes, J. (1982) Transformacoes recentes na geografia do futebol en Portugal. *Finisterra,* **17**, 34, 301–24.
30. Ingham, A., Howell, J. and Schilperoort, T. (1987) Professional sports and community: a review and exegesis. *Exercise and Sport Science Review,* **15**, 427–65.
31. Williams, G. (1983) From grand slam to grand slump; economy, society and rugby football in Wales during the depression. *The Welsh History Review,* **11**, 338–57.
32. Stepney, P. (1983) Towards a politics of football; the case of Bradford Park Avenue, in *Explorations in Football Culture* (ed. A. Tomlinson), Brighton Polytechnic.
33. Short, G. (1974) Sport and economic growth in the Windsor area, 1919–1939, in *Proceedings from the Third Canadian Symposium on History of Sport and Physical Education* (ed. L. Young), Dalhousie University, Halifax.
34. Lowerson, J. and Myerscough, J. (1977) *Time to Spare in Victorian England,* Harvester, Hassocks.
35. Lay, D. (1984) *The Migration of Scottish Footballers to the English Football League,* undergraduate dissertation (unpublished), Southampton University.
36. Korr, C. (1978) West Ham United Football Club and the beginnings of professional football in east London, 1895–1914. *Journal of Contemporary History,* **13**, 211–32.
37. Rupert, M. (1980) *A Geographic Analysis of Professional Baseball's First Year Signings, 1965–1977,* master's dissertation (unpublished), Oklahoma State University.
38. Bale, J. (1987) The muscle drain; foreign student-athletes in American universities. *Sport Place,* **1**, 2.
39. Bale, J. (1988) The international recruiting game (unpublished paper).
40. Redhead, S. (1986) You've really got a hold on me; footballers in the market, in *Off The Ball* (ed. A. Tomlinson and G. Whannell), Pluto Press, London, pp. 54–66.

Chapter 5

ECONOMIC GEOGRAPHICAL IMPACTS

Having considered some locational tendencies of modern sports we now consider the economic impact such locations and movements have on the communities and landscapes on which they take place. Such impacts are not necessarily positive; indeed, one of the most publicized spin-offs of sports events is the classic negative 'externality' of football hooliganism. In this chapter the geographical impacts, positive and negative, are described and mapped and where possible solutions to the negative impacts are considered. We also return to some of the ideas discussed in the previous chapter in our consideration of catchment areas of fans or 'fandoms'. In several respects this chapter adopts a more welfare-oriented approach to sports geography than previously as we observe that what might be sporting 'goods' for some people may be 'bads' for others.

5.1 SPIN-OFFS AND MULTIPLIERS

In an age of relatively easy inter-regional and international travel, sports events are able to generate substantial recurrent gatherings of peoples to what Gottman[1] calls 'collective rituals'. The historical religious pilgrimages have been replaced by modern international flows to such rites as the Olympic Games, the World Cup, national championships, cup finals and even smaller events. Gottman believes that such sporting occasions are among 'the important components of the centrality of large cities' the mega-structures which often contain them being not only symbolic of, and contributing to, the life and personality of places but, more importantly from an economic perspective, enlarging the movement of transients between cities and hence contributing to the wealth and economic dominance of the big city. Such focal points for major sports events are not restricted to the Occident or the 'developed' world.

Fig. 5.1 Although smaller than that of many small colleges in the USA, the National Stadium of Fiji is a symbol of nationhood and an assertion of modernity.

Indeed, the desire of the 'Third World' to host major sports events is already beginning to be satisfied. Rio de Janeiro possesses the largest stadium in the world, Mexico City has hosted an Olympic Games and two World Cup competitions, and Kingston (Jamaica) has accommodated the Commonwealth Games. Almost every Third World capital, from Suva to Santiago, houses the National Stadium, without which it would not be a real capital and without which it cannot assert its place in the world of international sport(Fig. 5.1).

Stadium construction in many modern cities results therefore, from more than simply a desire to improve facilities for spectator sports. Lipsitz[2] argues that the Dodger Stadium in Los Angeles, for example, drew attention to the city's transition from a regional centre to a national metropolis while the Houston Astrodome, built as an anchor for a hotel and convention centre complex, proved sufficiently newsworthy to advertise the growth of that city. Likewise the superdrome in New Orleans set the stage for a tourist-based growth programme for the city's downtown area.

To accommodate the transients who move to sporting rituals the city needs to supply transport, lodgings, and many other services. Existing businesses usually increase their takings from sports events; employment is created for the construction of stadiums and other facilities; travel agents set themselves up in business to specialize in sports tourism. The movements which are generated by sports events tend to contradict the view that the telephone and television have diminished the desire for geographical interaction.

Consider the economic benefits of, say, football to a large urban area. At the stadium itself, spectators spend money on tickets, concessions of various kinds, (e.g. food, rosettes, programmes) and parking. In addition, and in the USA in particular, a visit to a football game is often part of a visit to a city. Hence, lodgings, fuel for vehicles, shopping, outside-stadium parking, taxis, chartered buses, public buses and eating are all part of the expenditure generated by sport. Near British soccer grounds, pubs and other retail outlets may increase their revenue by as much as 500% on match days (though as we shall see later, some actually lose money on such occasions).

Even quite small sporting events can generate substantial amounts of revenue for the communities within which they are located. If these take place annually they become regular injections of income for the local economic system. Take, for example, a relatively modest event which occurs annually in Peterborough, Ontario, in Canada. The Peterborough Church League Atom Hockey Tournament has a twenty-three year history and is probably the largest recurrent sporting event in the Peterborough community. Today it attracts 3000 players, coaches, and spectators for four days of competitive ice hockey and associated social activities. Because competitors come from all over Ontario, parts of Quebec and the north-eastern USA, a considerable amount of money is

Table 5.1 Summary of total expenditure for the Peterborough Church League Atom Hockey Tournament, 1982

Distant teams	$130 637
Local teams	11 374
Spectators	2 704
Players' and spectators' children	8 481
Households supplying billets	2 666
Tournament team entry forms	9 303
	$165 165

(*Source:* Marsh[3].)

spent on things like accommodation, meals, parking, gasoline, drink and souvenirs. In 1982 over $165 000 was spent in these ways (Table 5.1).

Two further examples illustrate the impact of bigger sports events on local economies. Football at the University of Wisconsin at Madison is typical of American big-time college sports. The Greater Madison Chamber of Commerce attempted to establish the expenditure in Dane County by out-county football fans who came to watch Wisconsin games during the six weekends of football activity in 1975. Parents of students (who may have come to Dane anyway) were excluded but it was estimated that football visitors alone spent $4 680 000 during the period concerned. Restaurants and bars were the major beneficiaries of this spending (Table 5.2) but owners of many other retail outlets gained also. If locals and parent visitors were included the direct impact of football was estimated at a staggering $6 315 000. It will be clear from Table. 5.2 that payments to various university bodies (resulting from such things as the sale of programmes) were excluded. It was estimated that if indirect impacts were included the total would exceed $13 million!

A series of more detailed analyses have been undertaken into the expenditures generated by the Atlanta Falcons football team for the seasons 1966, 1972 and 1984. Attending Falcons' home games over 321 000 times in 1984, fans introduced nearly $12 million into the city's economic system. The nature of this expenditure is shown in Table 5.3.

Table 5.2 Estimated expenditure by non-parent football visitors to Dane County, Wisconsin, 1975

Object of expenditure	Amount
Restaurants and bars	$1 862 000
Apparel stores	871 000
Lodging places	677 000
Auto sales and service	519 000
General merchandise stores	387 000
Miscellaneous retail stores	120 000
Local government	97 000
Amusement places	46 000
Transportation services	39 000
Local households	25 000
Personal and business services	23 000
Furniture and appliance stores	12 000
Total	4 680 000

(*Source:* Cady[4].)

Table 5.3 Summary of expenditures by Atlanta Falcons' fans and visitors, 1984

Object of expenditures	Source of expenditures (thousands of dollars)				
	Local fans	Out-of-town fans	Teams	Visiting Press	Total
At Atlanta Stadium:					
Tickets	5040	2160	–	–	7200
Concessions	658	282	–	–	940
Parking	168	82	–	–	250
Food and drink	453	1092	32	30	1607
Other entertainment	–	322	6	9	337
Lodging	–	750	74	64	888
Gasoline	110	272	–	–	382
Shopping	–	239	–	–	239
Parking	37	15	–	–	52
Buses	47	11	16	–	74
Taxi	–	–	–	9	9
Total	6513	5225	128	112	11 978
Totals:					
Tickets (Falcons)	5040	2160	–	–	7200
At Atlanta Stadium	826	364	–	–	1190
In Atlanta	647	2701	128	112	3588
Total	6513	5225	128	112	11 978

(*Source:* Schaffer and Davidson, [5])

It is possible, of course, that money spent by local fans would have been spent in Atlanta anyway but the 96 000 out-of-town fans can be regarded as bringing new money into the Atlanta economic system. Furthermore, visiting press and visiting teams will spend money in the city in a variety of ways. In addition to the expenditures shown in Table 5.3 we must include the purchases and payments made by the Falcons football outfit itself. For many services an overwhelming proportion of expenditures and payments is made locally (e.g. transportation, construction, eating and drinking, employee payments) and in 1984 the total local expenditures made by the Falcons exceeded $15 051 000. However, this is not the end of the story because all this money is in turn spent by those who receive it and, in turn, by those who receive it from them so that the initial injection of money into the system is increased by a multiplier effect. The precise value of the multiplier will depend on the proportion of any increment of additional income spent in the local system – allowances being made for 'leakages' out of the local economy. When the multiplier works its way through the Atlanta system, Schaffer and Davidson[5] estimated that the extra money brought into Atlanta by the Falcons in 1984 amounted to $24.7 million. Of this, $17.3 million was spent locally and stimulated economic activity valued at $37.1 million. All this activity resulted in $16 million in incomes to local households while the local and state governments obtained revenues which together exceeded $1.6 million. If the multiplier applied to a seventeen year period of their presence in Atlanta, the $291 million spent by the Falcons and out-of-town fans stimulated $640.6 million in revenues and incomes to businesses, households and local governments.

In addition to the revenues and incomes generated by sports, the local community will be involved inevitably in expenditure to attract and provide for those attending sports events. The ratio between revenue and expenditure is therefore of importance. Such ratios will vary considerably depending on the extent to which fans make use of various local facilities. For example, when ratios of revenues to expenditures were calculated for the city of San Diego in California it was found that the city received 3.36 times more than it spent on sports visitors if they enjoyed hotel accommodation. However, as Table. 5.4 shows, this varied considerably if other forms of accommodation were used. In a sense, of course, the accommodation is a surrogate for income and the city naturally earns less if sports spectators stay at camp sites or are day trippers.

Professional sports teams can have a rather less obvious impact on the local economies of which they are part. The success of the English football club, Nottingham Forest, in the 1978/9 European Cup brought an estimated £880 000 of new business to the city's industries as a result of a promotional campaign running alongside the club's fixtures*.

Table 5.4 Revenue/expenditure ratios for non-residents attending spectator sports in San Diego, California

Accommodation used	Revenue/expenditure ratio
Hotel/motel	3.36
Rented cottage	2.50
Day trip	1.66
Campground	1.00

(Based on Murphy[6].)

* Quoted in Hoare[7].

In addition to the quantifiable benefits brought to cities through sports we have already noted that local pride and morale are boosted, sometimes merely through the presence – let alone the success – of sports clubs (see Section 2.3.1). In addition, a city itself obtains increasing publicity (what amounts to free advertising) through a professional sports club's media coverage. Other economic benefits include (a) the possible generation of extra employment, (b) new recreational opportunities for local residents, especially if going to a sports event replaces less desireable activities, and (c) the possible generation of interests in sports among young people[8].

We should not underestimate these external benefits of sports simply because we cannot quantify them. Many cities feel that they are not in the 'first division' or the 'big league' unless they have a professional sports team or (in America) a public stadium. As *The Economist* newspaper* put it in relation to the possibility of the Minnesota Twins baseball outfit leaving Minneapolis, 'a publicly owned domed stadium is a symbol of municipal machismo'. Faced with the possible loss of the team, unsold tickets for home games were bought up by 'phantom ticket holders' made up of civic-minded citizens, city councillors and local businesses – even though the seats themselves were never filled!

The presence of really major sporting events can have a huge impact on entire regions. The Olympic Games, for example, generate vast flows of international tourist traffic which stimulate the need for new hotels, parks, roads and various other aspects of the infrastructure. For the Munich Olympics of 1972 the Federal German government, the State of Bavaria and the city of Munich pooled enough investment to produce a new mass transportation system for the entire region, subsequently inducing the growth of population through migration into the region[9]. The French newspaper *Le Monde* noted in 1971 that:

> Munich lacked a stadium capable of seating 80,000 people and a cycling stadium always comes in useful. As for the underground system, every city dreams of having one and Munich would certainly have had to develop its transport system in the next decade. The new motorways had been planned for years . . . In short the Olympics enabled the Bavarian capital to jump ten years ahead in its development programme, and at less expense. For, since the Games were considered a matter of national interest, the federal state undertook 50 per cent of the investments and the Bavarian state financed another 25 per cent, leaving only a quarter of the bill to be met by the city itself. . . . The facilities will be put to good use after the Games. The stadium will be used for the 1974 World Cup Finals, the bungalows of the Olympic village will become university residences and the blocks of flats will be inhabited, indeed 60 per cent of them are already sold.

* Quoted in *The Economist*, 16 June 1984, p. 35.

In Brisbane the 1982 Commonwealth Games produced enough publicity for the city to attract housing and office development[11] while the 1968 Winter Olympics at Grenoble had the effect of promoting winter sports and tourism in the Alps[10]. They not only induce massive tourist flows at the time of their occurrence but a permanent expansion of tourist business may also have been generated by these special events[12]. At the level of the Olympics the expenditure before the event takes place runs into tens of millions. Even the promotion of the city during the bidding stage can cost around £7 million, if Birmingham's abortive bid for the 1992 Olympics was typical. If the city had succeeded in its bid it was estimated that the cost would have totalled £523.9 million between 1985 and 1993 – creating much needed employment in a recession-ravaged conurbation. At the same time the Birmingham boosters reckoned that the Games would generate an estimated £689 million*.

Such events involve regional, national and international bodies in the course of their organization. Such bodies, are, in effect, interest groups, each group being made up of 'actors' whose motives may differ. The different perspectives held by each group can have locational implications and can lead to public controversy and conflict. For example, in the planning of downhill events in the winter Olympics, the need for

Table 5.5 Key 'actors' involved in the development of the downhill events for the winter Olympics, 1988

Actors	Involvement
Calgary Olympic Development Association	Responsible to International Olympic Committee for organising Games, including selection of venues
International Ski Federation	Responsible for deciding if proposed sites meet Olympic standards
The Provincial Government	Control of the terms and conditions in which ski areas will be developed' also closely involved with the promotion of the Olympics
Private sector	Expected to undertake the development and operation of ski facilities; several consortia in active contention for the site of the Games
Several other private/public sector interest groups	Lobbying or otherwise working towards influencing the outcome of the selection process

(Based on Sadler[13].)

* I am grateful to Steve Thomas for these data.

(a)

(b)

Fig. 5.2 The 1984 Olympic Games mascot as seen (a) officially, in Los Angeles, and (b) by *Sovietsky Sport*, official organ of the USSR's Ministry of Sport. (Source: *The Sunday Times*, 21 November 1982.)

proposed sites to meet Olympic standards may conflict with the conservation or development needs of local or regional government or other interest groups. The infrastructure required for the development of such events is determined by several groups. Those involved following the selection of Calgary, Alberta, for the 1988 Winter Olympics are shown in Table 5.5. Interest groups, each with their own values and attitudes, are also principal actors at the national and local scale. In British soccer, local community groups, football supporters' clubs, local political parties and major developers are each pitched against each other when a club is faced with closure or merger. Analogous interest groups are evident in similar situations in North America and in some cases such sports developments serve to satisfy both the political ambitions of local mayors and city governments, and the economic ambitions of real estate and property developers.

A radical view of events such as The Olympics is to see them as being dominated by economics, profit and multi-national corporations. How such events are perceived will be dependent on ideological factors (Fig. 5.2).

Some sports facilities, designed ostensibly for special events such as the Olympic Games or World Cup, or simply for general use can develop over time, a sufficient mystique to become tourist attractions in their own right. They can continue in their primary roles as sporting venues but can also generate additional revenue as tourist foci. In some cases such revenue is generated in an 'off season' when the venue is not being used for sport; in other cases tours and visits are arranged during the sports season on non-game days. Wembley Stadium in London, for example, offers guided tours; the Holmenkollen ski jump in Oslo (see Fig. 6.6) offers tours by lift to the top of the ski jump to view Oslo and the land beyond, as well as having an excellent ski museum and memorabilia outlet as part of a ski complex. Other examples of sports venues which have become part of the tourist itinerary include the Berlin Olympic stadium, the Wimbledon tennis complex and the Athens Olympic stadium for the 1896 games.

Although it is possible to demonstrate that sport does indeed contribute to the urban economy in a significant way, the question of whether the benefits of successfully attracting a professional club to a new location outweigh the costs of getting the club there remains problematic. For example, Rosentraub[14] examined the costs and benefits of moving the Texas Ranger baseball network to the city of Arlington, located between the boom cities of Dallas and Fort Worth in Texas. A major initial cost item was the stadium, together with the necessary parking and roadways. In addition there was the need to pay compensation to the minor league team that already existed there and to purchase the broadcast rights of the Rangers' games. Finally, there would be the ongoing interest payments on stadium bonds. In order to attract the Rangers from Washington (where they had been the Senators) to Arlington, Rosentraub estimated that the total cost involved was at least $44 million over a thirty-year period. The revenue projected over the same period would come from the media networks, food and drink sales, parking, gate receipts, etc. This amount was estimated at $22 million – about half the cost estimate. The financial commitments which brought the Rangers from Washington to Texas amounted to about $36 per family in Arlington per annum. This analysis ignored the kinds of multiplier effects examined earlier for a single year for the Atlanta Falcons' football games, and the psychic benefits which virtually defy quantitative measurement. Nevertheless, the cost to Arlington's local government – and hence the local taxpayer – of attracting a professional sports franchise was substantial, though somewhat less than Seattle's $60 million facility and New York's $100 million expenditure to keep the Yankees there.

The suburbanization of much sporting activity in North America (which was noted in Chapter 4) has had a major influence on surrounding land use and traffic systems. Suburban stadium development has encouraged sprawl and polynucleation and requires massive car parking facilities in order to operate efficiently in a car-oriented society. At the same time the presence of suburban sports development has hindered the revival of the inner city.

It could be argued that stadium construction in the late twentieth century in the American central city has had an even greater landscape impact. Some have argued that the resurgence of downtown St Louis has

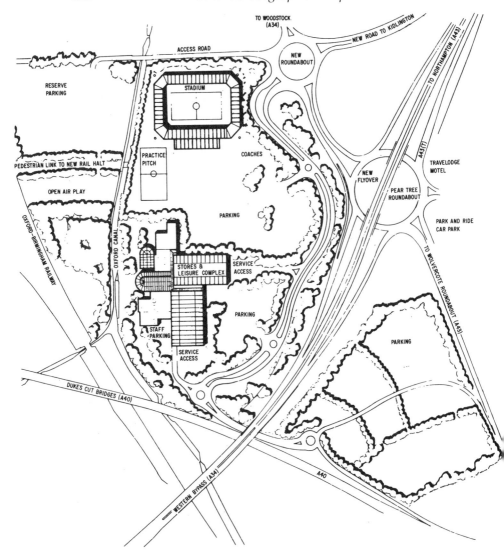

Fig. 5.3 Plan for a proposed multi-purpose retail and sports complex to be sited on the northern edge of the English city of Oxford. (Source: *Oxford Star*, 3 July 1986.)

been stimulated by the construction of the Busch Stadium. Its creation, along with parking, stores and restaurants, has replaced ramshackle buildings and marginal business establishments. Central business district (CBD) oriented sports facilities may make an important contribution to the urban tax base since the increased revenues from sport and its associated land uses help to offset the loss of inner city tax revenue resulting from the suburbanization of activities such as offices and manufacturing and of middle and upper income residents[15, 16].

An alternative view of such inner city sports complexes are that they are extravagant examples of urban monumentalism and greed. For example, the Busch Stadium probably did more for the Anheuser-Busch brewing company (who own the St Louis Cardinals baseball team) than for the people of St Louis; no slum housing was cleared or new residences built accompanying the construction of the stadium[2]. Likewise the 1976 loss-making Montreal Olympics were taking place at the same time as the largest stock of slum housing in Canada and the continued discharge of untreated effluent into the St Lawrence River were being ignored[17]. In Britain suburban and inner city redevelopments along such lines are but twinkles in the planners' eyes. This is not to say that no scenarios have been drawn up. A massive suburban sports complex for Leicester included a modern soccer stadium for Leicester City FC while in central Wolverhampton proposals which would transform the urban landscape with Molineux Stadium at it's centre have been mooted. It remains to be seen if Britain will follow the North American model; the blueprints have, however, already been drawn (Fig. 5.3).

5.2 FANDOMS

The physical artifacts which sport has given to the landscape are obvious impacts which are there for all to see; in many cases they will remain as permanent features of the landscape. However, many of sport's contributions to the landscape are temporary or irregular in nature but do, nevertheless, have tremendous effects on both people and places. This section deals with the spectator journeys to sports events which produce flows of humanity reaching peak intensity as the site of the sporting action approaches. The area over which a team draws its support is called a fan region or fandom, the size of which will vary from club to club. In general, however, three factors may be said to be of prime importance: first, as we saw in Chapter 4, the size of the city in which it is located; secondly, the existing quality of the club's performance since supporters are somewhat responsive to the win/loss record of their team; and thirdly the quality of the opposition. The fandom over which a club exerts its influence may be doubled during a period of a week if its opponents change from being a bottom to a top of division club.

Other factors affecting attendances include local intervening sporting, and other, opportunities, the nature of the facilities at the ground, and the weather[18]. When investigated empirically, the fan region can vary in size according to the method of delimitation which is adopted. For

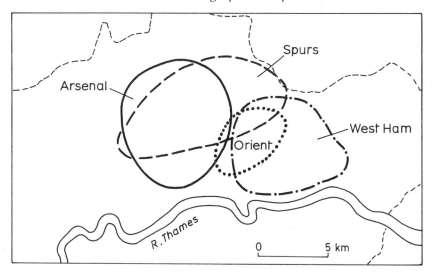

Fig. 5.4 Fandoms of North London football clubs based on interviewers with a hundred home supporters and plotting the homes of fans who said they would be likely to attend a majority of home matches. (Source: Thornes[18].)

example, the fandoms shown in Fig. 5.4 are based on what might be termed a sample of 'hard core' supporters who said that they would be likely to attend a majority of home matches. Other surveys, using a sample of all spectators at a given home match, reveal larger fan regions. For example, Fig. 5.5 indicates the distance of the journey to spectate for the London club, Chelsea FC, in the early 1970s[19]. This not only shows the declining intensity of movement away from the stadium (i.e. the distance decay curve to which we alluded in the previous chapter) but also an average distance of travel of over 18 miles. This is certainly somewhat less than that for top-flight USA pro football if the data generated by the aforementioned survey of the Atlanta Braves is typical. In 1984 local fans alone had an average journey-to-spectate distance of 18 miles and one quarter of all fans came from outside the greater Atlanta area. Again, it is worth reminding ourselves that given a spatial elasticity of demand for sport, this figure will vary somewhat from game to game. Also, the precise slope of the distance decay curve will be affected by the same kinds of factors influencing the spatial extent of the fandom.

It is therefore within the fandom that periodic landscape impacts are felt in the form of considerable movements of people across geographic space. However, in the 1980s support for a sports team does not necessarily involve any physical movement from home to stadium. The game can be brought to the home by means of television and in the USA, where live games are the norm, the size of the fan region is more a

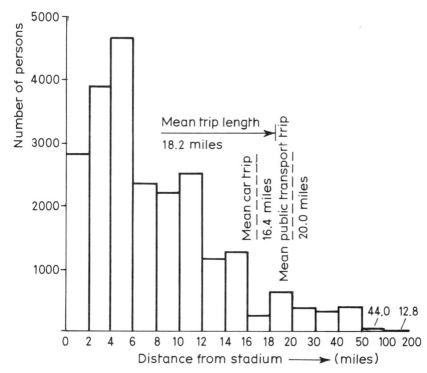

Fig. 5.5 The journey to spectate at Stamford Bridge, home of London's Chelsea Football Club, on 27 March 1971. (Source: Saunders[19].)

function of the spatial extent of television penetration of the team's games. Maynard Weston Dow[20], a geographer at Plymouth State College in New Hampshire, has mapped the spatial extent of the fandom of the Boston Red Sox baseball team by utilizing radio and television data.

The areas enclosed by the contours in Fig. 5.6 indicate that the cores of Red Sox fandom extend beyond the Canadian border. The value of each contour is defined as 'potential viewer games', i.e. the number of viewer game opportunities (viewers × games) that are possible within each contour. There is clearly a hierarchy of fandoms. Boston's core is three times that of Springfield's and fifteen times that of Portland and Burlington. Overall, Dow estimated that at least 22% of the population of New England were rabid Red Sox fans with others outside the state supporting the team as well as an unknown number who witnessed games via cable television.

Such an impact of sport over geographic space provides a benefit to those living within the fandom, especially if they are Red Sox fans. If they are not their accessibility does not provide any disadvantage – they do not

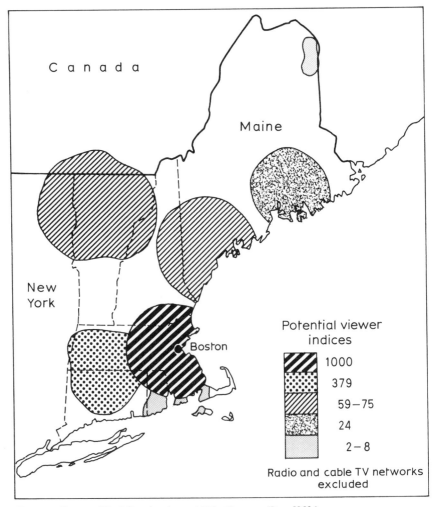

Fig. 5.6 Cores of Red Sox fandom, 1978. (Source: Dow[20].)

have to consume baseball (unlike those who might live in proximity to the stadium). Fans have accessibility to the sport without having to incur excess costs in travelling to see it. Even if they did go physically to the stadium they are at an obvious geographic advantage over Red Sox fans living in, say California, or indeed, much of New York state.

Some sports clubs are supported nationally, even internationally. When Manchester United soccer team play their matches, supporters from all over the UK converge in order to lend support. In the USA the support for the New York Yankees and Los Angeles Dodgers baseball teams reaches around 50% of the college population in parts of far away

The Grand Prix promoter's threat

For many of the people who were skeptical about St. Petersburg's first Grand Prix, the road race was an exciting surprise. Over three days, it brought more than 100,000 people to a downtown often aptly described as sleepy. It enlivened the city's image. It brought extra business to some, unfortunately not all, downtown merchants.

Not everything went smoothly, of course. Some businesses were damaged by the fences and loss of parking. Some residents along the race course were inconvenienced. Admission tickets were overpriced. On the whole, however, it was a fun weekend for thousands of street racing fans and many who were converted.

But St. Petersburg's first taste of life in the fast lane may be its last – if you believe Grand Prix president Harold J. Kelley Jr.'s threat: There will be no second St. Petersburg Grand Prix unless the city agrees to pay for all city services for the race.

Kelly's remark Monday was in response to City Manager Robert D. Obering's recommendation that the city provide free to the race up to $125,000 in police protection, fire protection and other services. Kelly said that is not enough, insisting that the city pick up the entire tab for these services – if the Grand Prix is to continue. Otherwise, he said, some potential investors will not help finance the race. (The Grand Prix was charged $223,000 last year for city services, but Obering expects that cost to decrease to $125,000 this year because city officials have a better idea of what is needed based on the inaugural race.)

Obering also has recommended that the city sign a five-year contract with the Grand Prix organizers, with an option for five more years. Kelly also objects to that arrangement; he wants a 15-year contract.

The City Council ought to approve Obering's recommendations Thursday because they are fair and reasonable. Other cities provide free services for Grand Prix events, and St. Petersburg already provides them to established community events such as the Festival of States. But Obering is right in insisting that there be some limit to the city's contribution.

To win the City Council's approval of the race, the Grand Prix promoters initially assured the council that the event would pay its own way and cost the city nothing. However, the promoters lost $500,000 running the first race and asked the city last December to bail them out of their financial plight by staking them up to $2-million. City officials wisely rejected that outrageous idea. But it hardly inspires confidence that the Grand Prix promoters would not somehow try to take advantage of a blank cheque from the city.

Obering also is right in calling for a five-year contract with an option for five more years. Many unforeseen things can happen in 15 years. The public waterfront is for everyone to enjoy in many different ways. An annual Grand Prix race may be one of those ways for many years to come. But it would not be wise to commit the use of public streets and property for a car race for the next decade and a half.

The City Council should back Obering's Grand Prix plan. If Kelly does not accept it, the council's only responsible response would be to bid the street race a regretful but firm farewell.

Vignette V The impact of auto racing on St Petersburg, Florida, has a number of implications as this leader article shows. (Source: *St Petersburg Times*, 2 April 1986.)

Texas and Tennessee respectively, the result not only of their playing success but also of their locations in media centres and the resulting large amount of media attention paid them[21].

The presence of fandoms which are separated from the home town of the team by many thousands of miles are a possibility given live television coverage of games. In Britain this has, until very recently, been vigorously resisted by the Football League, though it is commonplace for cricket and other sports. Should it become widespread in football, the national sport, it seems likely to create even more problems than already exist (see Section 4.4) for the small clubs who already find it difficult enough to survive without instantaneous transmission of games played by Liverpool or Manchester United.

We have seen, therefore, that fans and economic activities benefit from accessibility to sport. But some people incur negative impacts as a result, not of their accessibility, but because of their proximity to sport. Unlike the fans, such people are often consuming more sport than they would freely choose; they are victims of negative externalities of sport, a subject we consider in the next section.

5.3   NEGATIVE IMPACTS

The previous section showed how the presence of a sports team can bring benefits to the area, region or nation within which it is located. However, the multiplier effects which a new sports facility may bring to a locality will work backwards if the facility should decide to move elsewhere. Franchises are mobile but communities are not. When the Rams left Watts for Anaheim, the Los Angeles Coliseum lost $750 000 in rent since the Rams were the major tenant. Watts lost its income derived from the presence of the Rams and their fans. It also lost whatever civic pride the team provided. As Alan Ingham and his associates have put it, the Rams relocation served to 'materially and symbolically exacerbate the community deformation process'[22]. Losing a professional sports team may not only threaten the community's financial and psychological well-being but also serves to highlight how a facility with few alternative uses can become an economic (and local political) liability.

However, the most obvious negative impacts inflicted by sports are those which we might best describe as sport-induced nuisances. It is to these that we now turn and emphasize that such nuisances are essentially part of the journey to spectate, a subject which we consider first in our review of some of the negative impacts created by sports.

We have noted the significance of the spatial extent of the journey to spectate. It is this journey which directly and indirectly provides a major impact on urban areas. The journey to a football ground, in many

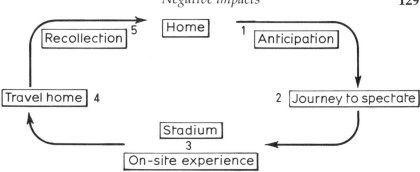

Fig. 5.7 The five stages of the sports spectator's experience. (Based on Clawson and Knetsh[23].)

countries often undertaken by car, is just one of what might be termed 'stages' in the spectating experience. Three of these – the journey to spectate, the in-stadium experience, and the journey home – possess the potential for major environmental impacts. The other two (Fig. 5.7), recollection and anticipation, are also important because it is upon these that the journey to the next game in part depends. If the recollection is satisfactory it is the best publicity a destination can achieve, for it promotes return visits[6]. Bad experiences, such as a boring game, a bad performance by the fan's team, harrassment from hooligans or police, or congestion and parking difficulties en route to the game may reduce the level of anticipation for a future visit. Such bad experiences are often cited as a partial contribution to the post war decline (from 77 million in 1949–50 to less than 20 million in 1985–6) in the numbers attending Football League matches in England.

Perhaps the major problem associated with sports facilities is the frequent inability of existing road networks to handle the traffic which they generate. Wepfer[16] notes that

CBD-located facilities tend to overtax the already-congested streets of the downtown and increase the off-street parking problem. CBD traffic congestion can be at least partially overcome, however, by special access ramps to the facility and by the construction of new parking lots (often, again, at the expense of inner city low-income housing) or by peripheral parking with mass transit shuttle service to the sports facility.

The main impacts generated by travel in relation to sports events tend to be felt after the events because crowds try to leave within a considerably shorter space of time than they take in arriving. In the Chelsea survey alluded to earlier, over half the spectators had arrived at least an hour before kick-off. In really big events the first spectators arrive many hours before the start. The concentration of 70 000 or more people leaving a stadium at once frequently puts impossible strains on public transport. Among suggestions to reduce such pressure have been that direct footways should link stadiums with railway stations, that extra mass transit systems should be provided, and that post-match entertainment should be available in the stadium to aid the spreading of departures over a longer time period[19].

Negative spillovers affecting the areas adjacent to sports events are not a new phenomenon. After a visit to a New York racetrack in 1842 it was felt that the 'crowd and dust and the danger and the difficulty of getting on and off the course with a carriage are scarcely compensated by any pleasure to be gained from the amusement'[24]. In Britain the negative aspects of football were felt in city centres in the years around the start of the present century. The destruction of virtually every street-lamp around Hampden was the way the *Glasgow Herald* described the aftermath of the 1909 Scottish Cup Final. Sociologist Eric Dunning[25] suggests that the less desirable spillovers from British soccer were widely felt around many football grounds at the turn of the century. Crowd violence at sports events is neither a recent phenomenon nor restricted only to Britain and football (Fig. 5.8).

Today the most well-publicized kinds of negative spillovers from British football are vandalism and hooliganism. However, several surveys suggest that not only are other nuisances such as traffic congestion and parked cars perceived as serious by more local residents (Table 5.6) but they are also perceived as such over a wider geographical area. Put in more explicit geographic terms, there are spatial variations in the extent of different sport-generated nuisances; the impact of some nuisances is very localized while that for others is more dispersed. Figure 5.9 shows the different geographic extent of four nuisances generated by Southampton Football Club, patterns probably typical of many British clubs. It is worth

Table 5.6 Ranking of the main problems, as perceived by residents, according to distance zone; the case of the 'Dell', Southampton

Zone A 0–500	Zone B 500–1000	Zone C 1000–1500
Traffic	Parked cars	Parked cars
Pedestrians	Traffic	Traffic
Parked cars	Pedestrians	Hooligans
Hooligans	Hooligans	Pedestrians
Noise	Noise	Noise

The distance from each zone to the 'Dell' is shown in m.

(Based on Humphreys *et al.*, [26], p. 407.)

Chinese fans in rampage

From Reuter
in Peking

ANGRY Chinese soccer fans stoned foreigners' cars and smashed buses last night after their national side was eliminated from the Asian qualifying section of the World Cup.

Thousands of people ran riot after China went down 2–1 to Hong Kong at the Peking Workers' Stadium.

The Hong Kong team was besieged in the stadium for over an hour and in the street nearby a taxi was overturned and buses had their windows smashed.

The car of the Tass correspondent Gazizulla Arslanov was surrounded and bombarded with bricks and bottles, showering his young daughter with glass and debris.

A Reuter reporter, Mr Anthony Barker, was threatened with death if he disagreed that the Chinese team was best and the Times correspondent, Ms Mary Lee, was covered in spittle.

● A 50lb car bomb was defused outside the football stadium in Victoria, northern Spain, yesterday after waiting fans were evacuated.

Cricket rivalry resulted in arrests

The trouble at the one-day international cricket match between Australia and New Zealand on Tuesday started at about 3.30 pm, according to police who were on duty at the Sydney Cricket Ground.

That was when people sitting in what is popularly known as the Doug Walters stand, perched above a group of about 200 vocal New Zealanders on The Hill, started raining empty beer cans onto the group.

Police made their first arrest at about 5 pm, but it wasn't until after the meal break at 6.30 pm that there were any "major incidents", police said. Some people had armed themselves with lumps of concrete, sticks and some pieces of metal from the construction site at the old Sheridan Stand.

Two constables suffered cuts and bruises when a man sitting in some scaffolding fought with them after allegedly refusing to obey their direction to come down. Police

allege that he lashed out with his feet and fists.

Constable Peta Blood, of Kings Cross station, and Constable Matthew O'Neil, of Redfern station, were sent to St Vincent's Hospital for treatment.

The 70 police at the ground continued to make arrests among the crowd of more than 36,000 during the night.

A total of 88 people were arrested and faced 96 charges.

All the arrests were made on or near The Hill, police said, and a number of people were arrested after the game as they left the ground or stood outside.

"It does escalate when there's New Zealanders around. There's a lot of New Zealanders here and they all seem to go to these events," said Sergeant Oakley.

"But really the liquor caused more trouble than anything else."

Fig. 5.8 Crowd violence in sport is a world problem. (Sources: *The Guardian*, 20 May 1985, and *Sydney Morning Herald*, 16 January 1986.)

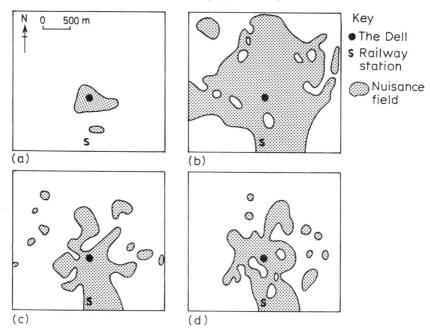

Fig. 5.9 Four 'nuisance fields' generated by football played at the 'Dell', Southampton; (a) noise, (b) traffic, (c) hooliganism and (d) pedestrians. Within the shaded area respondent residents perceived each of the football-induced effects to be a nuisance. (Based on Humphreys *et al.*[26].)

noting, in passing, the spatial extent of the auditory nuisance field, extending as much as 500 m beyond the stadium itself. Large crowds inside sports stadiums create major sound events in the auditory environment while some of the businesses associated with sports stadiums, notably hot food vendors, may make significant negative contributions to the 'olfactory environment'.

Generally speaking the perceived seriousness of the nuisance within a 'nuisance field' possesses a marked distance decay pattern. Figure 5.10 shows how for two turf clubs in Brisbane, Australia, local residents nearest the clubs perceived the sports nuisances (mainly parked cars) to be more serious than those living further away. The 'nuisance contours' were constructed following the interviewing of residents at sample locations around the racecourses[27]*. They were asked if living where they did they found the race meetings 'a serious nuisance', 'a nuisance' or 'no nuisance'. The location of each respondent was scored 2, 1 or 0 respectively and isopleths interpolated.

---

* See also references [26] and [28].

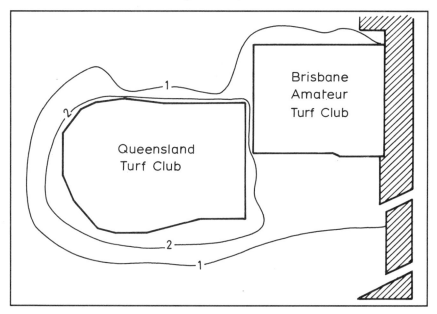

Fig. 5.10 The perceived seriousness of sport-induced nuisances, the example of two turf clubs in Brisbane. The values on the contours refer to (1) the limit of perceived nuisance, and (2) the limit of perceived serious nuisance. (After Fien and Lynn[27].)

While a distance decay pattern has been the traditional model used to represent such nuisances, a recent development, in Britain at least, has been the growth of nuisance outliers, some distance away from football grounds. This development has resulted from the intensification of policing in the immediate vicinity of the stadiums. In some cases potential nuisance outliers, such as motorway service stations, have responded by placing a ban on football supporters (Fig. 5.11). In the mid-1980s England's soccer supporters became what amounted to a mobile 'nuisance field', taking trouble with them to various European venues. The areas around stadiums in several capital cities temporarily became latter-day landscapes of fear. Following the horrendous disaster in the Heysel Stadium in Brussels in 1985, in which Liverpool supporters were held responsible for nearly forty deaths through riotous behaviour, English soccer clubs were banned from European competitions.

The costs of sport-induced nuisances to those who unwillingly consume them are difficult to estimate. Traditionally the community benefitted from a major sports stadium because rateable values (taxes) were high and the necessity for public services was low, thus creating savings to the ratepayers. Police were traditionally mainly deployed inside football grounds, the clubs bearing the costs of such policing.

On a par with pubs are football grounds. Tony Sandys has lived next to a couple of them. As though Arsenal wasn't enough, he then moved near to Chelsea. But Arsenal was the real horror. 'We lived about three yards away from Entrance Gate C so all the sausage, hot dog and Coke men sold their wares across the road from us and everyone queued up by the entrance to the flat. The mess, smell and filth were appalling, but there was nothing we could do to get rid of them.

'Parking was impossible once the police came and even towed my car away. I'm not interested in football at all so I never knew when there would be a match. If I caught the tube home when there was I couldn't get out of the station for hours because everyone gets channelled off into those little wire cages. It was easier to get off at a previous station and walk home.'

Katrina Baker found the football crowds a bit much for all of the two years she lived next to QPR football ground. 'The fans used to start walking down our little narrow road a few hours before the match. Manchester United were specially rough; I can now tell a United fan a mile off. Drunks would fool around jumping on the bonnets of all the cars. I used either to stay indoors or make sure I was shopping a long way away. There were hardly any buses running because the drivers were really worried. The fans are drunk you see.'

Peter and Jane Murray also live next to a football ground: Fulham. They can't let the children out while there's a match on and if the kids are going somewhere they'll take them early and leave them a couple of hours longer than usual to miss the struggle home.

Vignette VI Living next door to a stadium, as articulated by local residents. (Extracted from Phillips[29].)

During the past two decades, however, the policing of soccer matches outside grounds has increased dramatically as police have enforced the segregation of home and visiting fans. The costs of such police work is borne by the ratepayer. Whereas once retail outlets near grounds increased their takings on match days, today many put up shutters in order to prevent entry. The costs of nervous stress imposed on local residents is difficult, if not impossible, to quantify. In addition, the community around the ground will incur costs resulting from traffic delays, the loss of car parking space and the use of streets for children's play. All these nuisances rarely result in rate reductions or other forms of compensation, except, possibly, in the reduced cost of housing.

In the early 1970s it was estimated that a £5000 house located within ten miles of central London would, on average, experience a reduction in price of about 2½% as a result of its next-to-stadium location[30]. More expensive houses would suffer greater percentage reductions – a £20 000

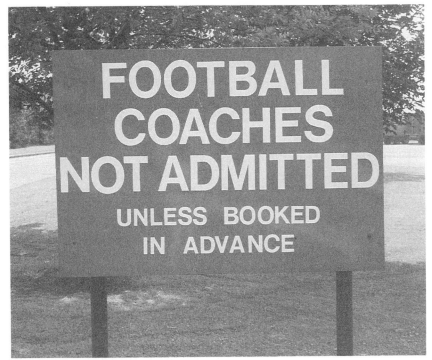

Fig. 5.11 Negative spillovers from football matches can be deterred. Signs such as this are common at service stations on Britain's motorway network.

house by as much as almost 12%* (Fig. 5.12). Some sportscapes, on the other hand, have a price-enhancing effect. The classic example is the golf-course effect, estimated for the early 1970s to increase the price of a £5000 house by about 14%. For playing fields the effect is rather different, as Fig. 5.12 illustrates. For the cheapest category of house the effect of being next to a playing field is price-enhancing but for the more expensive categories it is seen to be price-reducing.

The way to eliminate negative spillover effects is to locate the noxious sports facility in areas within which the externalities can be spread out over non-residential areas. Suburban locations may be the answer, though in Britain, as we have seen in Chapter 4, suburbanward movement has not even started to approach the extent reached in the USA. Where this has taken place amid complementary land use, sports facilities may be starting to have an impact on urban morphology[16], encouraging as they do the potential for increased growth and polynucleation of the

* The percentage changes quoted do not appear to have altered signficantly in the last decade or so.

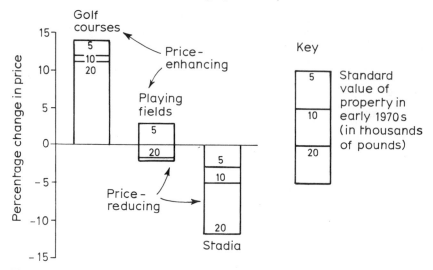

Fig. 5.12 Percentage change in price of three types of property within ten miles of central London when located next to different types of sports facility. (Based on Bowen[30].)

urban area. Given such expansion, the central business district (CBD) decreases in influence, and sometimes in viability.

Sport induces nuisances beyond the immediate impact of the stadium. In the case of the Montreal Olympics it has been suggested that the benefit/cost ratio was less than 1.0, resulting from the fact that the apartments in the Olympic Village were never occupied[31]. Indeed, the Montreal Games resulted in the postponment of housing, environmental and public transport projects and reductions in the social service budgets[32]. In Edmonton, Alberta, the location of the 1978 Common-wealth Games, it was recorded that 'facilities and related developments constructed for the "friendly" Commonwealth Games displaced 6000 people from their homes'[32].

The negative impacts on the environment (i.e. congestion, crowding, etc.,) were anticipated by the state of Colorado as being so serious that a decision was made not to bid for the Winter Olympics of 1976. The argument against state subsidization of the Games was that 'the Olympics would serve only to increase developer pressures in Colorado, creating that congestion the absence of which was one of the state's great virtues'[33] The case of the 1980 Winter Olympics is referred to by Shinnick[34] who reminds us of the way local residents at Lake Placid viewed with considerable alarm and hostility the suggestion that the Olympic village be converted into a prison once the games had finished.

Table 5.7 Selected ecological effects of sports

Type of sport	*Ecological effect*	
Stadium based sports	Removal of natural ecosystem; creation of artificial environment	Significant
Motor sports (land)	Chemical, including lead, pollution	
Motor sports (water)	Oil and gasoline spillages	
Alpine skiing	Damage to woodland, grass, soil	
Cross country skiing Orienteering	Some damage to undergrowth	
Wind surfing	Some damage to banks of water courses; nesting birds driven away	
White water canoeing	Insignificant (though artificial transport arrangements needed to get canoes to inaccessible locations)	
Running (in natural setting)	No significant effects	Insignificant

(Based on ideas in Mützelberg and Eichberg[38].)

5.4 AN ECOLOGICAL NOTE

We know relatively little about, and lack a conceptual framework for looking into, the impact of sport on the natural environment. We discuss the emergence of artificial sports landscapes in the next chapter but at this stage may note that ecological damage, while not especially significant by the standards of many modern-day activities, can nevertheless be brought about by sports. For example, sport-induced chemical pollution is far from unknown. In motor sports noxious fumes are emitted into the atmosphere in the case of auto-racing and into rivers, lakes or sea in the case of motor boat racing. In early 1987 a local environmental group in Italy successfully campaigned against holding the European bobsleigh championship at the artificially frozen track at Cortina because of the liquid ammonia used in the refrigeration plant. Such lobbying succeeded in getting the event switched to a natural track*.

In some cases the construction of a sporting landscape can produce negative geo-ecological effects, the costs of which are impossible to estimate. During ski piste construction, for example, the terrain is modified to such an extent that soil erosion occurs which in turn inhibits the regeneration of vegetation. The impact of artificial modification of

---

* Quoted in *The Guardian*, 14 January 1987.

mountain slopes for improved skiing facilities may affect as much as 15% of the surface area in some parts of the Swiss Alps[35]. As many of the growth sports are sometimes described as 'eco-sports' such impacts seem likely to continue at an accelerating rate.

Table 5.7 presents a tentative summary of direct ecological effects of well-known sports*. In addition it should be noted that the growth of major sports events such as the Olympic Games and the World Cup place pressure on the local energy systems of the centres in which they are located, while the growth of sports centres in mountainous and forested areas contributes to deforestation. Sport is also a user of natural resources in the sense that the rapidly expanding sports-equipment industries utilize plastics in the construction of many kinds of equipment and there is a substantial expenditure of energy for the heating and lighting of sports halls and stadiums. While we should not exaggerate the ecological impact of sports we should not ignore such an impact either, especially as sports, the sports goods industries and sports tourism are amongst the world's most rapidly growing industries.

5.5 CONCLUSIONS

This chapter has demonstrated that sporting activities can create what are widely regarded as positive spillovers, such as new employment, the provision of infrastructure and local economic multipliers. From another perspective it can be argued that this simply represents the increased packaging and commodification of sport. We have also seen that sport can create a number of negative externalities, both in terms of the costs it imposes on those who unwillingly consume more sport than they would freely choose, and in terms of its ecological effects. Given the state of spatial flux which characterizes much professional sport, it is hardly surprising that a recent report on the economic impact of sport in the UK stresses the need to establish local impact studies[39].

We have touched upon some of the landscape impacts of sport in this chapter and implicitly, in our discussion of relocation and suburbaniz-ation, in earlier chapters also. The chapter which follows considers in a more explicit way the kinds of landscapes and environments within which sports take place, illustrating the gradual transformation from landscape to sportscape and exploring the impact such changes have on the sporting experience.

* The growth of the 'green' political movement in the German Federal Republic may have contributed to a growing interest in sport and ecology among German academics. Apart from work by Eichberg (e.g. [36], [37]) most of this appears to be in German (e.g. Mützelberg and Eichberg[38]). Anglophonic sports geographers are at a major disadvantage with such literature, and I am grateful to Colin Wringe for an English summary of part of this work.

FURTHER READING

An excellent and wide-ranging critical review (with a very helpful bibliography) which explores and interprets the economic and symbolic place of professional sports in the (mainly) north American city is by Alan Ingham, Jeremy Howell and Todd Schilperoort, Professional sports and community: a review and exegesis, *Exercise and Sport Sciences Reviews*, **15**, 1987, pages 427–65. The methodology involved in analysing the impact of a professional sports team on an urban area is documented in William A. Schaffer and Lawrence S. Davidson's *Economic Impact of the Falcons on Atlanta: 1984*, The Atlanta Falcons, Suwanee, GA, 1985. European readers may find this somewhat inaccessible and are referred to the same authors' earlier work, The economic impact of professional football on Atlanta, in *Management Science Applications to Leisure-Time Operations* (ed. S. Ladany), North Holland Publishing Co., Amsterdam, 1975, pages 276–96. A brief introduction to 'nuisance fields' around sports stadiums is John Bale's Football clubs as neighbours, *Town and Country Planning*, **49**, 1980, pages 93–4 and this subject is covered in more detail in a case study by David Humphrys, Colin Mason and Stephen Pinch, The externality fields of football grounds: a case study of the Dell, Southampton, *Geoforum*, **14**, 4, 1983, pages 401–11. Detailed examinations of spheres of influence, catchment areas and fandoms are made in different ways by Maynard W. Dow, The impact of communications media on Red Sox fandom, *Proceedings of the New England St. Lawrence Valley Geographical Society*, 1978, pages 11–22 and R. Doyle, J. M. Lewis and M. Malmisur, A sociological application of Rooney's fan region concept, *Journal of Sports Behavior*, **3**, 1980, pages 51–60.

REFERENCES

1. Gottman, J. (1974) The dynamics of large cities. *The Geographical Journal*, **140**, 254–62.
2. Lipsitz, G. (1984) Sports stadia and urban development: a tale of three cities. *Journal of Sport and Social Issues*, **8**, 1–18.
3. Marsh, J. (1984) The economic impact of a small city annual sporting event; an initial case study of the Peterborough Church League Atom Hockey Tournament. *Recreational Research Review*, **11**, 48–55.
4. Cady, D. (1978) *The Big Game*, University of Tennessee Press, Knoxville, pp. 70–71.
5. Schaffer, W. and Davidson, L. (1985) *Economic impact of the Falcons on Atlanta: 1984*. The Atlanta Falcons, Suwanee, G.A.
6. Murphy, P. (1985) *Tourism; A Community Approach*, Methuen, London, p. 107.
7. Hoare, A. (1983) *The Location of Industry in Britain*, Cambridge University Press, Cambridge.
8. Okner, B. (1974) Subsidies of stadiums and arenas, in *Government and the Sports Business* (ed. R. Noll), Brookings Institute, Washington DC, p. 328.

9. Geipel, R. (1981) Which Munich for whom? in *Space and Time in Geography* (ed. A. Pred), Gleerup, Lund, pp. 160–82.
10. Brohm, J. (1978) *Sport; a Prison of Measured Time*, Ink Links, London.
11. Hammersley, R. (1982) Unexpected uses for a white elephant. *Town and Country Planning*, **51**, 185–6.
12. Williams, A. and Zelinsky, W. (1970) On some patterns of international tourist flows. *Economic Geography*, **46**, 549–67.
13. Sadler, B. (1983) Ski area development in the Canadian Rockies: past lessons future prospects, in *Tourism in Canada: Selected Issues and Options* (ed. P. Murphy), Western Geographical Series 21, Department of Geography, University of Victoria, British Columbia, pp. 309–29.
14. Rosentraub, M. (1977) Financial incentives, locational decision making and professional sports; the case of the Texas Ranger baseball network and the city of Arlington, Texas, in *Financing Local Government; New Approaches to Old Problems* (ed. M. Rosentraub), Western Social Sciences Association, Fort Collins, Col.
15. Rooney, J. (1974) *A Geography of American Sport; from Cabin Creek to Anaheim*, Addison-Wesley, Reading, Mass.
16. Wepfer, A. (1982) The impact of major sports facilities on urban morphology and function, unpublished revised version of paper read at the annual meeting of the Association of American Geographers, San Antonio.
17. Ley, D. (1983) *A Social Geography of the City*, Harper and Row, New York.
18. Thornes, J. (1983) The effect of weather on attendance at sporting events, in *Geographical Perspectives on Sport* (eds J. Bale and C. Jenkins), Department of PE, Birmingham University, pp. 182–90.
19. Saunders, L. (1972) The characteristics and impact of travel generated by Chelsea Football Club. *Research Memorandum*, 344, Department of Planning and Transportation, Greater London Council, London.
20. Dow, M. (1978) The impact of communications media on Red Sox fandom. *Proceedings of the New England–St. Lawrence Valley Geographical Society*, 11–22.
21. Shelley, F. and Cartin, K. (1984) The geography of baseball fan support in the United States. *North American Culture*, **1**, 77–95.
22. Ingham, A., Howell, J. and Schilperoort, T. (1987) Professional sports and community: a review and exegesis. *Exercise and Sport Sciences Reviews*, **15**, 427–65.
23. Clawson, M. and Knetsch, J. (1966) *The Economics of Outdoor Recreation*, Johns Hopkins Press, Baltimore.
24. Barth, G. (1980) *City People*, Oxford University Press, New York.
25. Dunning, E., Murphy, P. and Williams, J. (1983) Spectator violence at football matches; towards a sociological explanation. *The British Journal of Sociology*, **37**, 221–44.
26. Humphreys, D., Mason, C. and Pinch, S. (1983) The externality fields of football grounds; a case study of the Dell, Southampton. *Geoforum*, **14**, 401–11.
27. Fien, J. and Lynn, G. (1982) The racecourse next door; yea or neigh? *Geography Bulletin*, **14**, 155–60.
28. Bale, J. (1980) Football clubs as neighbours, *Town and Country Planning*, **49**, 93–4.
29. Phillips, B. (1977) Loathe thy neighbour. *The Observer*, 11 September.
30. Bowen, M. (1974) Outdoor recreation around large cities, in *Suburban Growth* (ed. J. Johnson), Wiley, London, pp. 225–48.

31. Loy, J., McPherson, B. and Kenyon, G. (1978) *Sport and Social Systems*, Addison-Wesley, Reading, Mass.
32. Kidd, B. (1979) *The Political Economy of Sport*, CAPHER, Ottawa.
33. Cox, K. (1979) *Location and Public Policy*, Blackwell, Oxford.
34. Shinnick, P. (1979) North-east regional development and the Olympic prison. *Arena Review*, **2**, 3–11.
35. Mossiman, T. (1985) Geo-ecological impacts of ski-piste construction in the Swiss Alps. *Applied Geography*, **5**, 29–38.
36. Eichberg, H. (1982) Stopwatch, horizontal bar, gymnasium: the technologizing of sport in the eighteenth and early nineteenth centuries. *Journal of the Philosophy of Sport*, **9**, 43–59.
37. Eichberg, H. (1986) The enclosure of the body – on the historical relativity of 'health', 'nature' and the environment of sport. *Journal of Contemporary History*, **21**, 99–121.
38. Mützelburg, D. and Eichberg, H. (eds) (1984) *Sport, Bewegung und Ökologie*, Studienganges sportswissenschaft der Universität Bremen, Bremen.
39. Henley Centre for Forecasting (1986) *The Economic Impact and Importance of Sport in the UK*, Sports Council, London.

Chapter 6

SPORT AND LANDSCAPE

Inevitably, the growth and continuing locational adjustments made by modern sports have created significant changes in the landscape. Some landscape changes are, as we have seen from the previous chapter, temporary in nature. The colours (and sometimes chaos) which marathon runners, cyclists and football spectators bring to the landscape disappear after a few hours. This chapter is more concerned with the permanent landscape impacts which sports have created – the golf course, race tracks and stadiums are obvious examples. The sports landscape is approached initially by considering two broad tendencies which have characterized its evolution. These are (a) the gradual artificialization of the sports environment, and (b) the increasing spatial confinement of the sites within which sport is practised. The chapter illustrates these two trends with examples from several sports and concludes with a consideration of whether such developments have, in any way, affected the overall sporting experience. The chapter is therefore rather more humanistic than those which have preceded it, dealing as it does with such notions as 'feelings' and 'values'.

6.1 FROM LANDSCAPE TO SPORTSCAPE

We have already noted (Section 3.1) that the folk game antecedents of modern sports were played on rough terrain without any standardized spatial limits. Commons, streets and fields – landscapes designed with things other than sports in mind – constituted the environment in which such sport-like activities were found. In the late 1500s and 1600s, however, there emerged a number of artificial and spatially confined sporting milieux in which the nobility practised games like tennis and physical recreations such as riding, gymnastics and fencing. For example, as many as 250 ballcourts were said to exist in Paris in 1596, although in 1615 London had only fourteen ('Real' tennis is a modern-day legacy of such activities). Indoor riding halls were popular in much of Europe as a form of 'social geometry' swept through the sport-like activities of the well-to-do, a sporting analogy of the landscape garden. Of course, the notion of the tennis 'court' may be interpreted not only as an area for sport but also as a way of marking the territorial bounds of the nobility at the expense of the commoners[1]*.

In Europe the court-oriented games began to lose their attraction from the end of the eighteenth century. Revolution and industry induced changes in the sport environment and, perhaps as a reaction to industrialization, sports and recreations saw a shift into the open air; a sort of 'green revolution' was taking place in sports. Gymnastics took to the fields and woods, and later to the 'turnplatz'. Sports played in the open air were showing increasing popularity: cricket in England, golf in Scotland, steeplechasing, rowing and swimming all having an impact on the outdoor environment. The indoor sports declined, so much so that only one of the indoor riding schools (that at Vienna) survived.

During the nineteenth century a series of developments took place which moved sports back indoors. Sport palaces and gymnastics halls made a return but by the late nineteenth century we again see a swing to outdoor activities – cycling and later motor sports, but also the continuation and intensification of the 'English' games of soccer, rugby and cricket. At the end of the century we witness the emergence – or re-emergence – of the stadium and the indoor swimming pool.

It is clear that what has been described in the previous paragraphs amounts to a cyclic interpretation (Fig. 6.1) of the evolution of the sports landscape, in contrast to a 'linear' interpretation which would infer a gradual transition from folk games to the highly confined and artificial environments of much of the present-day sports landscape. This cyclic approach derives from the work of Eichberg[2] who sees present-day sport moving in three different directions in terms of its relationships with the landscape and environment. On the one hand there are the continued tendencies to confine and artificialize the sporting environment. Windowless sport halls, keep fit studios, astroturf, concrete and domed stadiums and similar manifestations of modern technology make up industrial culture's technologized sportscape. At the same time a 'green' tendency is present in the form of the running, orienteering, and skiing revolutions. These sports take place in the open air but they are, nevertheless, quantified and competitive; they do not reject the basic ethos of sport. A third movement, however, does reject both competition and a special sport environment. This represents a return to the neutralization of space so that physical activities can be undertaken without recourse to specialist sites; yoga and tai-chi might be suggested as

* Much of the early part of this chapter is based on the work by German sports historian Henning Eichberg[1,2].

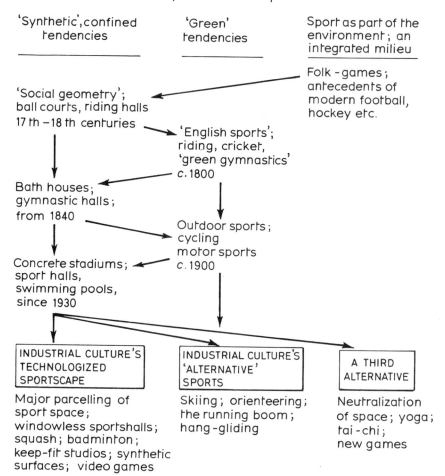

'Synthetic',confined
tendencies

'Green'
tendencies

Sport as part of the
environment; an
integrated milieu

Folk-games;
antecedents of
modern football,
hockey etc.

'Social geometry';
ball courts, riding halls
17 th –18 th centuries

'English sports';
riding, cricket,
'green gymnastics'
c.1800

Bath houses;
gymnastic halls;
from 1840

Outdoor sports;
cycling
motor sports
c.1900

Concrete stadiums;
sport halls,
swimming pools,
since 1930

INDUSTRIAL CULTURE'S
TECHNOLOGIZED
SPORTSCAPE

INDUSTRIAL CULTURE'S
'ALTERNATIVE'
SPORTS

A THIRD
ALTERNATIVE

Major parcelling of
sport space;
windowless sportshalls;
squash; badminton;
keep-fit studios; synthetic
surfaces; video games

Skiing; orienteering;
the running boom;
hang-gliding

Neutralization
of space; yoga;
tai-chi;
new games

Fig. 6.1 Changing relationships between sports and the environment. (Vertical lines indicate continuing trends, diagonal lines shifts in emphasis.) (After an idea by Eichberg[2].)

examples. Such activities could be interpreted as a reaction against the specialized sportscapes of modern industrial culture. Non-competitive, family-oriented walks (volksmarching) have also become relatively popular[3].

6.2 CONFINEMENT AND ARTIFICE

Let us look in a little more detail at the ways in which sports have become more spatially confined and have been 'played' on increasingly artificial surfaces. In the early days of modern sport racing took place on open country, cricket on fields with unmarked boundaries, golf on coastal dunes, gymnastics in fields, football often on land behind public houses and boxing inside the public houses. Sport was part of an existing landscape. Gradually, however, the emphasis shifted back to artificial landscapes (which had never totally disappeared) as spatial limits came to dominate the sporting scene.

Sports became increasingly refined and ordered in both time and space, mirroring the growing economic rationality of the world of work. Artifice and spatial confinement, though present in the 1600s, grew rapidly to characterize sports in the late nineteenth century. Whereas in the eighteenth century, cricket games usually had to wait for their fields until after the first haymaking (hence determining the latitudinal location of the season's first games)[4], by Victorian times the leading cricket scientists were the groundsmen[5], pitches becoming increasingly tended in order to reduce the chance element in the bounce of the ball. The first cinder running track was built in London in 1837; the first enclosed race course and artificial ice rink in the 1870s, the first floodlights at football in 1878; cricket boundaries were first established in 1885 and the dead ball line in rugby in 1891. It was an era of spatial delimitation and ordering in the world of sport. And as an increasing number of spectators became prepared to pay to watch team sports, banks and terraces were constructed around the pitches. The spatial separation of players from spectators and the identification of specific sites (to be filled and emptied at specified times) for sports, marked the end of folk games. The stadium, common in Roman times, had returned to the landscape after a gap of almost 2000 years.

In the twentieth century sportscapes rather than landscapes have tended to characterize the sports environment (Fig. 6.2). The current trend towards specifically designed sportscapes started in the nineteenth century. In the early 1950s the synthetic running track made its appearance and the first Astroturf pitch was constructed in 1966. New materials had changed the shape of the stadium and the texture of the surfaces; fields became carpets and parks became concrete bowls. Most sports require artificial settings, although the degree to which the natural environment needs to be changed varies between sports. Wagner[6] notes that even in sports like sailing and canoeing, in which only buoys or markers are used, it is not 'nature' which sets the challenge for the sports participant as it is for the outdoor recreationist. Instead, 'sport in all its varied forms needs specific kinds of places . . . and such places must be made.'

One interpretation of the manufactured nature of sports places is that because they are purpose-built 'with an overwhelming amount of

Fig. 6.2 Youthful and mature sportscapes. Contrast the overgrown rugby pitch in a forest clearing near Suva, Fiji (a) with the synthetic surface of Lewis Field, Oklahoma State University, USA (b).

concrete rather than just pure, uncontaminated, unmanipulated nature', they (and therefore sports *per se*) are inclined to be anti-nature. Galtung[7] stresses that this tendency results from the 'near-laboratory settings in which the unidimensionality of competitive sports can unfold itself under controlled conditions. Pure nature has too much variation in it; too much "noise" '.The following examples of the stadium, ski-jump and racecourse illustrate such a tendency in the transition from landscape to sportscape.

6.2.1 The stadium

The sports stadium has emerged as a spatially confined and increasingly artificial element of the landscape through a period of just over a hundred years, involving four stages of development (Fig. 6.3). In folk games no spatial limits were imposed and games were played on natural terrain, used normally for other purposes. Following the imposition of rules, spatial limits were placed on the area of play. The third stage emerged with the commodification of sport when people were required to pay money to watch. Initially only the principal clubs would have had enclosed fields. At first the pitch was simply roped off but subsequently pavilions, embankments, grandstands and turnstiles were required; social segregation was enforced as those willing to pay more were accommodated in superior style which, in the first instance, was simply a covered terrace. The date of commencement of each stage of course varied from sport to sport.

In the early twentieth century wooden structures, costing in the USA about $60 000 gradually gave way to fireproof stadiums costing $500 000. After about 1908 the largest US cities began to abandon the wooden edificies and the modern stadium had arrived[8]. Stadium capacity grew rapidly once money changed hands at the turnstiles. In the USA, for example, average stadium seating capacity for a sample of 135 college stadiums grew from under 7000 in 1920 to over 17 000 a decade later[9]. In the inter-war years stadiums on both sides of the Atlantic were erected to accommodate between 70 000 and 150 000 spectators, while in the post Second World War period the largest stadium capacity, for 200 000, has been achieved by the Maracana Stadium in Rio de Janeiro.

Technology has imposed itself on the stadium in recent decades in several ways. Glassed-in boxes have enclosed the most exclusive spectators; video screens have provided action replays, advertisements and even exhortations to cheer; synthetic playing surfaces such as Astroturf have replaced grass; floodlights have become almost ubiquitous. In the concrete structures which have replaced the wooden grandstands Neilson[10] avers that 'the closed circle of the bowl breaks

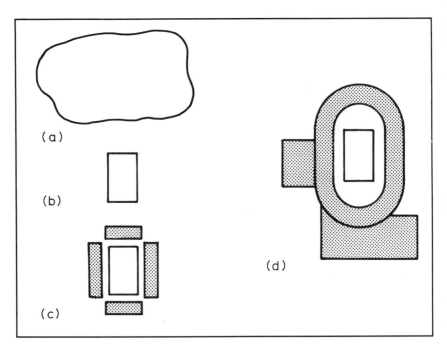

Fig. 6.3 A four-stage model of the evolution of the stadium. (a) Folk-game stage: no spatial limits; uneven terrain. (b) Spatial limits stage: formulation of rules; limits of pitch defined; all spectators standing. (c) Commodification stage: construction of embankments, terraces, pavilions and grandstands; payment required for entry; segregation of spectators by social class; minority of spectators seated. (d) Technologized stage: enclosed ground, concrete bowl, increased distance of spectators from pitch; synthetic playing area; TV replay screen; all spectators seated; associated sports hall and sports complex.

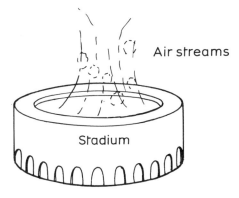

Air streams

Stadium

Fig. 6.4 A futuristic view of a sports stadium. The 'air roof' produced by continuous jets of air meeting above the centre of the playing area forms a protective ceiling which turns the elements aside. (Source: Ezersky and Theibert[11].)

the visual connection between the stadium and the town. The temporal and historical associations that say, "Here is a place connected to a landscape that grew out of a particular process" are severed'. The place becomes a 'non-place', almost identical to others of its type. Future developments hypothesized include stadiums with 'air roofs' where continuous jets of air meet and form a kind of 'volcanic cone' (Fig. 6.4) above the centre of the playing area. This forms a protective roof, turning the natural elements aside and at the same time eliminating the need for a membrane roof[11].

6.2.2 The ski jump

Technology has made equally significant impacts on the landscapes of individual, rather than team, sports. Consider, for example, ski jumping which initially took place for fun on natural slopes or from the roofs of houses. The changes induced by the introduction of first wooden and later concrete structures can be illustrated by the example of the famous Holmenkollen ski jump in Norway[12]. Here, on the northern outskirts of Oslo, the first ski jump was set up on the natural slope of the land in 1892, the only minor modification of the natural slope being the 'take off'. This initial jump was 9.5 m high. The subsequent development of Holmen-kollen has proceeded through a number of stages (Fig. 6.5), culminating in 1982 with a massive artificial slope constructed of concrete, 121 m high and dominating the Oslo townscape, being visible from many miles away. Today the ski slope can only be used for ski jumping. It attracts many thousands of tourists per year and has become part of a tourist

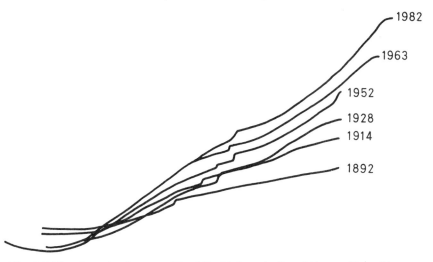

Fig. 6.5 The changing long profile of the Holmenkollen ski jump, Oslo, Norway, 1892–1982. (Based on Bergsland and Seim-Haugen[12].)

Fig. 6.6 The Holmenkollen complex, Oslo, Norway.

complex, possessing a neighbouring ski museum and providing tours of the ski jump and adjoining area (Fig. 6.6). Technological change has, of course, been accompanied by improved performances; whereas the best distance achieved on the initial slope was 33 m the present record stands at over 100 m.

Other ski-landscapes have been affected by technology in other ways. Where appropriately low temperatures and suitable slopes exist in the absence of snow, manufactured snow is produced at night by snow cannons. These eject water under high pressure which turns to snow on contact with the cold air, forming a narrow strip of snow surrounded by rocks and grass. Where neither slopes nor snow exist, artificial, plastic ski-slopes are constructed for so-called dry-skiing. When there is no daylight, forest ski trails in much of Scandinavia are floodlit so that cross-country skiing may continue in what would otherwise be sub-Arctic darkness.

A Japanese construction company has come up with an idea that takes the flying out of skiing – city centre indoor slopes. Why waste precious hours flying to Val d'Isère, Vail or Kashmir when you can be on the slopes in minutes without leaving the comfort of your BMW?

Kajima, which is best known for building nuclear power plants but is keen to move into urban redevelopment projects, is looking for clients for its brainchild: a six-storey shed which contains a 200 ft-high spiral slope, an artificial snow maker, gourmet restaurants, fashion shops and an aerobics centre. Kajima is now hawking the idea round companies owning redundant warehouses around Tokyo Bay. All a prospective client needs is a site of 16,500 sq metres and Y2 billion–10 billion ($14m–70m) depending on how deep in designer boutiques it wants its mini-resort to be.

The company reckons its scheme can provide skiing (of a sort) for 1,000–1,3000 people a day for a fee of Y4,000–5,000 on three courses of different difficulty up to 570m long. Skiing is fashionable among Tokyo's *shinjinrui*, affluent young adults who may one day grow up to be yuppies. Since the nearest real slopes are in the Japan Alps, a three-hour drive away, Kajima may be on to a winner, especially with those more concerned about showing off their designer ski-suits than in feeling the piste beneath their Italian ski boots.

Vignette VII *Indoor ski slopes for Tokyo?* (Source: *The Economist*, May 30th 1987, p. 73).

6.2.3 The racecourse

A space extensive sport which has obvious landscape impacts and which has developed distinctive sportscapes is horse racing. However, in the

Fig. 6.7 Epsom Downs, 1863. Aaron Green's oil painting provides an indication of the impact of sport on the landscape in mid-nineteenth century England.

eighteenth century racing in no way had exclusive use of the land on which races took place. The land was frequently meadow or common which for the rest of the year and was used for grazing[4]. By 1840 the number of racecourses in Britain totalled 137 but it was not until 1875 that the first 'enclosed course' was opened at Sandown Park[13]. Crowds at mid-nineteenth century races were substantial (Fig. 6.7), tens of thousands having attended the Epsom Derby[13].

Although the sixty or so race courses in Britain today are unstandardized, they nevertheless represent a major element of land use devoted primarily to sport. When located alongside or close to stables, gallops and training areas they not only take up a vast amount of space but can also generate a quite distinctive sportscape flavour. The total area associated with horse racing in Britain probably exceeds 100 000 acres[14]. In the town of Newmarket, racing has not only changed the landscape but has determined the unique character of the town. The early

'Rain stopped play,' one of the most disheartening announcements in British sport, could itself be wiped out by developments in artificial, all-weather sports surfaces.

The Jockey Club announced last week that it will this summer be spending around £750,000 on 18 furlongs of artificial all-weather gallops for Newmarket's training grounds. An intial nine-furlong artificial track was installed at Newmarket last summer with £500,000 donated by the Dubai racehorse owner, Sheik Hamdam Al Maktoum. It has since been used by between 500 and 1,000 horses a day, and was the only training ground to remain open in the extreme cold this January.

In addition, the Jockey Club in London is evaluating possible sites for a complete all-weather race track funded by the Betting Levy Board, which, two years ago, is thought to have lost £100 million in the space of two months due to race cancellations.

Newmarket's artificial surface, called Equi-track and manufactured under licence for Leicester-based firm En-tout-cas, consists of a sand and gravel mix coated in a water repellant visco-elastic polymer. Laid six inches deep, it makes a loose surface which, unlike turf, does not freeze and provides a cushioning effect. This, say trainers, reduces impact injuries and other common problems in wet or hard conditions.

Local authorities are also looking increasingly at all-weather sports surfaces in order to maximise the use of playing fields. The early synthetic tufted surfaces designed for football, such as Astroturf, had drawbacks. The most serious was 'footlock' – the foot is prevented from slipping on turning, resulting in jarring to the ankle, knee and groin. This was largely solved by brushing sand into the tufted surface to give it characteristics closer to grass.

Today the most sophisticated artificial soccer surfaces – such as Luton Town Football Club's ground – are a development of this formula. A tarmac foundation is laid with a shock pad of half an inch of granulated rubber, held with polyurethane and latex, and covered by a tufted surface with sand brushed into it.

The chief criticism of artificial sports surfaces, made most vociferously by the Football League, is that they give bad ball bounce and are not 'natural.' The game tends to be 'top of ground' – in other words, faster and demanding a different kind of playing. For local authorities, however, an all-weather surface which will cope with high demand means that football matches, for example, can be scheduled for every two hours at weekends.

Nottinghamshire County Council has come up with a grass reinforcement system which is seen as a compromise between the natural and the synthetic. Peter Drury, the county's playing fields officer, has adapted a commercial carpet-making technique called needle punching to produce a non-woven polypropylene wadding which resembles a giant green pan-scourer.

This construction is laid directly on to a soil base, filled with sand or soil, and then oversown with grass seed, the roots grow down into the base through the polypropylene fibres, which are masked by the sward. It is intended for entire areas as well as to strengthen patches – such as goal mouths – where grass experiences heaviest use. Once the grass has grown it can be cut and spiked (for drainage) as normal.

It has already been laid on the cliff tops at Great Yarmouth where the public were wearing away the turf. But critics of the system allege that if the grass needs top dressing the fabric is gradually buried underground, losing its effectiveness. Peter Drury, however, maintains that the structure reduces the need for top dressing. The wadding can also be used without grass, filled with sand or other particles such as rubber crumb, or as a shockpad under another surface; and it can be much cheaper than other artificial surfaces.

Vignette VIII *Where the going is always good*. (Source: Buxton[16]).

home of the sport's governing body, the Jockey Club, Newmarket is a rare example of a town which virtually owes it's *raison d'etre* to sport. As the novelist J. B. Priestley[15] put it, Newmarket is 'more like a place conjoured out of an old sporting print than any other in England'.

If spatial confinement in horse racing took place in the late 1870s, major artificialization of the racing environment is only just beginning. Although dirt, rather than grass tracks are more common in the USA (as is the standardization of courses), it is only in the late 1980s that experiments are taking place (by the Jockey Club in England) in the development of artificial surfaces. Such a development would enable flat racing to take place throughout the English winter.

Although show-jumping events are frequently held indoors it seems laughable to suggest that horse racing can also be held in the spatial confines of the indoor arena. However, in the late 1980s it appears that horse racing *is* being developed as an indoor sport. In the USA mounts half the weight of the average thoroughbred, and therefore more suited to indoor racing, are being fitted with 10 kilo (22 lb) glass fibre and metal 'super jock' robot riders, controlled off-course by a radio transmitter.*

6.3   GOLF: A CASE STUDY

A substantial amount of land today is consumed by monocultural golf courses. In the UK the estimated total is 80 000 ha (about 200 000 acres) while in the USA the area taken up by golf courses exceeds that of the state of Rhode Island[17]. In the early days of golf, courses were smaller than at present, but with the arrival of the rubber core golf ball players were able to drive the ball further and courses increased in size as a consequence. Initially golf courses utilized quite natural terrain, coastal sand dunes covered by grass (i.e. links) being the natural home of the sport. Undulating landscapes, natural bunkers, smooth turf and well drained soil provided the ideal environment out of which golf could grow. These conditions were ideally found in east-central Scotland – the home of British golf.

At the end of the nineteenth century there were sixty-one golf courses in Scotland compared with forty-six in the whole of England. In the 1880s inland golf was still played on what the chronicler of the sport, Bernard Darwin[18] described as 'glorified meadows of extreme muddiness'; inland golf was regarded as a very poor substitute for the real thing. However, by the 1890s it was discovered that landscapes of heather, bracken and sandy heath could be manufactured into inland golf courses. The tremendous demand for the sport meant that these landscapes were

* Quoted in the *Observer Magazine*, 23rd August 1987.

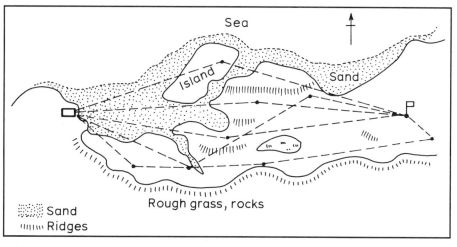

Fig. 6.8 Prize design for a hole by Dr A. Mackenzie, 1914. The hole was devised to make the player use his (sic) own judgement, according to his driving and the weather, as to which of the five routes he would adopt. (Source: Darwin[18], p. 12.)

insufficient and arable land began to be taken over for golf course construction; the average course of 100 acres was about the size of a small farm. Previously enclosed fields and woodland were metamorphosed into carefully simulated heathland. Contests were held in golf course design (Fig. 6.8) and the golf architect emerged as a kind of sub-Capability Brown figure.

Sometimes problems arose when golfers encroached on common land, usually with disdain and without permission. Violence between 'commoners' and golfers was not unknown and the solution was sometimes to 'incorporate' the commoners into an Artisans club, though this occurred less frequently than would ideally have been the case and in England (if not in Scotland) golf remains very much an upper and middle class sport[19].

Golf course design gradually became a sophisticated science – a long way from the situation in Yonkers, New York in 1892 when the St Andrews golfers moved from their original location and laid out their new six-hole course in a single day[20]. Between 1920 and 1930 the number of golf courses in Britain was growing at a rate of fifty per year[21], while in the USA between 1916 and 1930 the total grew from 742 to 5856[9]. Today's golf course architects have produced landscapes of fairway and green in parts of the Florida Everglades, the Nevada Desert, on a mountainside in Texas and on a strip coal mine in West Virginia. Robert Trent Jones and Peter Dye, two of the premier golf course architects of the

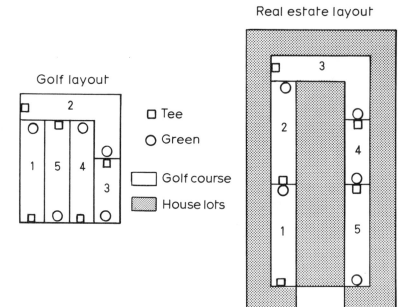

Fig. 6.9 Traditional and 'real estate' golf course models. Numbers refer to fairways whereas the traditional course was space-intensive, the 'real estate' model attempts to maximize residential frontage. (Source: Adams and Rooney[23].)

present day, have left their own distinctive sportscape signatures on their courses, the former providing 'lush velvet fairways, manicured roughs, tees the length of football pitches and giant undulating greens protected by lakes and contoured bunkers'[22]. Dye, on the other hand, has tried to return to the more rugged Scottish flavour which characterized the early British courses, though some have argued that by their severity they are more penal than rugged.

In urban and suburban areas, where they are mainly located, golf courses affect the nature of not only the land use but also the adjacent residential development. In the inter-war period the presence of a golf course often influenced the siting of the more affluent suburbs, large detached 'Tudor' style housing frequently abutting the suburban English course. Furthermore, golf courses are known to raise the value of houses sited next to them by around 11% (see Fig. 5.12).

Recent years have witnessed increased costs of golf course construction as the most appropriate types of landscapes become increasingly scarce. The traditional way of keeping costs down in cases where the prime motive of the developer was to construct a golf course was to build compact courses with a minimum of unused space (Fig. 6.9). However, in

Fig. 6.10 Announcing a residential golf community near Tarpon Springs, Florida.

order to counter cost increases a number of radical changes in golf course design are currently taking place, notably in the USA. In particular, new courses developed not solely for golf but as integral parts of real estate developments have emerged (Fig. 6.10). About one-half of golf courses under construction in the USA in early 1983 were of this type. Geographer Bob Adams* notes that 'in such cases the developer uses the golf course as a tool to enhance the attractiveness and value of the real estate, with golf itself being of secondary importance'[24]. In such cases, much more diffuse layouts result in the sides of each hole being lined with housing developments. An eighteen-hole course can, in this way, create as much as 9 miles of course-fronted property.

A second way of responding to the recent increases in construction costs is to change the interior design of the course. The traditional golf course was designed according to what Adams calls the 'turf-farm' concept – large areas of carefully manicured grass requiring substantial irrigation systems, and mammoth materials, equipment and labour

* See also Adams and Rooney[23].

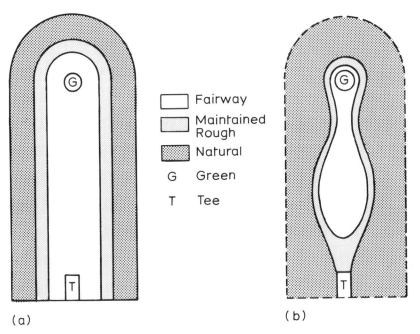

Fig. 6.11 Golf course design concepts; (a) turf-farm concept and (b) target concept. (Source: Adams and Rooney[23].)

budgets to maintain. In America a cost-saving tactic is to reduce the within-course area needing expensive maintenance by restricting the fairway and the maintained rough to an area where the golfers 'should' be hitting their shots. In this way the area requiring expensive maintainance is reduced (Fig. 6.11).

Another development is likely to be the emergence of what has become known as the Cayman facility – a new, more spatially efficient form of golf first tested by Jack Nicklaus's Golden Bear Corporation in the Cayman Islands. Cayman golf employs a ball which, when hit, travels only half the distance of a regulation ball. Hence, the course using this ball needs to be only half as long as a regulation course. In addition, the Cayman course is less expensive to build, a game takes nearly half as long and achieves a more intense use of land than the regulation course[25].

A further development in the landscape of golf is the construction of what might be termed 'grandstand' courses. On many golf courses it is difficult for spectators to get a good view of the game. With an improvement in this situation in mind, American initiatives have recently involved the construction of tiered spectator facilities alongside greens and fairways. What is more, football stadiums have recently accommodated golf in an attempt to provide fans with constant action. Johannesburg's 70 000 seater Ellis Park Stadium temporarily became a golf course in 1985 on which eight professionals played nine greens, with sand traps and water hazards cut into the turf to form eighteen par 3 holes. Tees were placed on platforms in the stands and while one foursome walked down the green the other teed off*. Stadium golf is likely to be followed by synthetic putting greens and even synthetic courses.

Whereas golf courses were once part of pasture or common land, with freedom of access to all, today it is not uncommon to see signs asking people to 'keep off' or impenetrable railings prohibiting entry. Golf courses are used today not merely to play golf but to sell real estate, industrial locations and conference venues (Fig. 6.12). At the same time as this is happening a firm in Salt Lake City is today offering an 'indoor golf course' which is a combination of slide projections (reproducing the golf course at Pebble Beach, California), special cameras and microprocessors to calculate the flight of the ball[2]. Add holography and the ultimate sportscape will have emerged.

Writing in the 1930s, the architect Clough Williams Ellis felt that the golf course was one of the things which most threatened the distinctiveness of the English scene†. The sameness, the artifice, or what Relph called 'disneyfication'[27] is certainly a characteristic of many sportscapes of the modern world. The synthetic running track, the standardized 50 m swimming pool, the synthetic astroturf, ice rinks and indoor sports halls make one sporting environment much the same as another. In few activities has there been so much pressure to make one place the same – exactly the same – as another. As sport has become a major user of land, the need for planning standards and the compatibility of land uses has arisen, the subject to which we now turn.

6.4 FINDING SPACE FOR SPORT

The inter-war years witnessed the emergence of a growing number of sports of a space-extensive nature which were to make an emphatic impression on the landscape. Motor racing, cycling, skiing and, later, orienteering, all required a considerable amount of space and, apart from the last named, created to varying degrees distinctive sportscapes out of pre-existing landscapes. At the same time both recreational and serious sports have increased their demands for urban and rural land.

Land requirements differ among the many space-extensive sports. For example, orienteering requires about 750 hectares of, ideally, undulating

* Quoted in *Golf*, 28 April 1986, p. 31.
† Quoted in Relph[26].

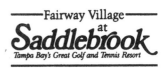
Fig. 6.12 Both residential and conference accommodation appear to need golf facilities, to judge from these advertisements.

wooded landscape with lakes, rivers and streams for variety. Uncultivated fields, commons, paths and parkland can also be utilized. On the other hand, downhill skiing needs a long gully of at least 18 m in width and 800 m long, with a drop in altitude over that stretch of about 300 m. The maximum and minimum slopes should be 25° and 2° respectively. Differing degrees of compatibility obviously exist, once particular requirements are prescribed for particular sports, even though they may be intrinsically capable of using the same area[28]. Compatible activities are those which can use the same area (of land or water) at the same time (e.g. canoeing and rowing); partially compatible sports can use the same area but not at the same time (e.g. orienteering and cyclocross) (Table 6.1); incompatible sports cannot use the same area of land and hence land

Table 6.1 Ranked relative compatibility of selected recreational sports

Sport	Ranked (overall) compatibility*
Orienteering	61
Cross country skiing	54
Downhill skiing	46
Cyclocross	45
Modern pentathlon	43
Grass skiing	40
Motor car sports	25
Motor cycle sports	25
Golf	9
Field archery	0

* High scores (over 50) indicate highly compatible sports; scores of under 25 indicate sports which are totally incompatible with at least half the other activities in the list from which this table is derived.

(*Source:* Hockin, Goodall and Whittow[28], p. 46.)

zoning is required. Compatibility of sports frequently leads to conflicts in the countryside about which sport should have the right of use. Resolving such conflicts may be easy enough when the land in question is managed by an independent agent (e.g. as in the case of country parks), but becomes more problematic when the owner of the land favours one particular sport[29, 30].

The less serious and less competitive the level of sporting activity, the more compatible with other sports it becomes. At the purely recreational (non-competitive) level, boating is compatible with canoeing; at the national championship level it is obviously not. In the case of serious top-class sport the sites and the sports have become so specialized that they are, at best, only partially compatible with other uses. In such cases, true sportscapes will exist.

Increasingly, various bodies set up what are regarded as 'standard' levels of provision for sport. For example the ideal area for a football pitch is regarded as 0.9 hectares (2.25 acres). In Britain the Sports Council suggested that an urban area of about 60 000 people should have about 141 acres devoted to sports use. About 50 acres would be given over to soccer pitches alone, 20 for cricket and the remainder to rugby, hockey and netball[31]. Given these conditions, vast tracts of urban land are today given over to mass-appeal sports and from some vantage points come to totally dominate the urban scene. The Sports Council also

Fig. 6.13 Long distance mass participatory running races put increasing pressure on a landscape designed with motor traffic in mind.

recommend sport centre provision at a rate of about one per 50 000. However, as Patmore[29] has pointed out, the rigid application of national norms may stifle much latent demand. Indeed, the figure of one per 50 000 may look somewhat low when compared with the present national provision of one per 75 000.

New sports, as they appear, affect the landscape in different ways. The marathon and distance running boom, with race fields exceeding 20 000 in some cases, has put pressure on municipal authorities to control and redirect traffic on racedays. As geographer-marathoner Christopher Winters[32] puts it, running in the USA can be understood in part as a reaction to, and an attempt to fit into, a landscape designed for the automobile (Fig. 6.13). Sports like hang gliding create pressure on rural hill and scarp country, surfing on beach areas, skiing has placed ecological pressure on mountain regions and water sports compete with one another for precious room on the limited amount of suitable inland water space.

Much sports action, especially of the space-extensive variety, inevitably takes place at the urban fringe, so much so that a peri-urban zone may be emerging – what Sommer[33] calls a 'zone of repose'. Within this girdle of recreational land he sees a futuristic belt accommodating nature trails, nudist camps, winter sports and big stadium complexes – the suburbia of Hedonopolis.

6.5 SPORT, ENVIRONMENT AND THE SENSES

It has been suggested that as the sporting landscape has changed over time, the potential for gratification (by both 'players' and spectators) from the sporting experience has become progressively reduced, the result of the increasing sameness in the sports landscape. In this section we consider two basic frameworks which might assist us in exploring experiential aspects of sport–landscape relations. The first is associated with the work of Appleton and is known as prospect-refuge theory but this has been less developed in a sports context than the second approach which views the sports landscape in terms of elements and ensembles.

6.5.1 Sport and prospect-refuge theory

It has been suggested by geographer Jay Appleton that it is an inborn necessity to hide and to seek. In the course of seeking, various views (prospects) are encountered while in the process of hiding a satisfactory refuge has to be found[34]. Appleton argued that the capacity of a landscape to ensure the achievement of seeing (prospect) without being seen (refuge) is a source of aesthetic satisfaction.

So what has prospect-refuge theory got to do with the sport landscape and the gratification derived therefrom? Although running, swimming, walking and interacting in other ways with the environment (from prospect to refuge) provide sources of satisfaction when leading to survival, they persist as a source of pleasure and gratification when the biological prerequisite for survival no longer applies. There are a large number of sporting activities 'which involve the fitting of bodily movements into a context in which they can more effectively evoke the satisfaction which comes with the creature's successful participation in his (sic) entire environment'[34]. In some sports environments such as a swimming pool, running track, gymnasium or boxing ring, the milieu may be subservient to the bodily movements as a source of satisfaction. Though satisfaction may be obtained in such relatively homogenized spaces from the spatial arrangement of the spectators *vis-à-vis* the 'players' (intimacy is frequently cited as contributing to the overall experience), when compared with sports like skiing or orienteering the environment is relatively unimportant as a source of enjoyment.

Although some enjoyment would probably be obtained from skiing on a featureless, sloping surface in a laboratory, satisfaction is greatly enhanced by the environment within which skiing normally takes place. In such landscapes the 'primitive' significance of the prospect becomes symbolically represented by the views, often from an elevated site (especially so in ski-jumping), the absence of hiding places in the open landscape, and the falling ground. The run transfers the skier from the world of prospect to that of refuge and rapid movement in such environments provides an exhilarating (hazardous) experience. Analogies might be made with sports like orienteering, cross-country running, hang-gliding and other such 'green' activities. Golf might seem quite different from downhill skiing but the notions of prospect and refuge can be invoked symbolically to aid an understanding of the sport–environment experience. We can take an extended quotation from Appleton's work[34] to illustrate this further:

A study of any golf course will reveal an extremely close parallel between the game and the experience of landscape as expressed in the terminology of prospect-refuge theory. The player takes his stance on the tee, an open and often somewhat elevated platform commanding a clear view (over falling ground) of the field through which he (represented by his ball) has to pass. From this prospect the goal can be seen as a clearing in a matrix of 'rough' to which a fairway (cf. vista) allows direct approach. Impediment hazards are introduced to right and left and very likely beyond the target. Other natural phenomena may influence his (or rather the ball's) passage, such as the wind, the wetness of the grass, the slope of the ground. That the player will reach his goal is almost certain – even a poor player is only occasionally denied that ultimate satisfaction – but the process may be achieved with a greater or lesser degree of efficiency which can be measured arithmetically by a simple criterion. When eventually he reaches this objective, he, through the medium of his representative, disappears into that most fundamental of refuges, a hole in the ground. Golf is a parody of primitive environmental experience in which the basic relationship of man to habitat is expressed in a system of stylized equivalents whose identity is very thinly disguised.

Further applications of prospect-refuge theory to the sports landscape have yet to be undertaken but if attempted might produce fascinating results.

6.5.2 Sport landscape elements and ensembles

Cultural geographer Karl Raitz has argued that the sporting landscape is made up of a number of 'landscape elements' which, in total, contribute to a 'landscape ensemble'[35]. He argues that the overall sporting experience is influenced by this ensemble, each element within it contributing to the sense of place experienced by the participants. The ensemble of a community baseball park in a small midwestern town might have elements which include:

the playing surface with a grass outfield and chalk-lined infield; the dugouts along the first and third base fences; the bleachers or grandstand; the concession stands; the board fence with painted advertisements that demarcate the limit of the outfield; the parking lot; the adjacent streets and houses[35].

The elimination of one or more elements subtracts from the distinctiveness or uniqueness of the place experience and the total replacement of the elements with what Neilson[10] calls a 'sports saucer' (or concrete bowl) results in a break between the sport and the broader landscape of which it is part. The argument is that if the landscape elements are reduced in number and one sport place becomes much the same as another, the overall experience will be reduced too because there will be less variety to experience. The English poet and cricket enthusiast, Edmund Blunden[36], was aware that in village cricket the landscape elements could, indeed, become more significant than the game itself. He recognized, however, that in top-class cricket 'where errors matter' there was a case to be made for 'austere cricket grounds, untouched by mysticism' so that players would not be distracted from their 'function'.

6.5.3 A paradox of modern sportscapes

The aim of such austerity and standardization of the sports environment is, of couse, to benefit participants both on the field of play and in the grandstands, terraces or bleachers. The treatment of the sports milieu is another example of the application of scientific humanism which we see around us in shopping malls, housing estates, holiday resorts and international airports. But as we have already noted some observers suggest that artificial environments actually detract from the sports experience. Eichberg[1] asked 'is the windowless hall, made of plastic and concrete, really something progressive when compared with the wilderness in which Jahn's gymnasts wrestled?' His question is rhetorical and he provides no evidence from those who have experienced such environments. Were such evidence unavailable we could interpret such questions as elitist but sports participants do comment on the apparent paradox of humanistic landscapes, i.e. that though the intention is to improve efficiency and comfort a sense of dissatisfaction somehow results. Let us consider some responses to the tendencies of confinement, artifice and standardization, first from 'players' and secondly from spectators.

Michael Oriard[37], one-time American footballer, refers to the dehumanizing aspects of the modern sports environment as 'the seeming

Torch songs

Our text for Olympic fortnight comes, curiously enough, from one of the few sports that has no part in the Games. In the Washington Post this week, Thomas Boswell looked back at the British Open Golf Championship. It was, he said, a truly wonderful, truly international event. Maybe America was the home of the greatest professional golf circuit. But golf "needs a great tournament on a neutral site – a place where Americans don't have home cooking, home crowds, and home conditions." Only four Americans finished in the top thirteen at St Andrews. And you needed, too, an "alternative to the kind of target golf played in the United States" – lush, windless, plasticated greens where "you pick a target and land the ball on it." You needed the "the lumps, mounds, pathways and pot bunkers." You needed the "brain-power and emotional resilience and creative shot-making and intuitive touch" to cope. In sum then: sport comes in many arenas and shapes and sizes. Venues and conditions across the world make beggars of domestic giants, and the mellow man learns and reflects rather than denounces. Sport is not some patriotic star war. Sport is a state of mind and a learning curve and a movable feast.

Fig. 6.14 Creativity and emotion are themes used in this leader from *The Guardian*, 27 July 1984.

lack of air in the semi-domed stadium in Dallas impressed on me a sense of unnatural stillness that was eerie as well as stifling. But playing in the Astrodome produced my ultimate non-experience'. Oriard felt a sense of constriction and an unsettling air of unreality, in great contrast to the feeling of freedom and the connotations of pastoralism in the city which had been generated by the more traditional forms of stadium. Howie Reed, a former pitcher with the Montreal Expos, told James Michener[38] 'I've pitched in those big, sterile stadiums in the States and believe me, it's much better to play a ball game in Jarry (a small, uneconomical ball park in Montreal). Intimacy is an asset. I'd not hesitate in calling it the best place in the world to play baseball. It actually adds to the enjoyment of the game'. In Britain, Inglis'[39] survey of the attitudes of British soccer players to different grounds revealed that 'the larger, more open grounds were all disliked'. Likewise, a survey of fans' favourite baseball stadiums in the USA revealed that the top five favourite ballparks were all built before 1930. The Metrodome at Minneapolis and the Kingdome in Seattle were rated 25th and 26th respectively[40].

In the case of golf, the American observer of the game, Herbert Warren Wind[41], noted that 'a new breed of golfers had forgotten that much of the game's satisfaction results from dealing resourcefully with the hazards' of nature. The US tree-lined course reduced the wind hazard and encouraged a distinctively American style of play, different from that

Fig. 6.15 Golfscape of modern America.

needed on the more 'natural' British course (Fig. 6.14). We have seen
(Section 6.3) that the golf landscape has gradually been transformed into
an artificial sportscape within which modern technology is an integral
part of the scene. Where bricks and mortar (the 'Condo canyon' type
course) are introduced the pleasure gained from playing is certainly
reduced; when the golfmobile (Fig. 6.15) or, as in Japan the 'monorail'
designed to carry clubs around the course, are introduced it is highly
arguable whether such an activity remains 'sport', though 'playing' and
'recreation' may continue. Could such phenomena be sporting analogues
of the commuter train, escalator or conveyer belt?

   Some sportscapes may be dehumanizing because they permit – indeed
they may be specifically constructed for – highly specialized, regularized
and rationalized training methods. Some sports take place in such
environments as to coerce the athlete into 'continued repetition of the
same precisely fixed and isolated narrow tasks'[42]. Synthetic running
tracks, for example, are designed not to make training easier but to avoid
deterioration in bad weather; they are designed not to interrupt the
training regimen. Although Astroturf is intended to provide benefits,
sliding tackles produce unpleasant 'astroburns', the rate of injury on
synthetic turf being 50% higher than on natural grass in the case of

American football. Given that two-thirds of gridiron 'fields' in the US are made of plastic horrible degrees of wear and tear on joints and tendons are the inevitable result. Heating of artificial surfaces also tends to increase player discomfort, artificial surfaces having on average summer temperatures 4.5°C higher than those of grass. Not surprisingly, players generally dislike such surfaces. Track and field athletics at the highest level are today exclusively confined to synthetic tracks, but the stiffness in these materials has again been implicated in joint and tendon injuries[43]. Grass, though less efficient, provides a more gentle surface. The marathon runner. Alberto Salazar, expressed a desire to get away from road and track and return to cross-country running, but even here artifice intrudes; at the world cross-country championships in New York in 1984 a racecourse was used and artificial 'hills' were temporarily constructed*.

In the modern artificial sportscape, the feelings of the fan may also be changed; 'the plushness of the theater seats and the extravagance of electronic scoreboards make the fan a passive observer of spectacle, rather than a vicarious participant in the re-enactment of ancient virtues'[37]. Oriard sees the traditional baseball park 'with its grassy spaciousness and sunlit diamond (as) a vestigial remnant of the rural landscape within the crowded, dirty, ashphalt city'. If such baseball environments provide the fan with feelings of 'peace and contentment, and intimations of unity with his (sic) environment'[37], the appliance of science to sport has made spectating more safe and comfortable but in some way less satisfying.

Several pressures have contributed to the desire to improve the comfort and safety of stadiums, notably in Britain where many football and cricket grounds are approaching a century of service. Three pressures in particular can be identified. First, there has been a desire to slow down, or halt, the declining number of spectators at soccer in particular, by increasing the proportion of seated accommodation. Secondly, there has been the implementation of certain safety standards and the reduction of capacity following very serious injuries and deaths resulting from fire (the Bradford incident in 1985 was the most serious) and crowding. Thirdly, there has been increased segregation of supporters on the terraces, visiting fans being separated from those of the home team. This practice is common in several European countries and is not restricted to Britain. Following the British experience a Swedish report recently advocated crowd control by police meeting visiting supporters outside the stadium[44]† (in Britain they are usually met at a rail or bus terminal) and escorted to the stadium to be placed in their designated 'pens'.

* Quoted in *Running*, March 1985.
† I am grateful to Bob Jones for this reference.

Traditionally crowds at Scandinavian sports events had not been viewed as a problem.

The economist Scitovsky[45] suggests that improved comfort should not be confused with a higher standard of living or, it might be added, progress. From the spectators' perspectives, sitting in a box may be more comfortable but lacks the greater sense of community which is obtained from standing on the more exposed and tiring terraces. It should be stressed that this is not a condemnation of comfort *per se* but an indication that dissatisfaction can result from more comfortable forms.

With glassed-in suites, closed circuit television, domed stadiums and synthetic pitches which eliminate the chance elements of nature, sport is reduced to theatrical spectacle. Indeed, 'improved' designs in football stadiums may have had the effect of alienating support. Simon Inglis[39] was told that at Tranmere and Chester (in north-west England), 'the most ardent supporters complained for years how cramped and inadequate the old stands were but once these were replaced by efficient but soulless steel structures, fans pined for the old wooden stand'. Inglis believes that 'the history of ground design is full of clubs who declined rapidly after building a new stand'. He rhetorically asks 'would we really want to see our local team perform in soulless concrete bowls that look much like any other concrete bowl?'

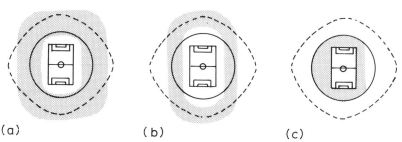

(a)   (b)   (c)

Fig. 6.16 Layout of stadiums and optimal viewing situations. (a) The Aztec Stadium was built especially for football yet still suffers from too many spectators too far from the action. It is built in the quadric plan, whereby each side is not parallel to the touchline, but curved slightly to allow better sight lines. The Greeks curved the seats of the arena with a chord of 3 m in a 200 m arc, a calculation also used at the Aztec Stadium. (b) Elliptical grounds such as Wembley show that the majority of spectators are outside the optimum viewing circle, and maybe one-fifth (20 000) are beyond the maximum viewing circle. Wembley also suffers from being a single-deck stadium, and having a wide perimeter track. (c) The ideal football ground follows the quadric plan but keeps all the stands within the optimum viewing circle. If space is limited the West Side should be larger, so that more view the game with the sun behind them. (Solid circle line is 90 m radius from the centre spot, or 150 m from the furthest corner – the optimum viewing distance. Broken line is 190 m from the furthest corner – the maximum viewing distance. (Source: Inglis[39].)

The closer people are to the sport action the greater their arousal and excitement, but the bigger the stadium the smaller the proportion of the total number of spectators who are exposed to the fine detail of what is happening on the field[46]. This is one of the prices we pay for giant stadiums which have had the effect of changing the relationship between spectators and the sport (Fig. 6.16). It has been suggested[39] that the spatial limits for viewing a football match is 90 m from the centre circle or about 150 m from the furthest corner flag. This optimal viewing distance for spectators was largely satisfied in the traditional English stadium with stands close to the pitch and the ground designed to a quartic plan. Newer stadiums, including both Wembley and the Aztec Stadium in Mexico City, may have been built specially for football but suffer from the fact that too many spectators are outside the optimal viewing circle. At Wembley an elliptical pattern means that the majority of spectators are actually outside the optimal viewing area. Despite the undoubted technical improvements associated with modern stadiums the spectators, while being more comfortable, are physically and emotionally distanced from the game they come to see. As Relph[26] would say, these stadiums have 'almost nothing in them that has not been concerned and planned so that it will serve those human needs which can be assessed in terms of efficiency and improved material conditions'. But spontaneity and the expression of human emotions are quietly and unobtrusively diminished, reducing the overall quality of the sport experience.

In some sports it might be argued that each stadium has its own idiosyncracies, hence defying the imposition of a general model. Such an assertion has been made for English cricket, for example[47]. To an extent this is obviously true, yet even in the gentle game of cricket, pressures for spatial confinement and artifice are undeniably present. In Australia commercial imperatives have led to the game being played under floodlights (in England, as an experiment, this was tried in downtown soccer stadiums) and in Australia there has been the substantial growth of indoor cricket. Such air-conditioned 'cricket centres' are often set amid industrial buildings, warehouses or filling stations (Fig. 6.17); the industrial landscape within which such places are located is reflected in the 'industrialization' of the sport environment.

The application of technology to sport does not inevitably reduce the sensations gained from relating closely to the environment. Indeed, those 'technosports' which take place in the open air (e.g. hang gliding, water skiing, motorbike racing) may heighten environmental awareness through the utilization of air currents, wind, waves, etc. The humanistic geographer, J. B. Jackson[48], drew attention to the fact that sport at speed 'shows nature shorn of gentler and human traits . . . To the perceptive individual there can be an almost mystical quality to the

Fig. 6.17 Brisbane Indoor Cricket Centre in its industrial environment.

experience'. But a heightened awareness and alertness to the surrounding environmental conditions may be best achieved in the absence of technology. Sports like running, skiing, cycling and orienteering 'directly exploit the pleasure-giving potential of nature by intimately incorporating the perceptual experience of the natural environment within the activity itself'[49]. On a still, warm summer evening, running in the countryside in preparation for a long distance race can provide an almost sensual feeling of oneness with nature[32]. Similar effects may be experienced by participants in other 'green' sports. The Scandinavian sport of orienteering, argues Appleton[49], integrates physical activity and environment to the farthest limits so far achieved in any recreational activity*. Similarly Janet Dunleavey[52] says that 'on cross country skis the human animal becomes a creature of wood and plain, kin to the deer, the ruffed goose, the otter, the snowshoe hare and other creatures who share the winter landscape'. At a time of year when other humans are indoors, the cross country skier emerges, 'rejoicing in the rythmic coordination of arms and legs, the spontaneous generation of ever-increasing energy, the exhilaration of breathing deeply in well-

* Otherwise, geographical allusions to orienteering have tended to refer to it as a basis for learning mapping and spatial skills, for example see Kirby[50] and Adams[51].

oxygenated air, . . . the sense of physical well-being with no hint of exhaustion, that is the skier's bounty'. Contrast these sentiments with those of sports participants who have been alienated by the bland environments in which they 'play'.

Picnic racing anywhere is one of the great Aussie institutions. There are little meetings on summer days all over Australia, in places with names like Tatura, Towong, and Yanko Creek. There is the Great Western meeting held where they make the local champagne; the racegoers usually go on winery tours first and afterwards behave accordingly. And there is a place called Bong-Bong, where the racing has passed into folklore as a byword.

Hanging Rock, though, is famously good-tempered. Perhaps people are inspired by the setting: the volcanic pinacles of the rock towering above them, the gum trees and hills of Victoria stretching ahead of them, and the sheer brooding resonance of the place, which is sacred to the Wurrunjerrie (or River Gum Grub) tribe as well as to the Australian film industry.

More likely, everyone behaves because the big meeting is held on New Year's Day, and they are all much too subdued after the night before to get too raucously drunk.

Technically, Hanging Rock is not really a picnic meeting because the jockeys are pros (if not exactly the local Edderys and Carsons) and the whole thing is run by the official stewards. But everyone thinks of it as picnic racing – a day out in the country, an hour's drive from Melbourne.

And if it were a normal meeting it would have been killed off years ago by bureaucratic officials as uneconomic, outdated and even dangerous – it's a very tight track and nasty and greasy if it rains. The meeting has been kept going by its enormous popularity and its sense of tradition. This year saw the 101st running of the Hanging Rock Cup.

Vignette IX Picnic racing in rural Australia. Although some of the races are professional (as in the case of those at Hanging Rock), the pleasure is in large part obtained from the natural environment in which such events are held. (Extracted from Engel[53].)

6.6 CONCLUSIONS

As sport emerged from its folk game origins it had a number of effects upon the landscape. In some central areas of cities and in some suburbs it is fair to say that sport has been the dominant factor influencing the character and shape of the landscape. At more periodic intervals we have seen how massive flows of fans change the landscapes of our cities. As technology has increasingly been embraced by sports, new forms of monoculture have emerged. Although developed and designed with improved satisfaction and performance in mind, it has been suggested that in some senses the overall sports experience is diminished in such environments and a partial response to this may have been a renewed 'greening' of sports and a return to non-sporting physical activities requiring no specialized site. Like the entertainment landscape of which it is part, the sports landscape is perhaps the most artificial, and hence the most human, of environments. As such it is worth recalling the words of geographer Peirce Lewis[54], that the landscape is part of our 'unwitting biography, reflecting our values, our aspirations, and even our fears in tangible, visible form'.

FURTHER READING

The sub-discipline of sports geography awaits the first book on the landscapes of sport. Until it is written readers wishing to go further can consult a number of fascinating papers by scholars from a variety of disciplines. Information on recreational land use is well covered in Allan Patmore's *Recreation and Resources*, Blackwell, Oxford, 1983, but references to sport *per se* tend to be incidental. Highly stimulating ideas on the growing spatial confinement and rationalization of the sports landscape are found in two papers by Henning Eichberg, Stopwatch, horizontal bar, gymnasium; the technologizing of sport in the eighteenth and early nineteenth centuries, *Journal of the Philosophy of Sport*, **9**, 1982, pages 43–59 and The enclosure of the body – on the historical relativity of 'health', 'nature' and the environment of sport, *Journal of Contemporary History*, **21**, 1986, pages 99–121. Many of the themes in these papers are given a twentieth century (and North American) treatment, see for example Brian Neilson's Dialogue with the city; the evolution of baseball parks, *Landscape*, **29**, 1, 1986, pages 39–47 and Karl Raitz's Perception of sports landscapes and gratification in the sport experience, *Sport Place*, **1**, 1, 1987, pages 4–19. Sensitive descriptions of the unique qualities of the environments of particular sports are typified by Aylwin Sampson's *Grounds of Appeal; the Homes of First Class Cricket*, Robert Hale, London, 1981 and Simon Inglis's *The Football Grounds of England and Wales*, Collins, London, 1983.

REFERENCES

1. Eichberg, H. (1982) Stopwatch, horizontal bar, gymnasium: the technologizing of sport in the eighteenth and early nineteenth centuries. *Journal of the Philosophy of Sport*, **9**, 43–59.
2. Eichberg, H. (1986) The enclosure of the body – on the historical relativity of 'health', 'nature' and the environment of sport. *Journal of Contemporary History*, **21**, 99–121.

3. Wepfer, A. (1984) The diffusion of volksmarching in the United States. *The Geographical Bulletin*, 9–28.
4. Brailsford, D. (1987) The geography of eighteenth century English Spectator Sports. *Sport Place*, **1**, 1, 41–56.
5. Sandiford, K. (1984) Victorian cricket techniques and industrial technology. *The British Journal of Sports History*, **1**, 272–85.
6. Wagner, P. (1981) Sport: culture and geography, in *Space and Time in Geography* (ed. A. Pred), Gleerup, Lund, 85–108.
7. Galtung, J. (1984) Sport and international understanding: sport as a carrier of deep culture and structure, in *Sport and International Understanding* (ed. M. Ilmarinen), Springer-Verlag, Berlin, 12–19.
8. Riess, S. (1978) The geography and economics of professional ball parks, 1971–1930. *Proceedings of the North American Society for Sports History*, 35–6.
9. Steiner, J. (1933) *America at Play*, McGraw Hill, New York.
10. Neilson, B. (1986) Dialogue with the city; the evolution of the baseball park. *Landscape*, **29**, 39–47.
11. Ezersky, E. and Theibert, P. (1976) *Facilities for Sport and Physical Education*, Mosby, St Louis.
12. Bergsland, E. and Seim-Haugen, O. (1983) Holmenkollbakken og Holmenkollrenne. *Sno og Ski*, **1**, 97–108.
13. Vamplew, W. (1976) *The Turf*, Allen Lane, London.
14. Coppock, T. (1966) The recreational use of land and water in rural Britain. *Tijdschrift voor Economische en Sociale Geografie*, **57**, 81–96.
15. Priestley, J. (1934) *English Journey*, Heinemann, London.
16. Buxton, A. (1987) Where the going is always good. *The Observer*, 17th May.
17. Adams, R. and Rooney, J. (1985) Evolution of American golf facilities. *The Geographical Review*, **75**, 419–38.
18. Darwin, B. (1951) *British Golf*, Collins, London.
19. Lowerson, J. and Myerscough, J. (1977) *Time to Spare in Victorian England*, Harvester, Hassocks.
20. Durrant, J. and Betterman, O. (1952) *Pictorial History of American Sport*, Barnes, New York.
21. Hawtree, F. (1983) *The Golf Course*, E. and F. N. Spon, London.
22. Barnes, J. (1984) The hole world in their hands. *Sunday Times Magazine*, 22 July, 32–5.
23. Adams, R. and Rooney, J. (1984) Condo Canyon; an examination of emerging golf landscapes in America. *North American Culture*, **1**, 65–75.
24. Adams, R. (1983) A geographic analysis of US golf facilities, paper read at the Annual Conference of the Society for the North American Cultural Survey, Lexington, Ky.
25. Hegarty, C. (1985) *An Analysis of the Geography of United States Golf with Particular Reference to a New Form of Golf, the Cayman Facility*, masters dissertation (unpublished), Oklahoma State University.
26. Relph, E. (1981) *Rational Landscapes and Humanistic Geography*, Croom Helm, London.
27. Relph, E. (1976) *Place and Placelessness*, Pion, London.
28. Hockin, R., Goodall, B. and Whittow, J. (1980) The site requirements of planning of outdoor recreation events. *Geographical Papers*, **43**, University of Reading.
29. Patmore, A. (1983) *Recreation and Resources*, Blackwell, Oxford.

30. Tanner, M. (1983) Governing bodies and the geography of water sports, in *Geographical Perspectives on Sport* (eds J. Bale and C. Jenkins), Department of PE, Birmingham University, pp. 173–200.
31. Patmore, A. (1970) *Land and Leisure*, David and Charles, Newton Abbot.
32. Winters, C. (1980) Running. *Landscape*, **24**, 19–22.
33. Sommer, J. (1975) Fat city and Hedonopolis; the American urban future? in *Human Geography in a Shrinking World* (eds R. Abler *et al.*), Duxbury Press, North Scituate, Mass.
34. Appleton, J. (1975) *The Experience of Landscape*, Wiley, London.
35. Raitz, K. (1985) Interpreting America's leisure landscapes, paper read at conference on Geographical Perspectives on Sport, London.
36. Blunden, E. (1985) *Cricket Country*, Pavilion Library, London.
37. Oriard, M. (1976) Sport and space. *Landscape*, **21**, 32–40.
38. Michener, J. (1976) *Sport in America*, Random House, New York.
39. Inglis, S. (1982) *The Football Grounds of England and Wales*, Collins, London.
40. Douglas, B. (1987) Fans rate major league baseball parks. *Sport Place*, **1**, 2, 36.
41. Wind, H. (1973) The lure of golf, in *Sport and Society* (eds J. Talimini and C. Page), Little, Brown and Co., Boston, pp. 397–412.
42. Rigauer, B. (1981) *Sport and Work*, Columbia University Press, New York.
43. Riley, T. (1981) *Sports Fitness and Sports Injuries*, Faber, London.
44. Svensson, B. (1986) Welfare and criminality in Sweden, in *Situational Crime Prevention; from Theory into Practice* (eds K. Heal and G. Laycock), HMSO, London.
45. Scitovsky, T. (1976) *The Joyless Economy*, Oxford University Press, New York.
46. Mehrabian, A. (1970) *Public Places and Private Spaces*, Basic Books, New York.
47. Sampson, A. (1981) *Grounds of Appeal*, Hale, London.
48. Jackson, J. (1957/8) The abstract world of the hot-rodder. *Landscape*, **7**, 22–7.
49. Appleton, J. (1982) Pleasure and the perception of habitat: a conceptual framework, in *Environmental Aesthetics: Essays in Interpretation* (eds B. Sadler and A. Carlson), Western Geographical series, 20, University of Victoria, pp. 27–45.
50. Kirby, R. (1970) The geographical sport of orienteering. *Geography*, **5**, 285–8.
51. Adams, W. (1972) Geography and orienteering. *Journal of Geography*, 71.
52. Dunleavey, J. (1981) Skiing; the worship of Ullr in America. *Journal of Popular Culture*, **4**, 74–85.
53. Engel, M. (1987) Horseplay at Hanging Rock. *The Guardian*, 10 January.
54. Lewis, P. (1979) Axioms for reading the landscape, in *The Interpretation of Ordinary Landscapes* (ed. D. Meinig), Oxford University Press, New York, 11–32.

Chapter 7

SPORTS
REGIONS

The outcome of the differing rates of adoption, the relocation and the landscape changes which have been described in the previous chapters is a mosaic of sports regions. A simple definition of a region is a number of spatially contiguous areas sharing a particular characteristic. In the case of scattered, non-contiguous areas sharing a particular characteristic we apply the term 'areal classification'. This chapter focuses on the concepts of regions and areal classifications in the context of sports.

For the average person the regions which are most meaningful are those of a 'vernacular' nature which they carry about inside their heads. Certain places are readily associated with certain sports in the mind's eye. Mention Texas and football comes to mind; talk of South Wales evokes images of rugby; Scotland and golf go together as much as do Canada and ice hockey. Despite our obvious familiarity with such sports-regional stereotypes, we know rather little about the public's cognitive involvement in sports. Little has been done, for example, to examine the strength of regional sports imagery or of the degree of congruence between the sports images people have of places and the sporting reality. This brings us to what might be called 'geographical' sports regions, in contrast to those of a vernacular variety described above. Geographers have made many attempts to identify sports regions using 'objective' measures of various kinds. This chapter explores both kinds of region at a variety of scales and suggests that the exploration of the degrees of congruence between regional sports images and actuality is one of the sports geographer's most important tasks.

7.1 MENTAL SPORTS MAPS

Sports-place images are communicated by a variety of media, including the press, television, radio, novels and even poetry (Fig. 7.1). Because we cannot visit personally all places and regions at which sports are practised we are dependent upon such secondary sources for images of the

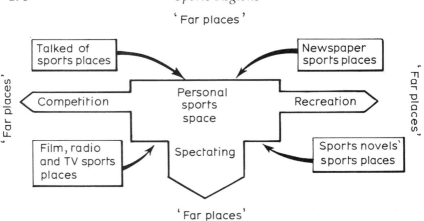

Fig. 7.1 Sources of information about sport-place images. (Source: Bale[1].)

sporting character of many parts of both our own country and the world. Bias frequently characterizes the media coverage of sports; certain regions receive greater coverage of say, soccer matches, than others; sports commentators on radio and television often link certain places to certain sporting attributes, labelling entire regions such as Eastern Europe as homogeneous entities. It is important that sports geography addresses itself to the accuracy of such images, something we proceed to do in the following pages.

The way in which sport is organized, i.e. on a team basis, stimulates local rivalries and local and regional identities. Nationalism, regionalism and localism, already built into many sports, are reinforced by one of the basic tools of sports coverage, namely the need to establish points of identification for the audience. As Whannell[2] has put it, 'television does not simply relay sport to us. It presents a particular view of sport'. Successful clubs often obtain greater media coverage than their unsuccessful colleagues, hence obtaining free advertising which serves to reinforce the link between sport and place. Places with teams which regularly win major events build up a mental link in people's minds between sport and place. Even novels about sports carry regional connotations. David Storey's *This Sporting Life* had, of necessity, to be set in the north of England. Centred as it was on the rugby league scene it would have been impossible to set it anywhere else. But Hugh de Selincourt's *The Cricket Match* did not have to be set in the south-east of England since cricket is played nationwide. Selincourt chose the south as his locale and in doing so passes on to the reader a sport-place association. Likewise Jilly Cooper, in her book *Class*, chooses Esher (in Surrey) to connote rugby union but each Saturday night the readers of the *South*

Fig. 7.2 The landscape of Welsh rugby as communicated each Saturday evening in the *South Wales Echo* by 'Gren'. Such media serve to reinforce images of sport and place. (Composite landscape based on several 'Gren' cartoons.)

Wales Echo are reminded via the cartoon strip by 'Gren' that it is the Valleys of Glamorgan and Gwent that are rugby's heartlands (Fig. 7.2).

In other words, a variety of media communicate sport-place images to the public who receive them as vernacular sports regions. These regions are not demarcated from their neighbours in any 'scientific' way; they are the taken-for-granted regions which people carry around in their heads as mental sports maps. Some examples of such perceptual regions are shown in Fig. 7.3. These represent the mapped responses of under-graduate students who were asked to indicate freely the areas of Britain which they associated with particular sports*. Areas identified with each sport by 60% of the respondents are enclosed by isolines (or, perhaps, 'isopercepts'). For example, it can be seen that football (soccer) is most strongly associated with England's industrial heartland – the 'axial belt' stretching from the metropolis, through the midlands to the north-west. Golf, on the other hand, is seen as a dominantly Scottish sport with an outlier in the south-east of England (40%). Tennis is very firmly associated with the south-east of England, no other part of the country being associated with the sport by more than 20% of the respondents. If tennis has a south-eastern image, rugby has a South Wales image with a minor outlier in southern Scotland (30%). Cricket approaches a bi-modal pattern in terms of its vernacular regionalization, with the south-east of England and much of Yorkshire being strongly associated with the game.

A similar example (Fig. 7.4) can be used to illustrate the idea at the continental level of scale, using the island continent of Australia and the three sports of cricket, soccer and Australian Rules football. Over a

* For greater details of these see references [1] and [4].

> At twelve-thirty it was decided not to wait for the missing pair, and the nine cricketers started off. At two-thirty, after halts at Catford, the White Hart at Sevenoaks, the Angel at Tunbridge Wells, and three smaller inns at tiny villages, the char-à-banc drew up triumphantly beside the cricket ground of the Kentish village of Fordenden.
>
> Donald was enchanted at his first sight of rural England. And rural England is the real England, unspoilt by factories and financiers and tourists and hustle. He sprang out of the char-à-banc . . . and gazed eagerly round. The sight was worth an eager gaze or two. It was a hot summer's afternoon. There was no wind, and the smoke from the red-roofed cottages curled slowly up into the golden haze. The clock on the flint tower of the church struck the half-hour, and the vibrations spread slowly across the shimmering hedge rows, spangled with white blossom of the convolvulus, and lost themselves tremulously among the orchards. Bees lazily drifted. White butterflies flapped their aimless way among the gardens. Delphiniums, larkspur, tiger-lillies, evening primrose, monk's hood, sweet peas, swaggered brilliantly above the box hedges, the wooden palings and the rickety gates. The cricket field itself was a mass of daisies and buttercups and dandelions, tall grasses and purple vetches and thistledown, and great clumps of dark red sorrel, except, of course, for the oblong patch in the centre – mown, rolled, watered – a smooth, shining emerald of grass, the Pride of Fordenden, the Wicket.

Vignette X Cricket in Kent. This extract conjures a rustic image of cricket in the 'Garden of England'. Indeed, the climax of the 'English country gardens' paragraph is the wicket itself. In fact, more cricket clubs per capita are found in industrial Yorkshire. (From Macdonnell[3].)

hundred geography teachers from all over the country were asked to undertake the mental mapping exercise and the resulting map of the 60% 'isopercepts' shows that cricket is perceived as being widely distributed throughout the populated parts of Australia. Australian Rules football, on the other hand, is viewed as being associated with Victoria and much of New South Wales while soccer is identified strongly with the former state only. The extent to which these maps reflect 'reality' (either in terms of the absolute number of participants, clubs, star players, or their per capita equivalents) remains to be seen and will require the attention of an Australian sports geographer.

Following the reception of mental sports maps it is not unusual for such images to be utilized by the places involved in order to boost their images in the form of promotional literature. Sport, therefore, helps advertising and, perhaps, assists the creation of new employment. A leaflet designed to attract industry to Wakefield, for example, suggested that the labour

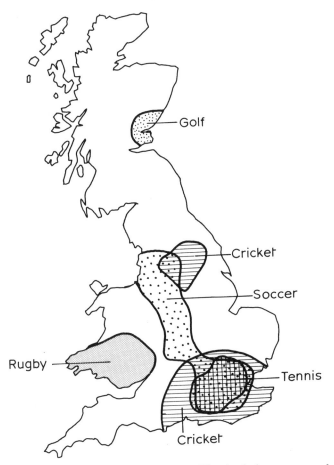

Fig. 7.3 Vernacular regions of six British sports. The shaded areas are enclosed by 60% 'isopercepts', i.e. the areas which 60% of respondents associated with each sport.

force gave as much on the shop floor as the town's rugby team did on the sports field[5]. Sometimes places are so strongly associated with sport that they have to stress that they do have other things to offer. Trafford, in Manchester, published an advertisement stressing that it was as good for industry as it was for cricket and soccer. On the tourist front, Ireland (Fig. 7.5) promotes itself through sport, by a sportsman, while in Brazil in 1970 the government announced plans for the development of the Trans-Amazonian Highway by utilizing the national mania for football by producing posters with the pro-government slogan 'There's No Holding Brazil' on a picture of the celebration of a goal by the soccer genius Pele[6].

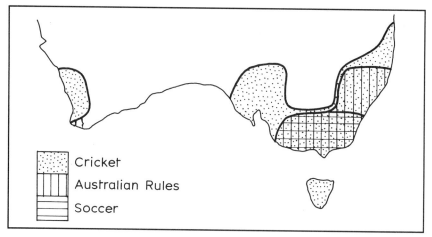

Fig. 7.4 A mental map of three sports in Australia, based on 60% 'isopercepts' of a group of geography teachers.

Sport is also prominent among the factors which contribute to national stereotyping and identity. One example comes from the work of Professor J. P. Cole[7], who asked a small sample of middle-class Mexican respondents to name the five aspects which first came to mind when the names of different countries were mentioned. For Britain, as many people mentioned Wembley Stadium as Trafalgar Square, as many Bobby Charlton as Sir Francis Drake. For Brazil Pele received twenty-three times as many mentions as any other Brazilian. Identical surveys requesting people's responses to China, USSR and France interestingly resulted in no mentions possessing sporting connotations. The fact that some countries seem to possess sporting connotations while others do not may indicate the differing impacts which sports have on societies and the ability of those sports to communicate 'favourable' images overseas.

What is more, it seems probable that if sports stars are the only members of a particular nation (or region or city for that matter) known to people from other places, the sportsmen or women in question may be taken to be representative of the whole nationality. Events like the World Cup or the Olympic Games may mould people's impressions of participating nations and nationalities. For example, Fig. 7.6 shows that football fans (if a sample of school students is typical) appear to view Brazilians as more skilful, creative and intelligent than non-fans who view them as more aggressive, unfriendly, nasty and dull. It is interesting that for those interested in football, Brazil is often regarded as synonymous with skill and excitement[8]. In other words, the perceived characteristics of nations may be derived from those of the sporting individuals who represent them.

Bill Beaumont's Ireland.

MEET the little people! Beaumont's own hurling heroes. I didn't know one end of a hurley from the other until I came here. Now I've reached local junior level! (Thanks to some fine coaching from my son, Daniel.)

Ireland's a place I find myself returning to, time after time. There's a real warmth here. It's amazing how you can feel completely at home, wherever you happen to end up.

And that's what makes it such great driving country. In no time at all you can be spirited from the heart of a big city to the wilds of Postcard Ireland.

And you know, for somewhere that seems a million miles away, it's not a long way to Tipperary!

The most interesting people go to Ireland.

For your free **Ireland 85** colour brochure, write to: **Ireland 85,** Irish Tourist Board, 150 New Bond Street, London W1Y 0AQ or dial 100 and ask for **FREEFONE IRELAND.**

Name _____

Address _____

_____ Postcode _____

🍀 Ireland

LONDON 150 NEW BOND STREET W1Y 0AQ (01 493 3201) BIRMINGHAM 6-8 TEMPLE ROW B2 5HG (021 236 9724) MANCHESTER 28 CROSS STREET M2 3NH (061 832 5981) GLASGOW 19 DIXON STREET G1 4AJ (041 221 2311)

Fig. 7.5 The image of Ireland as a hurling country is used to sell it to potential tourists by former rugby international, Bill Beaumont.

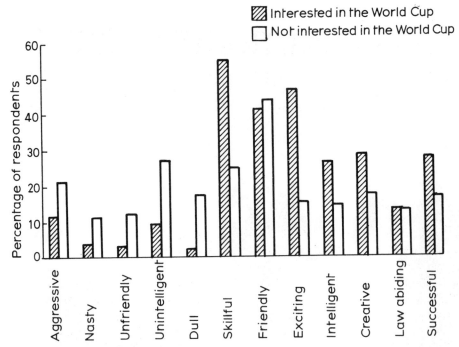

Fig. 7.6 Impressions of the Brazilian people held by soccer fans and non-fans. (After: Walton[8].)

What people think places, regions and countries are like is what is important in the way they form judgements of such places. However, there is likely to be a mis-match between perceived sports regions and those which we try to define objectively. It is those kinds of 'objective' sports regions ('geographical' regions, perhaps, to contrast them with 'vernacular' regions) that form the bulk of the remainder of this chapter.

Two kinds of sports region can be identified. First, there are those regions which are delimited on the basis of their apparent ability to 'produce' a disproportionate number of superior or elite athletes. These are often described as 'hotbeds' of player productivity or output. A second kind of region is defined by the emphasis it appears to place on mass participation in sport; in such regions there seem to be a larger number of clubs or a greater involvement by the population, either in their spectating or participation habits. In delimiting these sports regions we can compare our results with the vernacular regions or mental maps which we carry round in our heads. This is a particularly important function of a regional approach to sports geography since our 'objective' maps act as a yardstick against which we can compare our biased and untutored preconceptions. This may be especially important at the international scale, at which level our preconceptions might logically be regarded as being most at odds with 'reality'.

7.2 IDENTIFYING SPORTS REGIONS

One way of looking at the geographical differences in sporting or athletic 'production' would be simply to consider place to place variations in the birthplaces or school origins of elite participants in different sports. Such an approach is well illustrated by the geographic variation in the origins of major stock car drivers in 1970 (Fig. 7.7). Richard Pillsbury[9], a geographer at Georgia State University, used the residences of drivers as a surrogate measure of interest in stock car racing. He revealed that the sport's top professionals came from four main regions: the Carolina–Virginia Piedmont, a band of cities stretching from Wisconsin to Indiana, southern New England and adjacent upstate New York; and central and southern California.

Fascinating though such a distribution pattern may be, it does not take geographical differences in population into account. For this reason a more popular approach to the regional geography of sport is to look at relative differences in 'productivity' (i.e. numbers of players 'produced') or in the emphasis placed on particular sports. Rooney[10] has identified a large number of 'hotbeds' of sports activity in North America using an approach which compared regional variations with the national per capita level (of production or emphasis) which is calculated as an index of 1.00. This index provides a convenient yardstick against which the regional levels can be compared and is found by applying the following simple formula:

$$I = \frac{N}{P} \Big/ \frac{1}{n}$$

where I is the index, N is the number of athletes or clubs in the sub-region (county or state) under consideration, P is the population of the sub-region and n is the number of people in the region per athlete or per club. For example, if there were 23 000 people per rugby club in Britain as a whole $1/n$ would be 1/23 000. If a particular county had a population of 900 000 and also had 200 rugby clubs, the formula would read:

$$I = \frac{200}{900\ 000} \Big/ \frac{1}{23\ 000}$$

$$I = 5.11$$

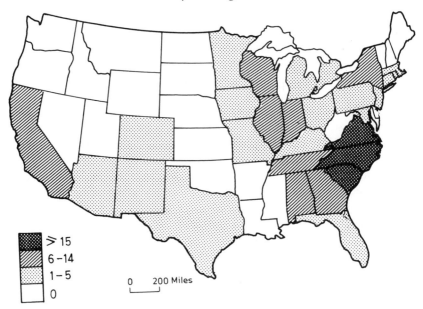

Fig. 7.7 Major stock car drivers, 1970. (Numbers refer to the number of drivers resident in the state). (Source: Pillsbury[9].)

In this case the county would have 5.11 times as many rugby clubs per capita as the country as a whole.

7.2.1 Some regional variations

Within a country such as the USA the ability of a region to produce elite athletes varies tremendously. In the late 1970s Louisiana had an index for the production of major college footballers of 2.98 compared with one of 0.06 for North Dakota[11]. Other states with high per capita scores were Missouri (2.32), and Texas (2.07). For basketball Rooney found that in the mid-1960s Utah had an index of 2.58, Kentucky 2.27 and Indianna 2.10. For baseball the leading three states in terms of the production of major league players were California (1.97), Oklahoma (1.94), and Nevada (1.75). Golf professionals come mainly from Texas (2.86), Oklahoma (2.76) and Wyoming (2.07)[10]. These scores obscure a good deal of intra-state variety and at the level of the individual county much higher scores will always be found to exist since the state scores are averages for a larger areal unit. For example, for footballer production Oucita, Louisiana, had an index of 6.43 with three other Louisiana counties having indicies of over 3.9.

In multi-event sports like track and field athletics different parts of the country appear to 'specialize' in the 'production' of different types of athletes. In Britain, for example, the south-east tends to have high per capita levels of sprinters while the long distance road runners tend to be most prolific in the north-west[4]. In the USA Goudge has identified Texas as a hotbed of sprinter production with Oregon similarly impressive for the output of elite high school distance runners[12]. Explaining why such geographic variations should exist in the production of elite athletes is not easy. The Texas football hotbed was attributed by Rooney[10] to the traditions of rugged individualism and militarism. In some cases sport provides an escape route from the ghetto or dole queue – a perceived route to employment and upward social mobility. Undoubtedly a multivariate explanation lies behind the regional differences in athletic productivity, Yetman and Eitzen[13] commenting that 'an unknown combination of variables predispose a county to overproduce or underproduce quality football players'. However, using multivariate statistical analysis of a number of social and economic variables they found that middle-class areas were highly productive but so too were those with large numbers of blacks.

When such geographical variations are mapped, it is often possible to discern regions of above average emphasis on the sporting attribute in question. Fig. 7.8 exemplifies professional footballer and boxer regions in England and Wales on the basis of those counties with 1.3 or more times the national average per capita output. In this example the regions are made up of contiguous counties of above average levels of 'production'. The map reveals that for football three regions and two outliers of high footballer productivity exist. The industrial north-east, long part of the folklore of British soccer, has counties such as Tyne and Wear, Cleveland, and Durham with indices of 2.64, 2.31 and 1.75 respectively. Further south, Clwyd, Merseyside and Greater Manchester have 1.92, 2.22 and 1.39 times the national average per capita output. The third region is made up of Humberside (1.43) and South Yorkshire (2.34). The two outliers in industrial South Wales are West (2.54) and South (1.62) Glamorgan – showing that Wales can produce soccer as well as rugby players.

The regions of above average boxer production are similar in some respects to the soccer regions. Professional boxers and footballers tend to come from traditional areas of heavy industry which today have relatively high levels of unemployment. Undoubtedly the major region of boxing activity in terms of 'production' of boxers is South Wales, a region which has produced a long line of illustrious fighters over many years. In the early 1980s very high per capita indices are found for South Glamorgan (4.25), Gwent (3.43), Mid Glamorgan (2.79), and West Glamorgan (2.75).

Fig. 7.8 Regions 'producing' more than 1.3 times the national per capita average number of professional footballers and boxers. (Source: Bale[4].)

A belt of industrial England running from West Yorkshire through South Yorkshire, Nottingham, Leicester and Northampton is another zone of high boxer productivity, the principal centre of activity in this region being Leicestershire and Nottinghamshire with respective indices of 2.41 and 1.55. For boxing three important outliers are worthy of mention. The metropolitan counties of Merseyside (2.41), Greater London (1.66) (the centre for the consumption of boxing) and the West Midlands (1.52) each produce at over one and a half times the national average. Interestingly, professional boxer production is noticeably absent from the major region of pro-soccer player production, the north-east. Likewise, London's relative ability to produce boxers is not matched by its supply of footballers, even though in this latter activity output has increased dramatically over the last thirty years[14].

Simplistic economic explanations about regional variations in the production of professionals in boxing and football may well need complementing by approaches which include an awareness of traditional regional popular culture, since areas of similar economic character differ in their response to the labour market for various sportsmen.

7.2.2 The effect of town size

A reasonably consistent finding from north American studies of regional variations in the 'production' of sports talent is that small towns produce

Table 7.1 Size of birthplace for ice hockey players and comparison data for distribution of boys in Canada, 1971

Community size	NHL players		Players in 3 pro leagues		Players in last 3 Olympiads		Boys 0–14 in the Canadian pop., 1971, for expected
	%	(N)	%	(N)	%	(N)	%
500 000 pop. and over	18.9	(48)	20.5	(74)	23.1	(15)	31.9
100 000–499 999	23.6	(60)	19.7	(71)	32.3	(21)	15.6
30 000–99 999	18.9	(48)	19.7	(72)	9.2	(6)	9.0
10 000–29 999	12.6	(32)	12.7	(46)	9.2	(6)	8.1
5000–9999	6.3	(16)	6.7	(24)	4.6	(3)	3.9
2500–4999	6.3	(16)	7.2	(26)	7.2	(6)	3.9
1000–2499	6.7	(17)	7.2	(26)	7.7	(5)	3.7
< 1000 and rural	6.7	(17)	6.1	(22)	4.6	(3)	23.9
Total	100.0	(254)	100.0	(361)	100.0	(65)	100.0

(After Curtis and Birch[15].)

relatively more professional sports personnel than large cities. This is not only a conventional wisdom of sports journalism but also an empirical generalization, derived from findings such as those in Table 7.1 which shows the percentage 'production' of superior Canadian ice hockey players for each size category of community in comparison with the expected percentages on the basis of the number of boys born in each size category. For example, places of over 500 000 produced 18.9% of NHL players when it would be expected that they would produce 31.9%; places of 1000 to 2499, however, produced 6.7% compared with the expected 3.7%.

Similar patterns have been found for American Olympic hockey players and at the state level, American college football and basketball players. However, it will be noted from Table 7.1 that hockey players are under-represented from the very smallest places, those of under 1000 people and in rural areas. In fact, it is the rural communities and the largest communities which are under-represented. The under-representation of the largest places might result from the large number of intervening opportunities for young people in large cities or from the fact that not enough teams exist in large cities to accommodate the latent talent which exists there. Rural places may be under-represented because of the lack of good facilities, lack of access to organized competition and the unavailability of good coaching. It is not known whether these kinds of relationships, common in some north American sports, are replicated in other countries and for other sports. Only further research will tell.

7.3 PLAYER MIGRATION PATTERNS

We touched on the movement of sports talent in Chapter 4 when it was noted that a feature of the more recent geography of sports was for clubs increasingly to widen their recruiting catchment for players, in many cases to embrace the world. Given the geographic imbalance in 'productivity' which is being discussed here it is inevitable, however, that some movement of talent will always take place between 'surplus' and 'deficit' regions. This is exacerbated when areas of high productivity have relatively small numbers of local sports outlets (clubs), or an insufficient number to accommodate the talent that they produce. In British professional football, for example, the north-east has always been a major source of talent but players from the region have invariably been forced to move to find employment. For example, in 1972 it was shown that 97% of all Northumberland-born players were engaged with clubs outside the county[16]. This is an extreme example but similar 'surplus' areas are found all over the world, in many sports, Missouri being a case in point for college footballer production in the USA[17].

What is of significance in any discussion of surplus and deficit regions is the rather predictable way in which the number of migrations decreases with distance from origin – another example of the distance decay curve (noted in a different context in Chapter 4). For the Northumberland example, mentioned above, although 97% of the players born there were exported, 61% were playing for clubs in the north of England; only 16.5% played for clubs in the south-east. Harold McConnell[18, 19], a sports geographer at Florida State University, has developed a simple model of migration for the 626 Floridian football players (65% of the state 'production') in out-of-state major colleges in 1981 which would statistically explain the resulting regional pattern of their destinations. His 'gravity model' was used to test the hypothesis that the number of Floridians varies directly with gravitational attraction. The model was generally successful, gravitational attraction explaining about 67% of the variation in the number of players from Florida.

Let us now look at the same kind of situation, not from the perspective of the source area of elite athletes but from that of the 'host' club for which such athletes perform. The same negative relationship between distance and numbers is found when we look at the numbers of players joining particular clubs. In South Africa Stellenbosch University has by far the largest number of registered (white) rugby players – about one quarter of all the nation's university players[20]. As Fig. 7.9 shows, there is a clear distance decay effect when the number of players from each region, per capita, is plotted against distance from Stellenbosch. However, it can also be noted that some regions, notably Calvinia, produce more rugby

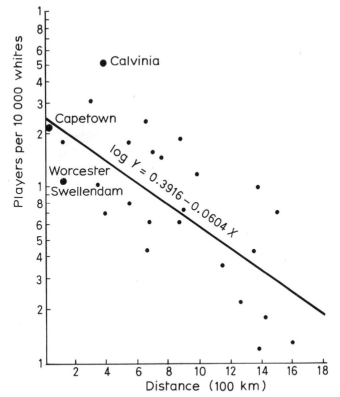

Fig. 7.9 Relationship between distance from Stellanbosch and per capita number of rugby players attending Stellenbosch University. (Source: Marais[20].)

players than would be expected, given their distance from the university, and can therefore be identified as rugby 'hotbeds'. It is worth speculating about the effect of distance of playing location from hometown on player performance. Homesickness and place-attachment are undeniably strong human emotions and the effect of this spatial dislocation is one which might be the subject of further research.

7.4 INTERNATIONAL PATTERNS OF ATHLETIC PRODUCTIVITY

So far we have been looking at regional differences in elite athletic production at the national level, but such regions can also be identified at the international level. The 'objective' identification of regional variations is arguably more important at this level since nations increasingly utilize their alleged success in turning out superior sportsmen and women as a

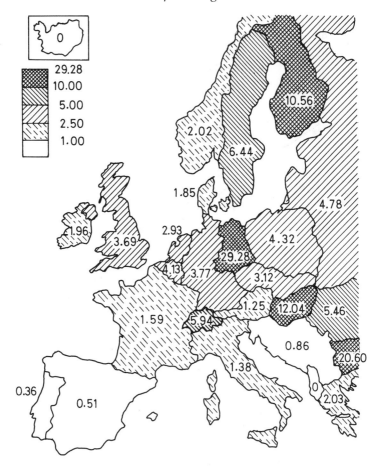

Fig. 7.10 Per capita 'production' of elite women track and field athletes, 1980. The key shows per capita indices; the European norm is 4.34 and the world norm is 1.00. (Source: Bale[22].)

means of propaganda. Let us look at some national differences in the 'production' of world-class (i.e. athletes able to rank in the top one hundred in the world in their event) women track and field athletes and swimmers at the continental scale. A frequently projected mental map of such sports is that of an Eastern European hotbed which produces world-class athletes at such levels as to overwhelm the countries of the West. For example, one observer of women's sports notes that 'the dominance of Eastern European women in general in many sports is quite astonishing – not just the occurrence of a few stars, but in-depth talent'[21]. Regional approaches to sports geography are helpful in exploring such stereotypes. Figure 7.10 shows the per capita scores for

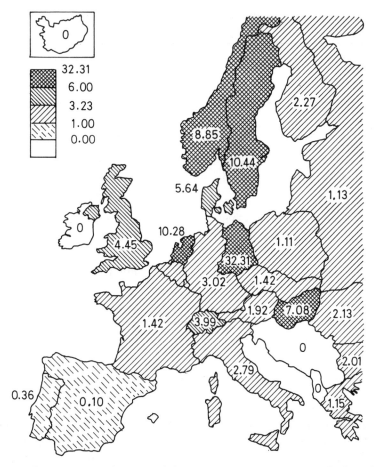

Fig. 7.11 Per capita 'production' of elite women swimmers 1982. The key shows per capita indices; the European norm is 3.23 and the world norm is 1.00. (Source: Bale[22].)

each European country in terms of the relative rate of production of elite women track and field athletes in 1980. The continental average was 4.34 and it is indeed true that five East European nations had indices greater than that figure. But so too did four West European nations. What is more, some countries in both East and Western Europe produce at below the world norm. It is noticeable also that Britain outproduced several Eastern states. Though the German Democratic Republic is (predictably perhaps) the continental and global leader with a spectacular per capita index of 29.28, there is very little evidence in Fig. 7.10 of an Eastern European bloc of highly productive nations.

Table 7.2 European 'production' of elite sportsmen in two sports, the top ten nations

Track and Field 1980		Swimming 1982	
Country	Index	Country	Index
Iceland	40.12	East Germany	15.10
Finland	22.56	Sweden	13.94
East Germany	13.81	Hungary	6.41
Hungary	10.04	Norway	6.21
Rumania	7.08	Switzerland	5.14
Eire	6.28	Netherlands	4.63
Luxembourg	6.25	Italy	3.74
Switzerland	5.98	Czechoslovakia	3.79
Sweden	5.66	United Kingdom	3.68
Norway	5.50	West Germany	3.02
Europe	4.53	Europe	2.73
USA	4.86	USA	6.83
World	1.00	World	1.00

(Based on data in Bale[22].)

Evidence of such macro-regional homogeneity is even less evident if a similar analysis is undertaken for women's swimming. Figure 7.11 shows that while East Germany is even more prolific in this case than in track and field, with a staggering index of 32.31, seven of the next eight major producers are from Western Europe. In this case Britain is a much more productive nation than the Soviet Union (indices of 4.45 and 1.13 respectively) and than most other Eastern European nations. Three Western states, Sweden, the Netherlands and Norway, are outproduced by only one nation from Eastern Europe.

If we consider the same two sports for men we find that Eastern European countries are even less prominent among the principal European nations. In track and field only East Germany, with an index of 13.81, Hungary and Rumania are ranked in the continental top ten. In swimming East Germany is the continental leader but only Hungary and Czechoslovakia among nations of Eastern Europe are superior in per capita terms to the United Kingdom. Table 7.2 shows this kind of information in greater detail.

We can analyse sport in exactly the same way at a global level. In 1976, for example, high levels of track and field 'productivity' were found in three macro-regions: Scandinavia, parts of Eastern Europe and some, but

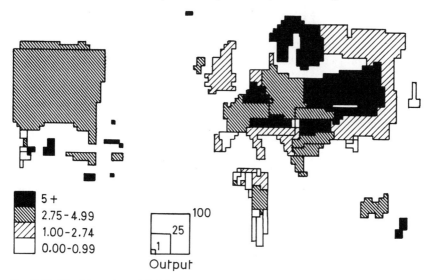

Fig. 7.12 World track and field space (men), 1976. The key shows the per capita index. (Source: Bale[23].)

certainly not all, of the islands of the Caribbean. Although the Soviet Union and the USA were major 'producers' in overall terms, their per capita output fell some way behind many other countries of the world. Figure 7.12 shows this kind of information in the form of a cartogram, the size of the countries of the world being drawn proportional to the number of world-class male track and field athletes 'produced' in 1976. Of course, most countries of the world produced no world-class athletes at all; South America, Africa and Asia are tiny in 'track and field space' and their share of world class athletic production seems to be increasing very slowly. While in 1956, Third World nations accounted for 7.4% of overall output, by 1980 the respective figure had only risen to 10.5%*.

These examples illustrate the danger of over-generalizing about sports regions at the macro-scale. Within both Western and Eastern Europe there are areas of both high and low athletic 'productivity'. A homogeneous bloc of Eastern (and Western) sports excellence is illusory when the per capita approach is adopted and maps such as Fig. 7.10–7.12 help identify the sporting character of the real world; as such they remove stereotypes and reduce the amount of bias in our view of the world of sport.

---

* Greater detail on global output of track and field athletes is found in Bale[23].

7.5 ANALYSING THE OLYMPICS

Arguably still the world's greatest sports festival, the Olympic Games are *de jure* a competition between individuals but media hype and government propaganda have combined to project the Olympics as contests between political and national ideologies. Essentially, an analysis of national and regional variations in success in the Olympics is an exercise in applied regional geography. In the popular press, sports journalists had started tabulating national 'winners' of the Olympics as early as 1928[24]. But it was really the 1936 'Games' at Berlin which generated the feeling that 'a stable of athletes . . . became necessary for national standing'. Richard Mandell[25], in his classic book, *The Nazi Olympics*, noted that it was from 1936 that 'the better an athlete was as an athlete, the less he was allowed individualism and the more he was cast as an allegorical, ideological batterer'. The 1936 Olympics were billed as 'the struggle of the two titans, Germany and the United States' and a trend that was strengthened by the results of the 1936 Olympics was to view athletes increasingly as national assets, procurable like fighter planes, submarines or synthetic rubber factories[25].

Such comments are invitations to social scientists to arrive at measures of Olympic 'success' which are more meaningful than the crude medal tally so frequently projected by the popular media. Indeed, although both Germany and USA were quick to point out that each had 'won' the 1936 Games, it needed a paper in the *Scientific Monthly* to emphasize that when population variations were taken into account the true 'winner' was Finland*. In the post-war period a number of studies have attempted to measure Olympic 'success', to build models of national Olympic performance and to identify characteristics of the most 'successful' nations[22].

Perhaps the most interesting and in-depth analysis was undertaken by Professor Ernst Jokl[27], of the University of Kentucky, into the 1952 Olympics held at Helsinki. These Games were particularly interesting because they marked the entry of the Soviet Union into the Olympic arena and pitted them against the traditional 'winner', the USA. However, what criteria should be used in assessing national performance at the Olympics? Jokl's approach was to assign a number of points to each athlete in each final of each event. The success of each nation was measured by a points system which was calculated using a formula derived from information theory. The formula was:

$$P = 100(1 - \log x / \log n)$$

where P is the number of points for a given nation, x is the placement of an

* Snyder[26], quoted in Mandell[25].

Table 7.3 Olympic participation and achievement of continents and regions, 1952

Continents and regions	Population in millions	Participations	Participation rate	Point share	Point rate	Point level
North America	166	289	1.74	10 722	64.6	37.1
Middle America	51	131	2.57	2 269	44.5	17.3
South America	111	239	2.15	4 437	40.0	18.6
Europe	396	2 038	5.15	49 293	124.5	24.2
USSR	193	209	1.08	8 690	45.0	41.6
Africa	198	145	0.73	3 331	16.8	23.0
Asia	1 272	290	0.23	5 977	4.7	20.6
Oceania	13	86	6.62	2 601	200.1	30.2
Total	2 400	3 427	1.43	87 320	36.4	25.5

(*Source:* Jokl[27.])

athlete or team, and n is the number of contestants in the event. Hence first place (i.e. an Olympic Gold medal) received 100 points (the log of 1 being zero) while last place received no points (since log n/log $n = 1$). So, fourth place out of five contestants received fewer points (14) than the more praiseworthy fourth out of twenty contestants (54 points). This approach is clearly a vast improvement on simply a count of medals.

The definition of some of Jokl's terms are worthy of brief consideration. A nation's point share was defined as simply the number of points collected by the country's athletes, the participation rate as the number of participations in Olympic events per million inhabitants, and the point level as the average number of points per participation. An important distinction is between the point rate and the point level. If we are considering the success of Olympic teams from each country then the point level is obviously more appropriate than the point rate, which measures success in relation to the population of the country as a whole.

On the basis of the 1952 Olympic results Jokl was able to reveal some particularly interesting findings. Table 7.3, for example, illustrates the global distribution of athletic performance on a continental and macro-regional basis. Consider the point rate criterion. In this case North America outscored the USSR. If the point level criterion is considered, however, the opposite is the case. In terms of team success (i.e. point level) the USSR was clearly more successful than any of the continents though in terms of point rate both Europe and Oceania outperformed her.

When participation and point rates were considered for individual countries, however, it was found that little relationship existed between

Table 7.4 Olympic participation and achievement of the temperature zones, 1952

Temperature zones*	Popula-tion in millions	Partici-pations	Partici-pation rate	Point share	Point rate	Point level
Cold	312	1 049	3.36	29 552	94.7	28.2
Cold and cool	246	417	1.70	14 979	60.9	35.9
Cool	401	1 395	3.48	32 472	81.0	23.3
Cool and warm	495	79	0.20	2 738	5.5	34.7
Warm	866	476	0.60	7 439	8.6	15.6
Warm and hot	64	11	0.20	146	2.3	13.3

* Annual isotherms of temperature zones:
 Cold: 0°–10°C or 32°C–50°F
 Cool: 10°–20°C or 50°–68°F
 Warm: 20°C–30°C or 68°–86°F
 Hot: More than 30°C or 86°F

(*Source:* Jokl[27].)

size of country and point level. Some very small countries were able to obtain high point scores, Jamaica on this criterion being almost as successful as the USA. Likewise, when Olympic achievement was related to the world's temperature zones it was found that it was possible for countries in warm and hot areas of the world to achieve success in sport, contrary to the somewhat environmentally deterministic view which tended to prevail at the time. The difference between point scores in the different temperature zones is shown in Table 7.4. It will be seen that the point rate, participation rate and point share for warm countries exceeded that of the cool and warm zones. Likewise, cold zones had a higher point rate than any other. This kind of research provides us with a much more objective and in-depth view of the Olympics than is possible by simply analysing the number of medals for each country. In view of the rigour provided by this approach it is somewhat surprising that it has not been repeated for subsequent Olympic Games.

Since the 1952 Olympics there has been a continuing argument about which countries in the world – communist or non-communist – are the most successful in the Olympic Games[21]. As we have seen, it is possible to ascribe victory to various countries or ideological groups of nations, depending on which indicators of 'success' are used. However, if it is Olympic success (and let us recall that only a small proportion of many countries' top athletes actually take part in the Olympics) we are concerned with then it does appear that communist countries do

Table 7.5 The most successful countries in the Summer Games in Montreal, 1976

Country	Type	Total points*	Success coefficient†
1. GDR	(Socialist)	195	38.3
2. Bulgaria	(Socialist)	46	17.3
3. Finland	(Protestant)	17	11.4
4. Cuba	(Socialist)	29	10.9
5. Hungary	(Socialist)	34	10.3
6. Trinidad	(Catholic)	3	8.0
7. Jamaica	(Catholic)	5	7.4
8. Rumania	(Socialist)	44	6.9
9. Mongolia	(Socialist)	2	6.9
10. Sweden	(Protestant)	14	6.0
11. Poland	(Socialist)	47	4.5
12. Norway	(Protestant)	5	4.1
13. Switzerland	(Mixed Protestant/Catholic)	7	4.1
14. FRG	(Mixed Protestant/Catholic)	71	3.8
15. USSR	(Socialist)	262	3.4
16. Denmark	(Protestant)	5	3.3
17. CSRR	(Socialist)	14	3.2
18. USA	(Mixed Protestant/Catholic)	195	3.1
19. Belgium	(Catholic)	9	2.8
20. Yugoslavia	(Socialist)	15	2.2

* Points based on number of medals won: 3 for gold, 2 for silver, 1 for bronze.
† Success coefficient is the ratio between the actual and the expected success of a nation.
(After: Seppänen[28].)

outperform non-communist states. In the 1976 Olympics at Montreal (the most recent to include both USA and USSR) six of the top ten countries in terms of Finnish sociologist Paavo Seppänen's[28] 'success coefficient' were socialist (Table 7.5). It is doubtful that even if the absent African nations had been in Canada they would have featured in the top ten. What is more, despite the very different cultural backgrounds of the various socialist states, they have been more successful since adopting socialism than before doing so (Table 7.6), although Albania and China must be excluded from this generalization because they had not taken part in the Olympic Games until 1984.

Why should communist countries do better in the Olympics than non-communist states? Part of the reason is that sport is regarded in such nations as a form of physical culture – rather than possessing the more

Table 7.6 Success coefficient of socialist countries in the Summer Olympic Games before and after the revolution according to the type of religion during the pre-revolution period (1896–1972)

Type of society before revolution	Before the socialist period	During the socialist period
Buddhist (Mongolia)	–	3.3
Confucian (China)*	–	–
Islam (Albania)	0.0	0.0
Orthodox-Islam-Catholic (Yugoslavia)	0.7	1.5
Orthodox (Bulgaria, Rumania, USSR)	0.0	2.9
Catholic (Cuba, Poland)	0.7	2.3
Catholic/Protestant (Czechoslovakia, Hungary)	5.0	10.2
Protestant (East Germany)†	3.1	14.3 (only 1968 and 1972)

* The achievements are not calculated because of the lack of information. Some occasional successes such as several world championships in table tennis and Chinese records in track and field refer, however, to the same tendency observed in the other socialist countries.
† Because of the joint team with West Germany only the Games of Mexico and Munich are taken into account. Coefficient for 'before socialist period' is that of undivided Germany.

(After: Seppänen[28].)

recreational connotations of the West. In addition, the status of women is different under communism – sport being intended as much for women as for men. Furthermore, elite individuals are spotted early and enrolled in special sports schools, in much the same way as we cultivate talented young musicians. All this is undertaken with the state in full control of the national sports system so that resources can be mobilized to greater levels of efficiency than in the West[29]. Success in the Olympics can be measured in a variety of ways. Communist states in general, and Eastern Germany in particular, are the most successful Olympic nations on earth. But as we have seen from our analyses of rather more in-depth performances (Figs. 7.10–7.12), it may well be the case that the communist states can 'deliver the goods' on the days of the Olympic finals better than other countries, but in terms of in-depth 'production' many of them are inferior to nations to the west of the 'iron curtain'.

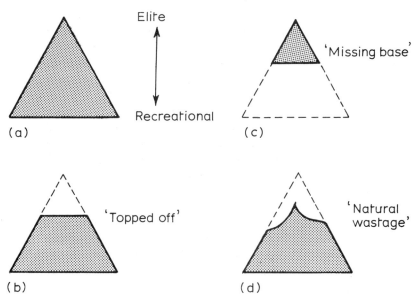

Fig. 7.13 Models of different national emphases on sports development. (Based on an idea in Cratty[30].)

7.6 SPORT FOR ALL OR FEW?

In promoting sport, or individual sports, different nations may adopt different emphases. Some may feel that most of their ideological eggs lie in the mass-participatory sport basket and they therefore devote a considerable effort towards engaging a large proportion of the population in sport, albeit at modest levels of performance when measured by the standards of the world's elite. In other countries their sports ministries may feel that they ought to put a disproportionate amount of investment and effort into producing a small number of highly visible world-class performers. In yet other cases a truly egalitarian approach may be adopted, each individual being provided with the motivation and resources to maximize his or her own sporting prowess.

The various national attitudes to sport and its development can be conceptualized by using a variation of the well known 'population pyramid' to describe diagrammatically the different theoretical 'outputs' of various sports systems. Figure 7.13 summarizes different model situations for four hypothetical countries. In the case of country (a) facilities may be available for every individual to reach his or her potential in sports. Such an output possesses both a broad base and a high peak with both internationally successful participation and a broad mass of lower level, recreational participation. In Cratty's words[30], such a country is at pains to 'remediate performance-blocking emotional problems in middle level competitors' so that few, if any, sporting stones are left unturned. However, in this model it is important to decide whether it is being applied to a population across or within sports. We might feel at first that this model applies to the German Democratic Republic but Carr[31] has stressed that because some sports offer the possibility of accumulating more Olympic medals than others, the GDR has concentrated on those sports which are most likely to boost the national medal tally. Hence the model might apply to swimming but not necessarily to sport in the GDR.

The second model, (b) is what might be called a 'topped-off' pyramid. A broad base may exist but talent fails to rise to the top because of a lack of suitable facilities, inadequate training and support personnel or a political philosophy which stifles the development of a nation's athletic potential. Widespread mass-participatory sport but weakly developed top-class sport would characterize such a country. Maoist China might be cited as coming close to this model.

The third model (c), would be typified by a nation which put a good deal of emphasis on a few, elite athletes at the expense of widespread participation at the lower end of the pyramid. Cratty suggests that speed skating in USA and diving in Canada are examples. To them could be added the case of long distance running in Ethiopia. In 1985, while the nation was starving, the Ethiopian men's senior and junior teams won world cross country championships.

It seems likely, however, that most countries in the western world can be applied to the fourth model, (d). This takes natural wastage into account. If natural selection of superior athletes occurs and the less capable, physically or emotionally, fall by the wayside, only a few will rise to the top of the sports pyramid and it will possess a steep upper slope. Britain and the USA are almost certainly overall examples of this system in which many potential champions are lost to sport despite relatively high levels of participation at the high school stage.

These pyramid models are attractive pedagogical and conceptual devices. But like the diffusion models in Chapter 3 and the central place model in Chapter 4 we need to ask whether they can be operationalized in a real world context. Certainly the actual construction of pyramids for sport *per se* would be difficult; it is, after all, well nigh impossible to compare a professional footballer with an international gymnast in terms of 'quality'. However, in individual sports where quantitative records of country's athletes are kept we might be able to make some progress in comparing countries.

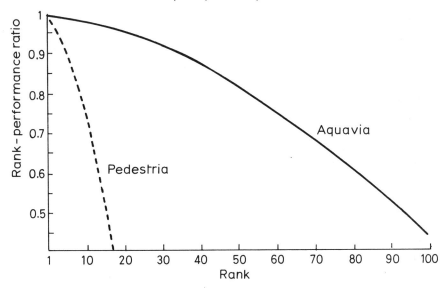

Fig. 7.14 Hypothetical rank-performance curves for two imaginary countries.

In sports like swimming, track and field, speed skating, weightlifting and others, we can construct 'rank-performance' curves* for individual events, each curve representing one country (or region). Such curves could be applied to elite or mass sport, depending on the appropriateness and depth of the available data sets. As many countries do, in fact, compile in-depth data in the form of ranking lists for sports such as track and field and swimming, the slopes of such rank-performance curves and the identification of any marked changes in them might serve to provide real world examples of the nature of 'output' from the systems. A comparison of curves would be most meaningful for countries of similar population sizes. Figure 7.14 provides a hypothetical example. Consider the case of two countries, Aquavia and Pedestria and their top one hundred 200-m backstroke swimmers. The rank-performance ratio is defined as R_n/R_1 where R_n is the performance of the nth ranked swimmer and R_1 that of the first ranked. In other words, each ranked athlete's performance is scored as a percentage of the first ranked. The hypothetical plot of the top one hundred for Aquavia is gently sloping, showing that after the nation's top ranked athlete a number of others have achieved performances of a comparably high standard (i.e. the 50th ranked has a ratio of 0.8). In the case of Pedestria, however, the curve is much steeper and in this case the tenth ranked swimmer has a ratio of 0.8 while the twentieth has one approaching 0.3.

* Geographers may recognize the well known rank-size 'rule' here. For a sports application, see Loy and Gudman[32].

Such curves provide a graphical indication of the extent to which the 'output' of a nation's sports system is dominated by one or two nationally outstanding performers or whether the system has been able to produce a number of comparable performers, and hence work towards the maximization of its potential – if this should be considered worthwhile. This approach can be used to illustrate in a dramatic way how Great Britain has been unable to achieve a level of output in one track and field event which is comparable with that of two smaller countries, Sweden and Finland. The event in this case is the javelin throw and only the top ten in each country are graphed. Figure 7.15 shows how Britain's curve is much steeper than that for the other two, much smaller, countries. In terms of their available resources, Sweden and Finland have each been much more efficient than Britain in producing elite javelin throwers.

Given suitable data, similar graphs could be drawn for all levels of sporting participation. The slopes of the curves will be a function of the kinds of factors discussed earlier in relation to the pyramid-type models.

7.7 REGIONS OF INTEREST AND INVOLVEMENT

So far in this chapter we have been looking at regional variations in either the 'production' of elite performers or the performances of different nations in the Olympics. We now turn to another kind of regional variation, that found at the recreational or mass participatory level of sport and concerned with variations in interest, participation or involvement. For the moment, we will stay with the international scale and return to the national level later.

It is clear that considerable differences exist in levels of recreational participation in sports between countries. In Norway and Sweden, for example, 50% and 30% of the respective national populations claim to participate in those countries' first ranked sports. In the UK and the German Federal Republic, on the other hand, it seems that only about 10% participate in the most popular sporting activity[33]. Some other national variations of this kind are shown in Fig. 7.16. However, this information tells us nothing about the frequency and the intensity of participation and in order to introduce these characteristics into international variations in sports, Manchester University geographer Brian Rodgers[33] defined three main indices of participation. These were (a) the index of penetration, which was represented by the percentage of the population who had ever played a particular sport; (b) the index of fidelity, which described the number of adults who still played a particular sport as a percentage of those who had ever played it; and (c) the index of intensity, which is the ratio between those who play at all and those who participate regularly. Sports widely practised at school will

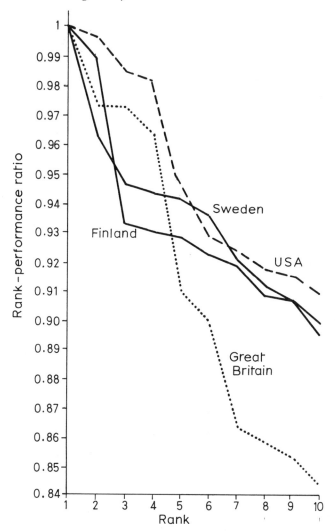

Fig. 7.15 Rank-performance curves for Britain, USA, Sweden and Finland, based on their top ten javelin throwers in 1984. Ideally, such curves should be drawn to compare countries of similar population bases.

tend to have high penetration levels. In the United Kingdom, for example, track and field athletics has a penetration index of 37; in France, on the other hand, it has an index of 15. However, the index of fidelity for this sport in these two countries is 8.1 and 7.3 respectively while the indices of intensity are also similar, 36 for the UK and 33 for France. Similar figures for other sports are shown in Table 7.7.

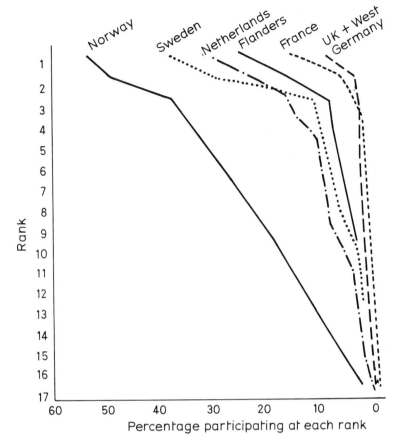

Fig. 7.16 Rank of individual sports related to participation rates in seven countries. (Source: Rodgers[33].)

Interesting though such data are, they cannot be used with very much reliability for comparing many countries because of the incompatibility of data collected by different countries and the variation in the definition of sport. It might be possible to use the per capita approach described earlier in relation to the production of superior participants and apply it to the international scale by using data collected by international sports governing bodies relating to club membership per country. Many such organizations keep quite precise records of club membership at the national scale. Of course, casual participation in sport by non-members would be excluded and such participation is likely to be sizeable.

We can return to the per capita approach by considering evidence and examples of regional differences in interest in different sports. Instead of

Table 7.7 Indices of sports participation in the UK and France

	Penetration		Fidelity		Intensity	
	France	*UK*	*France*	*UK*	*France*	*UK*
Athletics	15	37	7.3	8.1	36	33
Team sports	21	66	22	12	31	50
Swimming	36	50	55	12	13	52
Tennis	7.3	37	31	24	30	44

(*Source of data:* Rodgers[33].)

the number of players 'produced' we can use numbers of clubs or, better still, numbers of club members, in order to highlight parts of the country which appear to place greater emphasis on some sports than others, given the caveat given above. Consider some examples from Britain shown in Fig. 7.17. Tennis is clearly seen to be dominantly southern and suburban in location. Areas of limited emphasis on tennis are the great British conurbations, London being an 'island' of relative inactivity, the Merseyside and Greater Manchester areas adjoining a 'lobe' of tennis underdevelopment in the industrial midlands. Tennis is a middle-class sport found in its middle-class locations (i.e. broadly southern and suburban) but is not as strongly localized in the south-east as many people think (compare Figs 7.17 and 7.3.). Basketball and cycling display clear pattterns of Severnside–Wash and Lancashire–Essex axial spread respectively, but the pattern defies any obvious explanation. Auto cycling is dominantly peripheral and rural, located mainly in agricultural and non-urbanized areas where space is available for the noise and extensive courses which this sport demands.

Of course, the per capita approach to both the analysis of player production and popular, mass involvement is based upon only one variable, i.e. numbers of participants related to overall population. To obtain an indication of true intensity of involvement in a particular sport, a number of measures of involvement might be taken. For example, in the United States the Rooney-Adams golf involvement index involves a combination of per capita variables including facility supply, equipment purchases, golf magazine subscriptions, and support for the game in high school, to substantiate the premier status of the Midwest and Northeast as 'golfing regions'. By these criteria, Iowa, Michigan, Minnesota, Wisconsin, New Hampshire and Connecticut are the leading golf states. Much of the south had very low involvement[34]. Such an approach could obviously be applied to any number of sports and as well as being of cultural-geographic interest such findings are helpful in marketing and selling sports equipment and facilities.

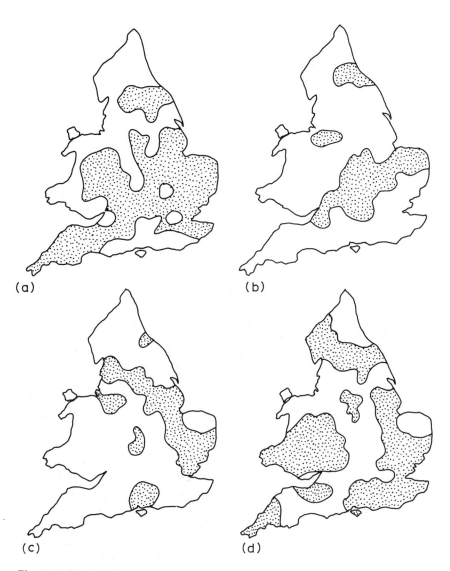

(a)   (b)   (c)   (d)

Fig. 7.17 Regions (more than 1.3 times the national average number of clubs) for (a) tennis, (b) basketball, (c) cycling and (d) auto cycling in the early 1980s. (After Bale[4].)

7.7.1 Cores and domains

In some cases it is possible to identify a kind of structure in sports regions. Figure 7.18 shows that for rugby union and golf the areas of greatest relative emphasis (i.e. those areas with more than twice the national per capita average number of clubs) are adjacent to, or surrounded by, areas of less emphasis but which still possess above average levels of club provision (i.e. indices greater than 1.3). In other words, the sports region appears to possess a core and a domain, beyond which might be said to exist a sphere of sports activity within which the sport exists at lower densities and with less intense local involvement*.

Three rugby cores are obvious from Fig. 7.18(a). First, several South Wales counties have very high per capita indices of over 3.5, confirming to a large degree the mental map of rugby (Fig. 7.3). The South Wales rugby region extends across the border into the English county of Gloucester. Beyond this core, north-west Wales, Avon and Warwickshire constitute a domain of above average rugby activity. The two other core regions are in south-east Scotland (the Border region has an index of 6.58, second only in Britain to Dyfed's 6.67) and Cornwall. In both cases a neighbouring domain exists. Two relatively isolated outliers of above average rugby activity are found in the sparsely populated parts of north-west Scotland and in the (perceived, see Section 7.1) 'rugger' county of Surrey.

In terms of regional structure a similar pattern is found for golf (Fig. 7.18(b)). The dominant core is central and south-eastern Scotland – the home of the game – where per capita scores exceed 4.0 in four of the Scottish regions. A minor regional core is found in north Wales with outliers of above average, but not spectacular, emphasis in Cornwall and south-east suburban England.

The distribution maps of sports preferences at the national scale are good examples of the geographical manifestation of popular culture. Tennis and rugby clubs, among others, are not simply dots on maps or parts of regional clusters, however. To many people they are the very things which distinguish their lifestyle from that of their regional (and sometimes local) neighbours. Association with such varying sports indicates that popular culture has not become homogenized; indeed, it may be one of the few such areas where a surprising degree of geographical variation continues to exist.

The patterns of player 'production' and of regional emphasis described so far are essentially snapshots taken at a point in time. It is now appropriate to begin to consider the dynamic nature of sports regions and provide examples of the way in which regional emphases change over time.

* This idea is derived from work by Meinig[35].

(a)   (b)

Fig. 7.18 Cores (heavy shading, indices >2.0) and domains (dotted areas, indices 1.3–1.99 times the national per capita norm) for (a) rugby union and (b) golf in Britain.

7.8 PATTERNS OF REGIONAL CHANGE

It would be an oversimplification to suggest that sports regions such as those we have been looking at were static and never changed. We have already observed the ways in which sports diffused across continents and countries and, in many places, they are continuing to do so. Over time, subtle, yet quite discernible changes take place in the geographical make-up of sports regions. In some cases the cores become intensified; in others they break up and the centre of the sport moves elsewhere. Let us consider two examples, illustrating different kinds of such regional change.

The case of the Dixie gridiron football region in the USA illustrates the spatial expansion and intensification of a region traditionally associated with football. Fig. 7.19 shows that in the early 1960s Texas and Missouri were above the national average per capita production level of elite college footballers but by the late 1960s and early 1970s Texas had become the core of the south-west football region. Whereas in 1960 Ohio had been the national per capita leader, that status had been assumed by the Lone

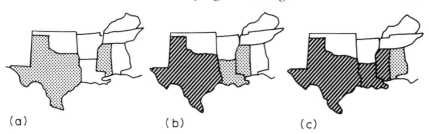

(a)   (b)   (c)

Fig. 7.19 The growth of the south-west gridiron region, (a) 1958–66, (b) 1968–72 and (c) 1973–6. (The heavy shaded regions indicate indices >2.0 times the national norm, while the dotted regions indicate indices >1.3 times the national norm.) (After Rooney[36].)

Star State by the end of the decade (from an index of 0.78 to one of 1.90). By the mid-1970s Louisiana had replaced Texas as the heart of the Dixie football region with neighbouring Missouri also exceeding the Texas index (see Section 7.2.1). Sports regions are clearly not static elements of culture; indeed, like other aspects of such culture, change may be the norm.

In the case of British football (soccer) one of the traditional hotbeds of player production has been the north of England[4, 16, 37]. In 1950 the northern region produced professional footballers at 2.45 times the national per capita norm. Within the region the county of Northumberland (see Section 7.2) produced at a level of 3.97 the national average, while Durham (2.74), Tyne and Wear (2.49) and Cleveland (2.02) were also prolific producers. At this time the south-east of England had a per capita index of 0.39. In 1980 the north was still the major producer in relative terms but with a reduced index of 2.06 (Table 7.8). In addition only two northern counties had per capita indices of greater than 2.0. The south-east of England, on the other hand had increased its index to 0.69 with Greater London changing from a production level of only 0.38 times the national level in 1950 to one which was slightly higher (1.12) than the national norm thirty years later. When mapped, two things seemed to have been taking place. first, there was a growing convergence between the highest and lowest producers and, as a result, a southern shift in player production (see Table 7.8) so that by 1980 it was the south-east, not the north-west or Scotland that was, in absolute terms, the national centre of footballer production. The second thing that had been happening over the thirty-year period was the growing metropolitanization of player output. Instead of a traditional north–south divide in player production it had become clear that soccer players were increasingly coming from urban centres, irrespective of location.

This growing regional convergence in soccer player production is probably the result of a number of factors. Three can be considered

Table 7.8 Per capita production of league professionals by standard regions, 1950 and 1980

Region	1950		1980	
	Number	Index	Number	Index
North	293	2.45	205	2.06
North-west	315	1.26	288	1.40
Wales	154	1.49	116	1.29
Yorks/Humberside	254	1.40	200	1.28
Scotland	300	1.48	182	1.11
Northern Ireland	54	0.99	36	0.75
West Midlands	160	0.97	145	0.95
East Midlands	106	0.85	120	0.98
South-west	88	0.64	82	0.59
East Anglia	22	0.40	34	0.57
South-east	232	0.39	372	0.69

(*Source:* Bale[14].)

seriously. First, we have noted from Chapter 5 that the recruiting catchments in virtually all sports have been widening in recent decades. Soccer in Britain is no exception and recruitment from areas such as parts of the south, hitherto relatively untouched, may have contributed to that region's increased contribution. Secondly, football has always been a way out of a dole queue and it is the cities which today form that repository of unemployed young men for whom sport can be an outlet. London is the single greatest centre of such unemployment; so too Merseyside has a major problem. Both have dramatically increased their contribution to British footballer output in recent decades. Thirdly, it is in the south that we have seen that the new entries to the Football League have been increasingly located (Chapter 5). It is in the south that both economic opportunities in general, and football growth in particular, have developed in the thirty-year period we have been considering. Connell[38] notes, therefore, that the trend of changes in the distribution of professional footballers parallelling changes in the national economy.

7.9 DEGREES OF DIVERSIFICATION

So far we have focused on output or emphasis using the per capita approach and this is clearly of value. However, in certain multi-event sports like track and field, swimming, weightlifting or speed skating the diversification of output might be of importance, not only for purposes of

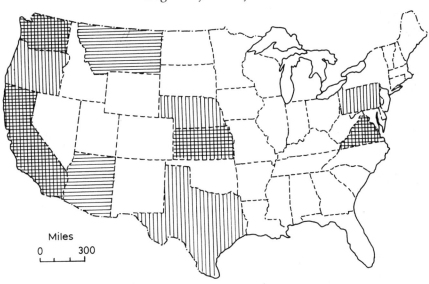

Fig. 7.20 Areas of high per capita output are not always the same as those which are highly diversified in their 'production', as this map of the geography of elite high school women track and field athletes clearly shows. (Horizontal lines indicate high per capita production, >2.0, and vertical lines indicate a high degree of diversification, <34.) (Source: Shepard[40].)

making international comparisons but also for the monitoring of national sports policy*. For example, it is arguably little good having an over-whelmingly powerful squad of hammer throwers if the nation's sprinters are of inferior quality. Balance in sporting excellence might be the aim of many countries wishing to develop their sporting prowess. For this reason it is useful to be able to identify geographical differences in diversification (or specialization) as well as in output. Let us consider first some examples at the national scale, showing how differences in the degree of specialization of 'production' of superior girl track and field athletes varies within the USA. The per capita high is 4.75 for the state of Oregon, with two other Pacific states, Washington (4.15) and California (2.31) also of importance, outproducing all other states except Wash-ington DC (3.23). Other states with scores over 2.0 for the period 1980–83 are shown in Fig. 7.20. However, the states with high per capita scores are not necessarily well diversified.

We can measure diversification by a number of methods but perhaps the most simple is to calculate the percentage of a state's (nation's) athletes in each event (100 metres, 200 metres, high jump, discus, etc.)

* For a larger number of countries see Bale[22]. See also Bale[39].

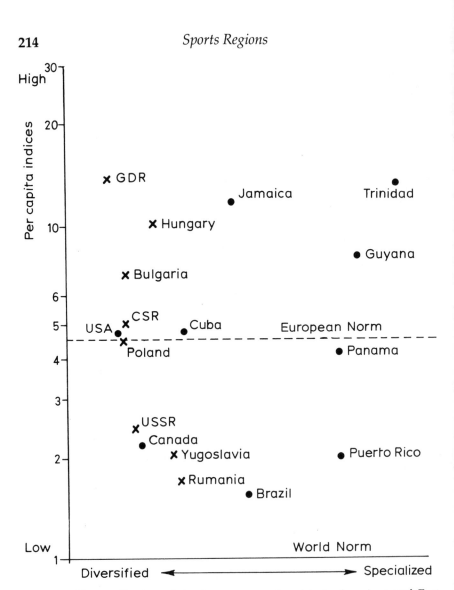

Fig. 7.21 The application of the 'success space' matrix to American and East European nations, in men's track and field athletics, 1980. The latter nations generally appear the most 'successful', although on these criteria USA outperforms USSR.

and apply the following simple formula to find the specialization index (SI):

$$SI = \sqrt{P_1^2 + P_2^2 + P_3^2 + \ldots P_n^2}$$

where P_1 is the percentage of the total number of athletes in event 1, P_2 the

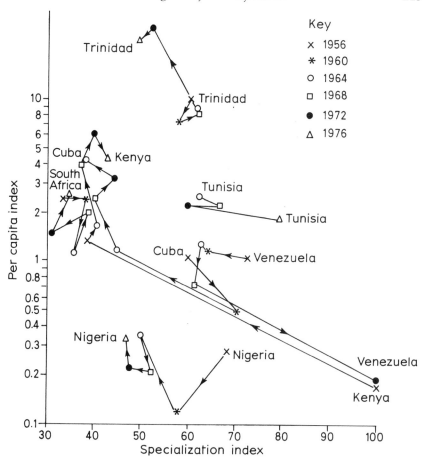

Fig. 7.22 Application of the 'success space' matrix to selected African and Latin American countries, 1956–76. (Source: Bale[23].)

percentage in event 2, etc. The maximum score is always 100, indicating extreme specialization with all athletes in one event. The lowest score will depend on the number of events. When this is thirteen (as in the present examination of women's track and field) it is 27.73; for eighteen events it is 23.59.

In the present case study the most diversified output comes from California (29.31), DC (30.15), Virginia (31.87) and Pennsylvania (31.88). Clearly places are not necessarily well diversified, even though they may be highly productive (Fig. 7.20). As we have seen, Oregon has a high per capita score but is somewhat specialized with an SI of 43.01. Texas, on the other hand, is an average per capita producer (1.12) but Texan output is quite well distributed across the thirteen events (SI = 32.59).

We return to the international scale to consider the implications of the SI to one of the analyses we examined earlier. In Table 7.2 it was noted that East Germany was the global per capita leader in men's swimming with an index of 15.10; the respective score for the USA was 6.83. Although obviously inferior in per capita terms, the USA's output was more diversified than that of the GDR, the former having an SI of 28.87 (with Australia, the most diversified of the men's swimming nations) while the East German SI was 32.26, a reflection of her relative paucity of elite performers in medley and butterfly events.

It is possible to integrate the two indices for output and specialization respectively to arrive at a measure of 'success' which can be displayed graphically. For each state or nation their position on a two-dimensional graph can be plotted according to each score, such as is shown in Fig. 7.21 for the nations of Eastern Europe and the Americas in terms of 'success space' for men's track and field athletics in 1980. The nearer the top left-hand corner of the graph, the more 'successful' the country on the two criteria. Nations with high specialization and modest per capita output, on the other hand, are near the bottom right-hand corner. If time series data are available patterns over time can be easily plotted.

The dynamic element in the world of sport is illustrated in the example of the success space matrix shown in Fig. 7.22. In this case a number of countries from the Third World are shown 'moving' in success space for the period 1956–76. The chosen sport is track and field athletics and it is abundantly clear that in this sport both Cuba and Kenya have 'taken off' since the early 1960s. In the case of Venezuela, on the other hand, the opposite is the case. South Africa shows a situation of relative stagnation, barely having moved around on the graph since 1956. This type of approach can clearly be used to monitor national standings in sport for those who wish to make international comparisons. Indeed, given that the Olympics no longer represent all the nations of the world, an approach such as that described above might be a better way of assessing international variations in sports success – for those sports for which it is appropriate.

7.10 CONCLUSIONS

Sports regions can be identified for any and every sport. A huge number of regions exist, based on a vast number of criteria. For example, regions identifying strongly with the production of not sporting humans but sporting animals could be identified. Thus Kildare has been identified as the centre of the Irish racing industry, based on the geographical distribution of stud fees[41]. Likewise, it is probable that the regional origins of sports coaches and managers are far from random and display some kind of geographical pattern. We find, for example, that on a per capita basis the New England States and the Plains states are the leading 'producers' of US college basketball coaches while in the case of football the Midwestern states and the Rocky mountain area are the leading areas of coach 'production'[42].

Simply mapping regional differences in the origins of professional sports players, for example, has recently been criticized by David Ley[43] on the grounds that 'description takes place over interpretation'. This is to ignore the fact that the identification of regional variations is, in itself, intrinsically interesting to many people but, more important perhaps, is the fact that the identification of such differences acts as a base line against which media-generated stereotypes (particularly important for propaganda purposes at the international level) can be gauged. It is this rationale that has formed the basis for this chapter and it is the search for a comparison between 'vernacular' and 'geographical' sports regions which might best justify further involvement in the regional approach to sports. This is not to deny, of course, the need for the kind of interpretive accounts for which Ley argues.

FURTHER READING

The regional approach to sports is applied to the USA and UK scene respectively in John Rooney's *A Geography of American Sport: from Cabin Creek to Anaheim*, Addison-Wesley, Reading, Mass., 1974 and John Bale's *Sport and Place*, Hurst, London, 1982. A large number of articles dealing with sports regions has been written and are well exemplified by Carl Ojala and Elwood Kureth's From Saskatoon to Parry Sound; a geography of skates and sticks in North America, *The Geographical Survey*, **4**, 4, 1979, pages 22–34 and John Harmon's, Bowling regions in North America, *Journal of Cultural Geography*, **6**, 1, 1986, pages 109–24. Sports regions at an international scale are explored in John Bale's Towards a Geography of International Sport, *Occasional Paper*, **9**, Department of Geography, Loughborough University, 1985. Several excellent books describe the nature of sport systems in various countries; different approaches are adopted in the classic by James Michener, *Sport in America*, Random House, New York, 1976, from those in the collection edited by James Riordan, *Sport Under Communism*, Hurst, London, 1978.

REFERENCES

1. Bale, J. (1986) Sport and national identity; a geographical view, *British Journal of Sports History*, **3**, 18–41.
2. Whannell, G. (1983) *Blowing the Whistle; the Politics of Sport*, Pluto, London.

3. Macdonnell, A. (1935) *England their England*, Macmillan, London.
4. Bale, J. (1982b) *Sport and Place*, Hurst, London.
5. Burgess, J. (1982) Selling places; environmental images for the executive. *Regional Studies*, **16**, 1–17.
6. Humphrey, J. (1986) No holding Brazil; football, nationalism and politics, in *Off The Ball* (eds A. Tomlinson and G. Whannell), Pluto Press, London.
7. Cole, J. (1972) A Mexican view of Mexico and the World. *Ideas in Geography*, 45.
8. Walton, M. (1984) The influence of the World Cup on international stereotypes. *Teaching Geography*, **9**, 203–7.
9. Pillsbury, R. (1974) Carolina Thunder; a geography of southern stock-car racing. *Journal of Geography*, **22**, 39–46.
10. Rooney, J. (1974) *A Geography of American Sport; from Cabin Creek to Anaheim*, Addison-Wesley, Reading, Mass.
11. Rooney, J. (1980) *The Recruiting Game*, University of Nebraska Press, Lincoln.
12. Goudge, T. (1983) Interscholastic athletic participation; a geographical analysis of opportunity and development. *Proceedings, US Olympic Academy*, **7**, 165–202.
13. Yetman, H. and Eitzen, S. (1973) Some social and demographic correlates of football productivity. *The Geographical Review*, 63.
14. Bale, J. (1983) The changing regional origins of an occupation; the case of professional footballers in 1950 and 1980. *Geography*, **68**, 140–8.
15. Curtis, J. and Birch, J. (1987) Size of community of origin and recruitment to professional and Olympic hockey in North America. *Sociology of Sport Journal*, **4**, 229–44.
16. Konig, E. (1972) *A Geography of Football in England and Wales*, undergraduate dissertation (unpublished), Portsmouth Polytechnic.
17. McConnell, H. (1983) Southern major college football: supply, demand, and migration of players. *Southeastern Geographer*, **23**, 78–106.
18. McConnell, H. (1983) Floridians in major college football 1981. *Florida Geographer*, **17**, 17–31.
19. McConnell, H. (1984) Recruiting patterns in Midwestern major college football. *Geographical Perspectives*, **53**, 27–43.
20. Marais, H. (1979) Herkomspatrone van Stellenbosch se toprugbyspelers. *Geo-Stel*, **3**, 45–53.
21. Dyer, K. (1982) *Catching up the Men*, Junction Books, London.
22. Bale, J. (1985) Towards a geography of international sport. *Occasional Paper*, 8, Department of Geography, Loughborough University.
23. Bale, J. (1979a) A geography of world class track and field athletics, *Sports Exchange World*, **4**, 26–31.
24. Lowe, B. (1977) Sport prestige; the politicization of winning in international sport. *Arena Newsletter*, **1**, 11–13.
25. Mandell, R. (1972) *The Nazi Olympics*, Souvenir Press, London.
26. Snyder, C. (1936) Real winners of the 1936 Olympic Games. *Scientific Monthly*, **63**, 372–4.
27. Jokl, E. (1964) *Medical Sociology and Cultural Anthropology of Sport and Physical Education*, Thomas, Springfield, NJ.
28. Seppänen, P. (1981) Olympic success; a cross national perspective, in *Handbook of Social Sciences in Sport* (eds G. Luschen and G. Sage), Stipes, Champaign, Ill.
29. Riordan, J. (1977) *Sport in Soviet Society*, Cambridge University Press, Cambridge.

30. Cratty, B. (1973) *Psychology in Contemporary Sport*, Prentice Hall, Englewood Cliffs, NJ.
31. Carr, G. (1974) The use of sport in the German Democratic Republic for the promotion of national consciousness and international prestige. *Journal of Sport History*, **1**, 123–36.
32. Loy, J. and Gudman, W. (1984) An analysis of sport pattern involvement using Zipf's law. *North American Culture*, **1**, 35–6.
33. Rodgers, B. (1977) *Rationalising Sports Policies; Sport in its Social Context*, Council of Europe, Strasbourg.
34. Rooney, J. (1986) The demand for golf in the year 2000, in *Golf Projections 2000*, National Golf Foundation, Jupiter, Fla., 1–8.
35. Meinig, D. (1967) Cultural geography, in *Introductory Geography; Viewpoints and Themes* (Association of American Geographers), AAG, Washington DC.
36. Rooney, J. (1981) Football in the new southwest (1958–1976). *Journal of Regional Cultures*, 149–61.
37. Gavin, T. (1979) Up from the mines and out from the steelworks? A study of regional variations in the production of top-flight professional footballers in Great Britain. *South Hampshire Geographer*, **11**, 22–34.
38. Connell, J. (1985) Football and regional decline: some reflections. *Geography*, **70**, 240–2.
39. Bale, J. (1979) Track and field regions of Europe. *Physical Education Review*, **3**, 137–45.
40. Shepard, J. (1980, 1983) *High School Track*, Shepard, Westminster, California.
41. Lewis, C. and McCarthy, M. (1977) The horse racing industry in Ireland. *Irish Geography*, **10**, 72–89.
42. Sage, G. and Loy, J. (1978) Geographical mobility patterns of college coaches. *Urban Life*, **7**, 253–76.
43. Ley, D. (1985) Cultural-humanistic geography. *Progress in Human Geography*, **9**, 415–23.

Chapter 8

THE SPATIAL REORGANIZATION OF SPORTS

So far this book has been largely concerned with interpretations of what is rather than with what ought to be. It is now time to turn to this latter theme and this chapter focuses on a number of examples in which attempts have been made geographically to reorganize sport according to certain norms or principles.

The locational and regional patterns found in modern sports are neither random nor regular. It will be clear from several earlier chapters that 'gaps' exist in the geographical provision of sports teams and sports facilities and that some places appear to be denied facilities for certain sports. In some cases teams might appear to be simply in the wrong place; in other cases the spatial organization may appear to be wrong because fixture lists have been structured incorrectly. However, terms like 'incorrect' or 'wrong' are value judgements and there is a need to specify the criteria or norms upon which our geographical judgements are based. For example, are location patterns in sport designed with profit or welfare maximization in mind? There is also the problem of deciding whether such inequalities result from inadequacies in the supply of facilities or whether they relate to people's own regional aspirations and tastes[1]. For example, in Britain rugby league is strongly concentrated in the north of England and is widely regarded as an element of regional popular culture; the paucity of provision of rugby league facilities in the cocktail belts of south-east England hardly leaves the residents of such regions feeling deprived!

In attempting to select the optimal distribution of sports facilities the two criteria chiefly employed are profit and welfare maximization. In the USA it is widely argued that profit maximization dominates the motivation of those who run both leagues and clubs and we have exemplified this theme in Chapter 4. In recreational sport, on the other hand, local authorities may be more concerned with the maximization of welfare and hence seek to fill gaps in regional or local provision.

This chapter seeks to illustrate examples of some ways in which prescriptions have been made for the spatial reorganization of sports. Both elite and mass sports are included and efforts are made, as previously, to provide examples from both Europe and North America. Because the number of applied-geographical studies of sports is somewhat small (in the early stage in any sub-discipline the emphasis tends to be on description rather than application) this chapter is necessarily brief. Indeed, about half of the studies described in what follows have been undertaken by non-geographers, in a strict disciplinary sense. This is not to say, however, that the problems they have been concerned with have been in any way non-geographical. The aim of what follows is to show the kinds of sports-oriented problems with which geographers might be expected to become increasingly involved. Technical details are omitted and those readers wishing to pursue these are referred to the original papers.

8.1 REORGANIZING AN EXISTING SPORT PATTERN

The patterns of points which make up spatial distributions of individual sports facilities or clubs are not necessarily those which are the most optimal – either from the viewpoint of maximizing revenue from sport or from the perspective of providing a fairer distribution pattern for the consumers of sport. Let us consider, in the first instance, a computer model which simulates the reorganization of North American professional football franchises. If the locations were based mainly on the distribution of population and the geographical organization of television market areas (so important in US sport, as we have seen in Section 5.2) the 26-team league would differ in some respects from the actual pattern. Although in many cases the actual and the optimal locations were the same, it was revealed in one of John Rooney's studies of US sport[2] that the south, south-west and north-western parts of the USA are currently under-represented and that the present distribution did not maximize its potential audience (Fig. 8.1). When the distribution of teams is reallocated according to population distribution we can see that while the actual location of Florida professional football in 1974 was in Miami, the optimal location would have been in Tampa. Likewise, Montreal and Albany 'should' have teams whereas Buffalo and Cincinnati should not. It would be possible to apply the same model to an increased population of North American football teams in order to arrange the spatial pattern of the league if it were to expand to fifty or a hundred teams.

In the case of the English football league the situation also exists where there is an apparent over-supply of clubs in some places and a rather obvious 'gap' in provision elsewhere. For example, in the north-west of

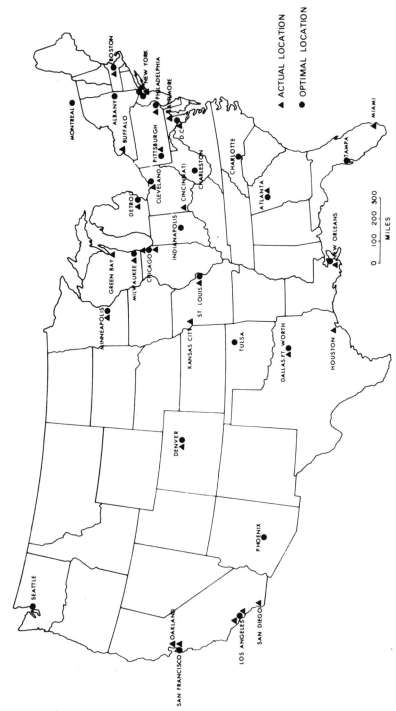

Fig. 8.1 Optimal and actual location of professional sports franchises based on population distribution, 1974. (Source: Rooney[2].)

England there is 1.31 times the average per capita number of league clubs (i.e. one per 534 000 of the population) whereas in the south-east the respective figure is 0.73. If the percentage of the population which watches soccer is the same, it is clear that the south-east has less than its 'fair share' of clubs.

Traditionally the last four ranked clubs in the football league have had to seek annual re-election to the league and, at the same time, non-league clubs made bids for election. Although this situation has now changed (the top non-league club now enters the football league) it does not affect the discussion which follows. By and large the geography of the football league is a fossil of what existed at the end of the first quarter of this century. Although some new entries have taken place (see Section 4.5) a good deal of spatial competition exists for support in the absence of any regionally based franchise system (see Section 4.1). The question asked by Paul Rivett[3], of Sussex University, was where would the best place be for two new entries to the league, assuming that the sole criterion was the maximization of home crowds and that the entries would be fourth division clubs of average success. It was recognized that for lowly clubs, the visiting club had no significant effect on crowd attendance* but that population variations and the differing regional emphasis (i.e. interest) in football had to be taken into account in the prediction of the two most suitable locations.

Predicting these locations was not easy because some non-league clubs, which on the basis of their playing performances were suitable applicants to the league, were located in parts of the country which were already well-served by league clubs. Corby in Northamptonshire, for example, would steal supporters from existing league clubs like North-ampton and Peterborough. According to a model developed by Rivett, it was concluded that the best locations would be Crawley in Sussex and somewhere in south-east Kent (e.g. Dover). This part of England has traditionally been a football 'desert' and the two locations would generate crowds of 9000 and 6000 respectively – well above the average gates of many third (let alone fourth) division clubs.

Exactly the same kind of problem can be encountered at the intra-urban level. Consider the example of the geographical distribution of swimming pools in the city of Edinburgh (Fig. 8.2). In this case we can compare the actual location of pools with the pattern which would be obtained if the aggregate travel distance to any pool was to be minimized. Figure 8.2 shows clearly that the central area of Edinburgh is probably over-provided with pools and that a rather more peripheral location pattern would be the optimal arrangement. Indeed, it has been estimated by

* See Walker[4], however, who notes that the 'local derby' effect is more pronounced in the lower divisions.

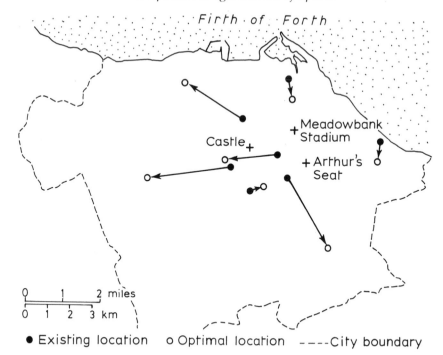

Fig. 8.2 Comparison of acutal locations of public swimming pools in Edinburgh in 1971 with locations which minimize aggregate travel. (Based on Hodgart[5].)

Edinburgh geographer R. L. Hodgart[5], that the aggregate travel to the present public swimming pools was 42% greater than to the optimal locations. It is therefore surprising that when the only pool constructed in the city since 1939 was built for the 1970 Commonwealth Games it was sited in an area which was already relatively well provided for.

In some sports it is not so much a point pattern which might require reorganization, but a pattern made up of areal units such as English counties. In Britain top-class cricket is organised on a county basis, seventeen 'first class' counties forming the apex of the English cricketing scene (Fig. 8.3). The location of the counties which qualify as 'first class' was more or less laid down before 1900, the entire system having evolved in a somewhat haphazard way during the nineteenth century. For the first sixty years of this century these first class clubs played their matches almost exclusively at locations within their county boundaries, engaging in a kind of 'periodic marketing' (see Section 4.2) of the sport at a number of locations. Rarely were the home games of a 'first class' county team played outside, its county boundaries.

Since 1963 there has been a growth of one-day cricket matches,

Fig. 8.3 The seventeen 'first class' counties and their original areas.

following the decline in popularity of the three-day games which had traditionally characterized the county championship. As a result of sponsored knock-out games of a limited number of overs, the number of games per season has increased. Clubs were faced with a locational problem, either to maintain their traditional locational arrangements, 'hawking' their games around their administrative county, or, in some cases, 'colonizing' areas outside their own county but inside 'minor counties' who were not provided with top-class cricket themselves. For example, Northampton played several games in Bedfordshire, Hertfordshire and Buckinghamshire; Somerset played some games in Devon while Gloucestershire played in Wiltshire. In effect, such counties are 'colonizing' the no-man's land of the minor counties without possessing any geographical logic for so doing. Why, for example, should it be Northants which has played games in Hertfordshire and not Middlesex? What if Middlesex wanted to play games in Herts? Would a conflict of interest arise between Middlesex and Northants should such an issue arise?

At the same time the geographical character of the English counties has changed drastically since the reorganization of county boundaries in 1974. In effect, historic boundaries are now being used to govern the geography of cricket. As a result certain paradoxes have resulted. Gloucestershire's headquarters ground at Bristol is now in the 'new' county of Avon; likewise, Warwickshire's ground is in the meteropolitan

Fig. 8.4 Possible demarcation of spheres of influence for first class counties with strong emphasis on population equalization. (Source: Walford[6].)

Fig. 8.5 Possible demarcation of spheres of influence of first class counties with strong emphasis on regional identity. The areas identical to those demarcated by the population equalization model are unshaded. (Source: Walford[6].)

county of the West Midlands. Hampshire play at Bournemouth, a town which is now in Dorset.

As a result of both out-county 'colonization' and the redrawn map of the English counties Walford[6] was led to speculate about possible moves towards the demarcation of 'spheres of influence' for the first class counties. Even though it is not in the minds of cricket legislators at present, it is possible that some distant dispute may eventually raise the whole issue. Two alternative models of such spheres of influence are suggested in Figs. 8.4 and 8.5. The former derives from a primary emphasis on population equalization; the latter from the force of historical linkages and the realities of regional identity.

The suggestion basic to the two models is that England and Wales could be conveniently demarcated into eighteen cricketing areas, with the present set of counties joined by a new one in the north based on Northumberland, Tyne and Wear and Durham. The present historic counties would continue as the heartlands and as the identifiable symbol and name of these areas, but the demarcation of the wider areas would effectively create the possiblity of first class cricket for all parts of England and Wales in a statutory way. The legitimation of such wider areas would call the historic counties to their missionary responsibility as well as act as a clear territorial treaty in relation to the selection of venues, the registration of players and the search for membership. They would also rationalize the eccentricities of history without obliterating the past.

8.2 GEOGRAPHICAL REORGANIZATION OF FIXTURE LISTS

Spatial reorganization of fixture lists may be required if (a) the distances involved in completing the existing fixtures in a sports league are too great, and hence too costly, and (b) the order of fixtures could be rearranged in order to produce a more equitable overall result, e.g. where climatic interference is more likely to occur if the fixture is arranged at one time rather than another in the season. Each of these problems will be illustrated in turn.

Let us take the case of a sports conference in the USA which consists of ten universities, each located in one major region of the country. If each university basketball team plays each other team in the conference twice, then each team will play eighteen conference games. In doing so a considerable amount of travel is inevitably involved. The patterns of movement would become much more complex at the professional level where many more games are played in each season but in principle the description of what follows could be applied to such situations.

Table 8.1 Comparison of 1973/4 schedule with optimal schedule, for a ten-team basketball conference

Team	1973–4		Optimal		Percentage mileage reduction
	Miles	Tours	Miles	Tours	
1	4554	8	3569	5	21.6
2	5278	8	3880	5	26.5
3	8925	8	5741	5	35.7
4	5516	7	4154	5	24.7
5	7746	8	5338	5	31.1
6	8340	8	5566	5	33.3
7	5539	7	4096	5	26.1
8	5300	8	3801	5	28.3
9	6098	8	4303	5	29.4
10	5595	8	4026	5	28.0
Mean	6289	7.8	4447	5	29.3

(*Source:* Campbell and Chen[7].)

For the south-eastern conference each team travelled, on average, 6289 miles in fulfilling its conference obligations for the 1973/4 season. One travelled almost 9000 miles while another travelled 'only' 4500. Mileages were higher than theoretically necessary because of the number of trips from home which involved one-day game visits. If two games were combined on a tour, the mileages and costs would be reduced. How the total number of tours and mileage travelled could be minimized was the problem facing mathematicians Robert Campbell and Dar-San Chen[7]. The solution to such a problem of spatial analysis involved producing an 'ideal' schedule for the ten-team conference which satisfied a number of constraints. These included such things as no team being allowed to play more than one game on a given day, no team being allowed to play away on two consecutive weekends, and a two-game tour having to take place on the same weekend. The problem was solved by applying a computer algorithm which produced a schedule which reduced the number of tours per team from 7.8 to 5 and the average mileage from over 6200 to under 4500. On average the total mileage reduction was 29.3%, the reduction for individual teams ranging from 35.7 to 21.6% (Table 8.1) All this was achieved with each team having five Saturday home games.

This kind of problem is common in many sports. Pressures to reduce transport costs are severe and the application of distance minimizing solutions could mean the difference between viability and demise in the case of some professional sports clubs.

Another case for the reorganization of fixture lists occurs when matches played at a particular point in a sequence (i.e. at a particular time of the year) are more likely to be affected by weather variables than if they had been played at another time. The effects of weather on sports are many and varied[8]. Some sports, like skiing or gliding, require specific kinds of weather. In other cases weather affects, rather than makes possible, the sporting action. In the USA baseball games can be 'rained off' but wet grass and wind can influence the action also[9]. In the case of English cricket Thornes[10] has not only analysed in detail the effect of rain on the outcome of games for a single season (1974) but has suggested certain solutions to the problem. In cricket rain in particular affects play in a number of ways. It can lead to the abandonment of a game without a single ball being bowled; in such cases a draw is awarded. Rain can also affect the nature of the wicket upon which the game is played, sometimes producing astonishing feats of bowling. Not unrelated to rain is the possibility of 'bad light' which can prematurely terminate play. In the 1974 season some English county teams lost over 70 hours play as a result of inclement weather.

Because some locations in the United Kingdom are more likely to be subject to heavy rainfall than others, and in order to reduce the number of matches spoilt by rain, it might be better if counties played more of their home games in months which were statistically 'dry'. As Thornes[10] pointed out, this would ideally require the search for a rainfall pattern in which a drier month for one county corresponds to a wetter month in another. This is a difficult problem, not least because any one year is likely to differ greatly from the long-term average. Although in principle this idea seems sound, Thornes was led to conclude that a more appropriate solution would be to offer 'wet bonus points' as compensation for rain-affected games. The Thornes analysis met with an interesting response from Morgan[11] who noted that because uncertainty and luck have traditionally been accepted as major factors contributing to interest in the game, they should be retained. In addition, the implementation of the Thornes approach would, Morgan argued, make the game even more complex than it already was!

8.3   RATIONALIZING RECRUITING

To a large degree, the football and basketball activities of American universities and colleges are part of the entertainment business. Many of the top-flight US sports-oriented universities contain stadiums which would shame many professional sports clubs in Europe and other parts of

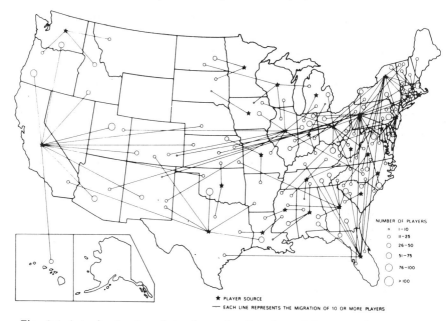

Fig. 8.6 Actual migratory behaviour of college-bound football players (major colleges, as designated by the NCAA and NAIA and including a 100% sample from each state) (data base: 1971–2, 1976–7 rosters). (Source: Rooney[12].)

the world (see Section 6.2). In small towns and sparsely populated regions which have no access to a professional sports team, the university (or in some cases, even the high school) team takes its place and serves as a vehicle for enhancing local and regional pride – as well as adding substantially to the coffers of the Athletic Department.

Because of the pressure placed on university football teams to win (and hence attract large crowds and revenue) most of the major institutions engage in nationwide recruiting for elite high school talent. What is available locally may not be good enough; what is more, some parts of America produce more superior talent than those regions can 'consume' themselves. It is to those areas that college coaches and scouts flock to try and lure the 'blue chip' athletes to their institutions, a process which Rooney[12, 13] has graphically described as the 'recruiting game'. Not surprisingly, such a hectic scramble for talent encourages abuse of NCAA rules on recruiting. Indeed, recruiting is regarded by many as the bane of college sports. A very brief list of recruiting violations includes:

● threatening to bomb the home of a high school principal who refused to alter a student's academic transcripts;
● offering a job to the parents of a good football player;

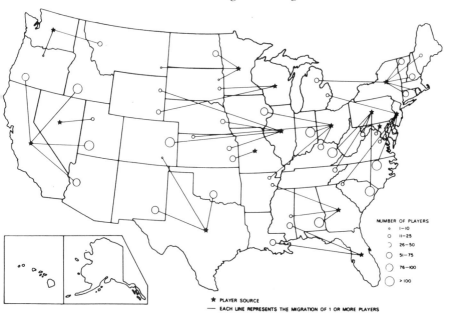

Fig. 8.7 Optimizing migratory behaviour of college-bound football players (major colleges, as designated by the NCAA and NAIA and including a 100% sample from each state) (data base: 1971–2, 1976–7 rosters). (Source: Rooney[12].)

- firing from a state job the father of a prospect who enrolled at other than the state's university;
- getting grades for athletes on university courses they never attended;
- providing a footballer with a new car every year;
- providing a college basketball player with an apartment.

Penalties imposed by the NCAA seem insufficiently stiff to dissuade the rule breakers. The fact that national recruiting is taken for granted exacerbates the cheating problem and for this reason Rooney[12] came up with some alternative suggestions. In essence he called for an end to national recruiting. With his Oklahoma State colleague Steve Tweedie, Rooney sought to redistribute athletic talent in such a way that long-distance recruiting would be eliminated. A computer program produced an optimizing pattern of talent migration which was based on two operating principles. The first was that the big universities in each state recruit players from that state as needed to make up their numbers. The second was that any surplus of talent is distributed to adjacent states so as to minimize the overall travel distance of the player surplus. If this system was adopted the geography of college football recruiting would change dramatically (Figs 8.6 and 8.7). In fact the amount of inter-state move-

Table 8.2 Prime candidates for a collegiate football super-league

Alabama	Kansas	Oklahoma State
Arizona	Kentucky	Penn State
Arizona State	LSU	Pittsburgh
Arkansas	Maryland	Purdue
Auburn	Michigan	Rutgers
Baylor	Michigan State	South Carolina
California	Minnesota	Stanford
Clemson	Mississippi	Tennessee
Colorada	Mississippi State	Texas
Florida	Missouri	Texas A and M
Georgia	Nebraska	Texas Tech
Georgia Tech	North Carolina	UCLA
Houston	North Carolina State	USC
Illinois	Notre Dame	Washington
Iowa	Ohio State	West Virginia
Iowa State	Oklahoma	Wisconsin

(*Source:* Rooney[12], p. 181.)

ment would be reduced by about 80%! A similar procedure was applied to basketball with equally dramatic results.

If such a plan was actually put into operation the most obvious benefit would be that the competition (and hence the recruiting abuses) for the best high school talent would be substantially curtailed. Costs of obtaining players would also therefore be cut. However, the fundamental disadvantage of such a system would be that it would also curtail academic freedom to move to whichever college or university a student wished. Such a system would impose unacceptable constraints in a free society. For this reason, Rooney provided alternative scenarios to the existing system. In the final analysis he realized that a super league of top university sports teams (Table 8.2) might be the best way out of the existing jungle of double standards. The criteria for inclusion in the super league were again based on geographical principles. A computer program was used to predict those institutions which would qualify for inclusion based on home game attendances, tradition, interest in the sport in question, and the location of existing professional franchises. In football-crazy Texas, for example, five institutions would be candidates for the super league; other prime candidates would come from states such as Nebraska and Arkansas – far removed from professional football franchises, but possessing powerful university football teams in their own states.

Rooney's powerful plea for an end to the abuse of inter-collegiate sports is founded on the application of geographical principles, applied to recruiting patterns. For this reason it is an excellent example of problem solving in a sports-geographic context.

FURTHER READING

Works on applied sports geography are few in number. One of the best books on applied sports geography, which has only been briefly alluded to in this chapter, is J. Rooney's *The Recruiting Game* (2nd edn), University of Nebraska Press, 1980. Many of this book's conclusions are succinctly reviewed in Rooney's Athletic recruiting, in *National Forum*, LXII, 1982, 32–6. For an example of a study which is concerned with rationalizing, rather than relocating, a sports activity see R. Le Heron's Rationalising the location of the New Zealand Horse Racing and Trotting Industry, in *Proceedings of the New Zealand Geography Conference*, Dunedin, 1977, New Zealand Geographical Society, Conference Series, 9, 1978. A quite different kind of article, which applies a technique called morphometric analysis in order to summarize numerically the terrain of long distance road races, is Ronald Eyton's Morphometrics of the Chasquis Invitational Rocky Mountain Road Race, *Sport Place*, 1, 2, 1987, 38–47.

REFERENCES

1. Patmore, A. (1983) *Recreation and Resources*, Blackwell, Oxford.
2. Rooney, J. (1975) Sports from a geographic perspective, in *Sport and Social Order* (eds D. Ball and J. Loy), Addison-Wesley, Reading, Mass.
3. Rivett, P. (1975) The structure of league football, *Operational Research Quarterly*, **26**, 801–12.
4. Walker, B. (1986) The demand for professional football and the success of football league teams; some city size effects. *Urban Studies*, **23**, 209–20.
5. Hodgart, R. L. (1978) Optimizing access to public services, *Progress in Human Geography*, **2**, 17–48.
6. Walford, R. (1983) The spread of first class cricket venues since 1945; a study in "colonial expansion", in *Geographical Perspectives on Sport* (eds J. Bale and C. Jenkins), Department of PE, Birmingham University, pp. 127–46.
7. Campbell, K. and Chen, D. (1976) A minimum distance basketball scheduling algorithm, in *Management Science in Sports* (eds S. Ladany, R. Machol and D. Morrison), North-Holland, Amsterdam.
8. Thornes, J. (1977) The effect of weather on sport. *Weather*, **32**, 258–67.
9. Shaw, E. (1963) Geography and baseball. *Journal of Geography*, **62**, 74–6.
10. Thornes, J. (1976) Rain starts play. *Area*, **8**, 105–12.
11. Morgan, R. (1976) Rain starts play. *Area*, **8**, 257–8.
12. Rooney, J. (1980) *The Recruiting Game*, University of Nebraska Press, Lincoln.
13. Rooney, J. (1985) America needs a new intercollegiate sports system. *Journal of Geography*, **84**, 139–43.

Chapter 9

CONCLUDING
COMMENTS

What criteria should be used in deciding if a subject is worth studying or not? Its pervasiveness in society as a whole? Its degree of media coverage? Its economic and landscape impact? Its political and social significance? If the answer to any of these questions is 'yes' then there is little obvious reason for excluding the study of sport from the academic curriculum. Because functional academic disciplines of the future will probably differ from those of today it is very possible that future curricula will give rather more attention to sports studies than is presently the case[1]. If this is so, then it should be clear from the contents of this book that geography has a strong case for having a position within such studies. But the discipline itself will need to accept that sport is a valid area of geographic enquiry: that football is as appropriate for geographical study as footpaths, hockey as appropriate as holidays, and sports as appropriate as recreation and leisure.

This book has explored a variety of situations in which geography is related to sport and vice versa. Although previous books have focused on the sports geographies of particular places or of particular problems, the present book represents the first attempt to integrate the broad spectrum of sports-geographic literature, taking examples from a number of continents and from a wide variety of sporting activities.

From the start we argued that space and place, two concepts basic to geography, are also central to the phenomenon of modern sport. We went on to show how sports grew geographically as well as historically, using well-known geographical models of innovation diffusion to aid an appreciation of the growth of sport. We noted the continuing state of locational flux which characterizes modern sports and the way sport possesses considerable economic impacts upon cities and regions. It was pointed out that some of these impacts were of a negative nature, sport producing social costs as well as benefits. Sports landscapes were explored and it was stressed how totally new monocultural landscapes have emerged. Our review of sports regions ranged from modern cultural regions made up of states, as in the Dixie football region in the USA, to smaller areas made up of English counties such as the north-east soccer region. Such regions were delimited on their ability to produce elite participants but others were based on levels of sporting activity, defined by numbers of clubs or participants. Areal classifications were adopted in our review of Olympic success where we stressed the prevailing dominance of communist states. As with the diffusion and location pattern of sports, regional patterns are constantly changing, again emphasizing the dynamic nature of the world of sport. We concluded our review with the kinds of prescriptions geographers make for a new spatial organization of sports.

The basic purpose of this book has been to provide an overview of a burgeoning sub-discipline. However, apart from the pervasiveness of space and place in sport studies, two other themes have featured frequently in the previous pages. The first is the strong linkages which exist between sport and political-economy. Sport grew with the growth of industrialization; it penetrated continents as urbanization and industrialization also penetrated them; and many of the innovations in sports were of an economic character. Today top-class sport is essentially an industry in itself, its raw materials being athletes who are carefully recruited from an international resource base and its processing plants being the clubs (and, in the USA, the colleges and universities) which provide an increasingly theatrical spectacle for a sports-crazy public. Economic spillovers, of a positive and negative nature, are generated by sport. Sociologists may study the social origins of a phenomenon such as football hooliganism but geographers are concerned with the environmental and spatial impacts which such fans bring to the localities within which they operate. Economic rationality is frequently assumed by sports entrepreneurs, even in nations such as the UK where sport has traditionally been viewed as being concerned with maximizing utility rather than profits.

A second theme which has featured in many of the preceding pages is the growing rationality which is found in sport. Rationality is increasingly assumed, not just in an economic sense but also in terms of the landscapes in which sport is played (or, in many cases, worked). The landscape upon which sport was occasionally played has given way to monocultural sportscape of a carefully territorialized nature. Sport spaces have become spaces to fill and empty at specified times, set off from other land uses and sited in particular zones of the city. It has been debated whether such increased rationality is reflected in progress or whether, in some cases, alienation is the result. We have seen that sport has increasingly become an economically rationalized activity; the sports geographer is interested in exploring the locations, landscapes and regions associated with such activity.

9.1 ALTERNATIVE FRAMEWORKS?

The framework suggested in this book is essentially that proposed by Rooney[2] who suggests that either a topical or regional approach can be applied to the geography of sports. The topical approach is convenient for organizing material about sport, but it may not necessarily be the best way of thinking about how we should explore sports-geography relations. A way forward towards a firmer conceptual base may be to first recognize the significance of sport in the contemporary analysis of modern society and then ask what a geography of sport can tell us about this relationship*. The centrality of place in sport was stressed early on in this book; a merging of the notions of localism and popular culture may be one way forward since there can be little doubt that it is through sport that current manifestations of localism (and regionalism and nationalism) are most visible. Relating sociological work on localism and popular culture to sport and geography might be placed near the top of the agenda for sports geographers in the deacde ahead. It has been noted that 'there is a substantial literature in the sociology of sport . . . and cultural geography would be strengthened by drawing on it[3].

It is not only by drawing on and relating to other disciplinary approaches that a geography of sport might develop. The sub-discipline needs to move further than it has done into philosophical approaches other than empiricism and postivism which have characterized most work in the field. Parts of the present book have implied that there are rich insights to be obtained from adopting more humanistic and structuralist philosophies, recognizing the human feelings derived from sport, place and environment (for example) on the one hand, and the fact (for example) that the reality (Table 2.1) of modern top-class sport is that of a global system on the other. The latter approach has been touched on in several places in the present book; in Chapter 3 attention was paid to the emergence of international governing bodies; in Chapter 5 we talked about the international 'trade' in sporting talent. Such interaction could simply not take place if sport was not a global system. Yet the experience of sport in one country is different from that in another. Although the rules of basketball, for example, are the same in both the UK and the USA, the experience of a college basketball match in each country is totally different. In America the razzmatazz, number of fans, the win-at-all-costs philosophy and the media coverage contrast with the low-key, handful of spectators and play-for-fun ethos in Britain. This distinction can be interpreted via an approach adopted by political geographer, Peter Taylor[4]. Reality (i.e. modern, global sport) has passed through two sets of ideological filters to make the local experiences different. What we

* I am grateful to Roger Lee for this point.

make of sport in particular places may depend upon the ideologies within which sport is embedded*.

9.2 SOME AVENUES TO EXPLORE

Nearly two decades ago Rooney wrote that there was much to be done if the full potential in the geographical approach to sport was to be realized[6]. Sports geography has developed since his exhortation; more papers are being written, more conferences being addressed by sports geographers, and more non-geographers are recognizing the value of a geographic view of sports. The role of the Society for the North American Cultural Survey should not be underestimated in spreading an interest in sports geography in the USA and the massive atlas, *This Remarkable Continent*, produced by the survey places sport firmly within the context of North American culture[7]. It is also good to see a section on 'sport' in an *Atlas of Industrializing Britain*[8], though its brevity totally fails to do justice to one of the most enduring innovations of Victorian Britain. Sports geography is also beginning to appear in American undergraduate cultural geography texts, for example Jordan and Rowntree's *The Human Mosaic*[9], hence providing a more balanced treatment of culture than hitherto.

However, despite these advances a number of avenues remain unexplored. For example, sport is essentially a commodity[10], but it creates further commodities. Sports events create linked activities in construction, publishing, clothing and manufactures of many kinds. It is significant that we have said virtually nothing in this book about one of the most rapidly expanding areas of sports, the sports goods industries, and this is a subject to which economic geographers with a penchant for sports could begin to address themselves†. Certainly, sports goods production typifies the rapid shift from local to global forms of industrial organization.

A second area which has barely been addressed by the present book is the physical geography of sport. We have touched on the effects of certain physical factors in our early discussion of how place may affect sporting outcomes, but physical geographers have a great deal more to contribute to sports studies. Thirdly, there is a strong case to be made for geographic explorations of certain aspects of international sports, the surface of which has barely been scratched in the present book. Geographical replications of Jokl's early work would be rewarding, as would a clearer picture of the phenomenon of sports tourism, encouraged not only by

* This approach is used in Bale[5].
† About the only example I know is Hammond[11].

events like the Olympics and World Cup but also by the whole host of more modest international soccer matches, mass marathons and other such activities.

It is also clear that while some subjects have been quite rigorously researched in some countries, the same is not true in others. For example, the kinds of economic-geographical impact studies of sports involving the application of regional multipliers are almost entirely American in origin and there is an obvious need for such studies to be applied in a wide variety of other sporting contexts.

This book has been written in order to alert students in sports studies and geography to the presence of a fertile field of academic enquiry. The book's contents have charted the route; it is to be hoped that others will explore newer frontiers and horizons.

FURTHER READING

There is little which has been written to assist teachers wishing to integrate a geographical component to sport studies courses, or to develop courses on the geography of sport. A book which outlines a course in sports studies but omits any explicit reference to geography is by Harold J. Vanderzwaag and Thomas J. Sheehan: *Introduction to Sport Studies; from the Classroom to the Ball Park*, Brown, Dubuque, Iowa, 1978. A paper which argues strongly for the inclusion of sport in the curriculum is Keith Thompson's Culture, sport and the curriculum, in *British Journal of Educational Studies*, **28**, 1980, 136–41. Some practical strategies for teaching sports geography are found in John Bale's Sport and the Environment, in *Bulletin of Environmental Education* (1987), 187–8, and his Sport in geography, in J. Fien and R. Gerber (eds) *Teaching Geography for a Better World*, Oliver and Boyd, Edinburgh, 1988. Essential reading for all students interested in sport is the thrice yearly journal *Sport Place*.

REFERENCES

1. Vanderzwaag, H. and Sheehan, G. (1979) *Introduction to Sports Studies*, Brown, Dubuque, Iowa.
2. Rooney, J. (1975) Sports for a geographic perspective, in *Sport and Social Order* (eds D. Ball and J. Loy), Addison-Wesley, Reading, Mass., pp. 55–115.
3. Ley, D. (1985) Cultural-humanistic geography. *Progress in Human Geography*, **9**, 415–23.
4. Taylor, P. (1985) *Political Geography*, Arnold, London.
5. Bale, J. (1987) The muscle drain; foreign student-athletes in American universities. *Sport Place*, **1**, 2.
6. Rooney, J. (1974) *A Geography of American Sport: from Cabin Creek to Anaheim*, Addison Wesley, Reading, Mass.

7. Rooney, J. and McDonald, J. (1982) Sports and games, in *This Remarkable Continent* (eds J. Rooney, W. Zelinsky and D. Louder), Texas A and M University Press, College Station.
8. Vamplew, W. (1986) Sport, in *Atlas of Industrializing Britain 1780–1914* (eds J. Langton and R. Morris), Methuen, London, pp. 198–201.
9 .Jordan, T. and Rowntree, L. (1982) *The Human Mosaic*, Harper and Row, New York.
10. Kirby, A. (1985) Leisure as commodity: the role of the state in leisure provision. *Progress in Human Geography*, **9**, 64–84.
11. Hammond, R. (1983) Valley canoes; a case study in industrial geography. *Trent Geographer*, 8–15.

APPENDIX

Suggestions for practical work

Teachers using this book as a course text may wish to use the following discussion questions, practical exercises and suggestions for projects to complement the further reading sections at the end of each chapter.

PROJECTS/TOPICS FOR DISCUSSION

Chapter 2

1. Attempt a classification of sports based on the degree of rigidity of the spatial constraints (e.g. squash is highly constrained, orienteering is relatively unconstrained).

2. Undertake a study of the 'home field advantage' for (a) three different team sports and (b) team sports at three different levels (e.g. top-class, amateur, high school). Evaluate the extent to which playing at home appears to constitute an advantage.

3. Evaluate the varying effects of climate, relief and weather on sports.

4. Undertake a field project on sports-oriented graffiti. Does it serve to boost the local team, denigrate opponents, or mark the limits of a club's 'turf'?

5. Early on in Chapter 2 we noted that sport could be regarded as work, or work-like. The six most unsatisfactory aspects of work which are most frequently cited are shown in the left hand column on p. 241.

   To what extent do you think any of these sources of dissatisfaction might apply to sport? Take examples from sports which illustrate (a)–(f) below. You should be able to find several examples for most of them. Record them in a table like the one below. If there are unsatisfactory aspects to sports, why do people take part in them?

Unsatisfactory Aspects	Examples from work	Examples from sports
a. Harmfulness of environment	Dust in coal mining	Steep slopes in downhill skiing
b. Physical fatigue and stress		
c. Risk of accidents		
d. Repetitive work		
e. Subordination		
f. Time spent at place of work		

6. We noted in Chapter 2 that sport is a data rich subject. The information below is extracted from one source of British sports data, *Rothman's Football Yearbook 1973–4* which is typical of the genre. Have a look at the data included in the extract on Bristol City Football Club. Comparable data exist for each of the other Football league clubs.

BRISTOL CITY

Year Formed: 1984.
Turned Professional: 1897.
Limited Company: 1897.
Previous Grounds: 1894, St. John's Lane; 1904, Ashton Gate.
Previous Name: 1894–97, Bristol South End.

BRISTOL CITY – PLAYERS

Player and position	Ht.	Wt.	Birthplace	Clubs
Goalkeepers				
Len Bond	5 9	12 0	Ilminster	Bristol C.
Ray Cashley	5 10	11 0	Bristol	Bristol C.
Full backs				
David Bruton	6 2	14 0	Gloucester	Bristol C.
Brian Drysdale	5 7	11 0	Wingate	Lincoln C.
				Hartlepool
				Bristol C.
Trevor Jacobs	5 9	11 10	Bristol	Bristol C.
Geoff Merrick	5 9	11 0	Bristol	Bristol C.
Geoff Merrington	5 11½	12 5	Newcastle	Burnley
				Bristol C.
Stephen Ritchie	5 11	13 3	Scotland	Bristol C.
Half backs				
John Emanuel	5 11	13 7	Ferndale	Bristol C.
David Rodgers	6 1¼	13 2	Bristol	Bristol C.
Gerry Sweeney				Celtic
				Morton
				Bristol C.
Les Wilson	5 8	10 11	Liverpool	Wolverhampton W.
				Bristol C.
Forwards				
Danny Bartley	5 8	10 10	Paulton	Bristol C.
Ian Broomfield	6 0	11 1	Bristol	Bristol C.
Keith Fear	5 7	10 8	Bristol	Bristol C.
John Galley	6 1	12 7	Clowne	Wolverhampton W.
				Rotherham U.
				Bristol C.
Gerry Gow	5 8	10 8	Glasgow	Bristol C.
Kevin Griffin	5 9	12 0	Plymouth	Bristol C.
Tom Ritchie	5 11	12 8	Scotland	Bristol C.
Gerry Sharpe	5 8	10 7	Gloucester	Bristol C.
Peter Spiring	5 8	11 0	Glastonbury	Bristol C.
Trevor Tainton	5 8	11 7	Bristol	Bristol C.
Edward Woods	6 0	15 0	Ferndale	Bristol C.

(a) Identify which data you regard as potentially valuable in geographical enquiry.
(b) How could the data illustrated above be used to explore (i) geographical aspects of the club itself, (ii) the club's players, and (iii) as part of a study of national patterns of geographical growth and change in soccer?

Chapter 3

1. Using secondary sources such as association handbooks, trace the diffusion pattern of selected sports and establish whether the sport exemplifies the S-shaped curve, the neighbourhood and the hierarchical effects.

2. Using similar sources to 1. above, examine the geographical diffusion of innovations in sport (e.g. county championships, professionalism, specialized facilities). Do the last areas to adopt the innovations share any common characteristics?

3. Consider the kinds of people who introduced sports to places, both regional and national, and the kinds of people who initially played them there. To what extent do you feel your examples confirm the social control function attributed to sports?

4. Explore sports which have (as yet) failed to gain a footing in particular countries. What do you think are the barriers to adoption?

Chapter 4

1. Map the birthplaces of players starting their careers with (a) four successful professional sports teams and (b) four unsuccessful ones. Is there any difference in the patterns?

2. Plot the relocation patterns of clubs in selected sports. What factors have influenced their decision to relocate?

3. Relate town size to success in selected sports. How do you explain any anomalous cases which you may discover?

4. Review the conflicting interests which might be expected to be revealed following a decision to relocate an inner city sports stadium in the suburbs.

5. Debate the pros and cons concerning the international recruitment of sports talent.

Chapter 5

1. Attempt to obtain data from which you can map the fandoms of your local professional club or the catchment area of your local sports club.

2. By undertaking a survey of local residents, establish the spatial extent of the 'nuisances' generated by your local professional sports club. Establish the nature of the nuisances and whether the residents are compensated in any way.

3. By using data collected from estate agents attempt to establish the effect of proximity to sports grounds of various kinds on house prices.

4. Undertake an interview survey with retailers of various kinds located around sports outlets in order to discover whether, and to what extent, revenues increase on match days. Is there a distance effect in relation to the stadium?

5. (a) Read the news item on p. 245 taken from the *Fresno Bee* (8 April 1986). Identify the principal 'actors' who might be involved in the race track location scenario.
   (b) Divide your class into groups, each group identifying with one of the interest groups. Prepare a case for your group's viewpoint and elect a spokesperson to present it at a simulated planning tribunal. You might summarize the overall presentation as shown in the table below.
   (c) On the basis of the article, to what extent do you sympathize with the plan to develop the racetrack?
   (d) What further information might you require in order to arrive at a more informed judgement?

Interests involved	Reactions and viewpoints	Major area of concern

Race track plan revived
Application refiled for auto racing in Malaga

By WANDA COYLE
Bee staff writer

A new attempt to get approval for an auto race track in Malaga is on its way through Fresno County planning procedures.

Businessman Jerry Turner, whose application for the track was turned down by the Board of Supervisors in March 1985, refiled the request on March 27, after the expiration of the one-year waiting period required when an application is denied.

The county Planning Commission, which recommended approval of the first application on a split vote, is tentatively scheduled to rehear the issue May 8.

Margie McHenry of the county resources and development department staff said that whether that hearing date is kept depends on whether all of the environmental assessment and other staff procedures can be completed in time.

However the commission votes this time, the final decision again will be in the hands of the supervisors.

The planning staff last year had recommended that an environmental impact report be prepared for the project. The planning commission rejected that recommendation, and instead directed the staff to develop a list of conditions to deal with the environmental and other concerns raised by neighbors.

The supervisors never dealt specifically with the impact report issue, voting to deny the application without considering directly the environmental questions.

McHenry said the new application incorporates the approximately 30 conditions proposed by the staff and it is possible that the inclusion of those mitigation measures might eliminate the need for an impact report. That will be decided after the comments of other public agencies about the new application have been considered, she said.

The site proposed for the track is 24 acres on the south side of East Central Avenue between South Willow and South Peach avenues, bordered on three sides by additional property owned by Turner. It is in an area designated by the county General Plan for industrial uses.

The operational statement calls for a one-third-mile dirt track, seating for 3,500 spectators and parking for 1,400 vehicles. The track would operate from 6 to 10 pm Saturdays and 1 to 5 pm Sundays from May to September, with food and refreshments, including beer, available on the premises.

Jerome Behrens, Turner's attorney, said the new application is the same as the previous one except for the inclusion of the mitigation measures designed to deal with the concerns raised by neighbors at the earlier hearings.

He wouldn't predict how the hearings might turn out this time, but said, "Maybe the time is right, now, for a race track here."

The track would be the third in the central San Joaquin Valley. The others are in Hanford and Madera.

Turner had submitted a petition bearing 11,000 signatures in favor of the track, and foes had countered with a 315-name petition in opposition.

The opponents were especially worried about the effects of noise and traffic on nearby residential neighborhoods.

Behrens said the mitigation measures included in the new operational statement, including nosie abatement measures and the employment of traffic control officers, "are designed to take care of every environmental concern. I can't imagine anything new being raised now."

Chapter 6

1. By comparing old and new maps calculate the extent to which formalized places designed specifically for sports have grown in the last fifty years.

2. Draw up a classification of sports based on the extent to which they are undertaken in natural and artificial environments. Do you think people of different personalities take part in different sports?

3. Identify top-class sports which range from those which can still be played on landscape to those which require a sportscape. Try to find the key points in time when landscape gave way to sportscape for particular sports.

4. To what extent do you feel that sport in its present form is anti-nature? Does it deplete resources, use renewable sources of energy or add to pollution in any way?

5. *Sports landscape elements and ensembles*
   In Chapter 6 it was noted that landscape elements contribute to a sports landscape ensemble. This learning experience involves students in the creation of their own 'model' landscape ensembles for selected sports. As an example, the landscape ensemble of the English cricket ground has been chosen but the idea could be applied to any sports landscape.
   The following outline shows the barest detail of a cricket ground with wicket and boundary only marked. In the form of an annotated sketch map add to a larger version of this outline the various sports landscape elements which together contribute to the traditional cricket landscape ensemble. This will be essentially a model of the English cricket ground. Landscape elements can be collected from various media such as cricket novels (in which the landscape within which cricket grounds are found is often described), cricket histories, anthologies, 'coffee table' books on the English landscape, etc.
   If the ensemble was replaced with a concrete bowl would the sporting experience differ? In what ways?

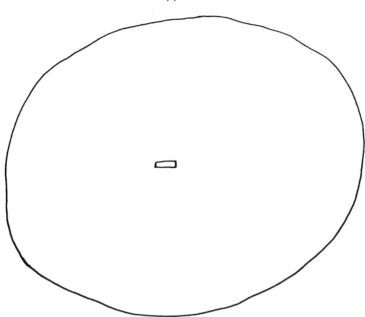

6. *Sport 1993*

    Chapter 4 looked at some locational aspects of sports and Chapter 6 has explored the sports landscape. The next learning experience adopts a 'futures studies' approach to each of these themes. The following information sheet includes some stimulus materials about what sport might be like in 1993. Essentially, it is an invention of a future, not a prediction of the future.

    Read the 'Sport 1993' sheet on p. 248.

    (a) What does 'Sport 1993' tell you about changes which have taken place in sports since the present time?

    (b) How far, if at all, do you feel that the invented changes which are described, are already underway?

    (c) At the end of this century what other aspects of sports geography might be very different from the way they are today?

Sport 1993

1993 was a momentous year in sport. Australian cricketers reverted to wearing white clothing – like their fathers did – and the President of VFL Inc., Sir Ronald Barassi, was rumoured to be preparing for a football comeback. Oil was discovered at the Melbourne Cricket Ground, and King Charles presented Bjorn Borg with the Wimbledon crown – yet again.

Here veteran sports reporter GEOFF SLATTERY, reviews the highlight of 1993, a classic year in sport.

New golf venue

The 1993 Australian Open Golf Championship will be held at the Sydney Showgrounds, following a 20-year, $62-thousand million deal between the Australian Golf Union and Lord Packer.

Lord Packer has just secured the Australian rights to the amazing American invention – the portable golf course. The new system allows holes to be placed in whichever venue an entrepreneur desires. Lord Packer has secured 36 separate holes from the US distributor.

'This is a great system,' said Lord Packer. 'We can roll the holes one after the other into the Showgrounds. As one hole is completed, it will be removed, and replaced by the next. It's a revolutionary system, and allows spectators to watch 18 holes of golf from the one vantage point.'

Tennis move to New York

The 1993 Australian Open tennis championships will be held in New York from 26 December to 31 December, in an effort to attract the world's top players.

The decision to change venues was made by the Lawn Tennis Association of Australia, following last year's Open at Kooyong, won by Alice Springs blacksmith Jack Knight.

MCG strikes oil

The Melbourne Cricket Ground will be reconstructed at Wallan, 40 kilometres north of Melbourne, following the discovery of oil at the Jolimont Ground, Melbourne's cricket headquarters for almost 150 years.

Oil gushed from the surface of the ground minutes after workmen began digging up the MCG pitch – the last grass cricket pitch in Australia – to replace it with a regulation aluminium pitch.

Esso–BHP geologists believe there is sufficient oil under the MCG and Yarra Park to maintain Australian oil self-sufficiency until the year 3000.

'The discovery of oil certainly explains why the wickets played so low in the early eighties,' said newly appointed MCC secretary, Mr Jack Lyons.

(After N. Gough. Alternative futures in education, in *Teaching Geography for a Better World* (ed. J. Fien and R. Gerber), Jacaranda, Brisbane, 280.)

Chapter 7

1. Attempt to chart the migratory pattern of professional sports players between clubs during the course of their careers. Do any patterns emerge which suggest any tendency for players to have regional preferences?
2. Undertake a mental mapping exercise which attempts to identify people's perceptual sport-place associations.
3. Using ranking lists from multi-event sports such as track and field or swimming, calculate per capita and specialization indices for selected countries and locate each on a 'success space' matrix. If possible, chart the changes in location within the matrix over time.
4. *Athletic superpowers or sporting stereotypes?*
   This is an exercise in sports geography at the global scale. It tries to identify national variations in 'sports productivity' for one sport, namely track and field athletics. It uses data on the top twenty athletes for each Olympic event in 1987 and indicates the extent to which the 'productivity' of different nations deviated from the global average level of production. It should be noted that the definition of 'national output' (i.e. the number of each country's athletes in the world 'top 20') is only one of many possible definitions. For example, much deeper ranking lists were used in the construction of Figs. 7.10 and 7.11.
   From the following data on (i) the 1987 world rankings and (ii) the populations of the countries from which the ranked athletes came, we can:
   (a) select countries for analysis (e.g. from one continent, from the 'Third World'):
   (b) count the number of rankings for each country (this need not be a daunting task if this is used as a group project). This will give you the absolute levels of 'production', and
   (c) calculate a per capita index. This will compare countries with the global average, represented as an index of 1.00. For example, there are 667 rankings and 4400 million people in the world; therefore there is one world class athlete per 6.6 million people. This is the world average per capita which we can represent as an index of 1.00 by using the following formula:

$$\text{index value} = \frac{\text{number or rankings } (n)}{\substack{\text{total population} \\ \text{(in millions)}(t)}} \div \frac{1}{6.6}$$

$$\left(\text{or } \frac{n}{t} \times 6.6\right)$$

(d) Do this for each of the countries you have selected. Record your data in the following table and map your results. Does any regional pattern emerge?

Name of country	Absolute total	Per capita index

(Note: Because some athletes appear in more than one event, the absolute totals refer to numbers of rankings, not numbers of athletes.)

World Best Performers In 1987*

MEN'S EVENTS

100 METRES

Ben Johnson	(Can)	Dennis Mitchell	(USA)
Carl Lewis	(USA)	Viktor Bryzgin	(USSR)
Linford Christie	(UK)	Harvey Glance	(USA)
Mark Witherspoon	(USA)	Lee McNeill	(USA)
Lee McRae	(USA)	Henry Thomas	(USA)
Calvin Smith	(USA)	Vladimir Krylov	(USSR)
Ray Stewart	(Jam)	Stanley Floyd	(USA)
Max Moriniere	(Fra)	Chidi Imoh	(Nig)
Attila Kovacs	(Hun)	Floyd Heard	(USA)
Vadim Davyov	(USSR)	Thomas Jefferson	(USA)

200 METRES

Carl Lewis	(USA)	Henry Thomas	(USA)
Floyd Heard	(USA)	Wallace Spearman	(USA)
Dwayne Evans	(USA)	Tony Jones	(USA)
Calvin Smith	(USA)	Stanley Kerr	(USA)
Attila Kovacs	(Hun)	Thomas Jefferson	(USA)
Gilles Queneherve	(Fra)	Bruno Marie-Rose	(Fra)
John Regis	(UK)	James Butler	(USA)
Robson da Silva	(Bra)	Dennis Mitchell	(USA)
Harvey McSwain	(USA)	Roberto Hernandez	(Cub)
Vladimir Krylov	(USSR)	Pierfrancesco Pavoni	(Ita)

400 METRES

Butch Reynolds	(USA)	David Kitur	(Ken)
Innocent Igbunike	(Nig)	Roddie Haley	(USA)
Thomas Schonlebe	(GDR)	Michael Franks	(USA)
Danny Everett	(USA)	Andrew Valmon	(USA)
Derek Redmond	(UK)	Jens Carlowitz	(GDR)
Raymond Pierre	(USA)	Darren Clark	(Aus)
Roberto Hernandez	(Cub)	Roger Black	(UK)
Antonio McKay	(USA)	Mathias Schersing	(GDR)
Gabriel Tiacoh	(Iv C)	Kevin Robinzine	(USA)
Bert Cameron	(Jam)	Henry Thomas	(USA)

800 METRES

Billy Konchellah	(Ken)	Said Aouita	(Mor)
Peter Elliott	(UK)	Moussa Fall	(Sen)
Jose Luis Barbosa	(Bra)	Harald Schmid	(FRG)
Philippe Collard	(Fra)	Stephen Marai	(Ken)
Johnny Gray	(USA)	Sammy Koskei	(Ken)
Tom McKean	(UK)	Babacar Niang	(Sen)
Abdi Bile	(Som)	David Mack	(USA)
Ryszard Ostrowski	(Pol)	Dieudonne Kwizera	(Bur)
William Wuyke	(Ven)	Slobodan Popovic	(Yug)
Faouzi Lahbi	(Mor)	Peter Braun	(FRG)

1500 METRES

Said Aouita	(Mor)	Johan Fourie	(SA)
Steve Cram	(UK)	Markus Hacksteiner	(Swi)
Abdi Bile	(Som)	Jim Spivey	(USA)
Jose Luis Gonzalez	(Spa)	Adrian Passey	(UK)
Peter Elliott	(UK)	Tim Hacker	(USA)
Jens-Peter Herold	(GDR)	Philippe Collard	(Fra)
Sydney Maree	(USA)	John Walker	(NZ)
Steve Crabb	(UK)	Mike Hillardt	(Aus)
Dieter Baumann	(FRG)	Chuck Aragon	(USA)
Jose Abascal	(Spa)	Pierre Deleze	(Swi)

5000 METRES

Said Aouita	(Mor)	Brahim Boutaib	(Mor)
Jack Buckner	(UK)	Domingos Castro	(Por)
Jose Luis Gonzalez	(Spa)	Gary Staines	(UK)
Jose Abascal	(Spa)	Eamonn Coghlan	(Irl)
Frank O'Mara	(Irl)	Peter Koech	(Ken)
Arturo Barrios	(Mex)	John Treacy	(Irl)
Fethi Baccouche	(Tun)	Abel Anton	(Spa)
Pascal Thiebaut	(Fra)	Herbert Stephan	(FRG)
Sydney Maree	(USA)	Doug Padilla	(USA)
John Gregorek	(USA)	Joao Campos	(Por)

10 000 METRES

Francesco Panetta	(Ita)	Mark Nenow	(USA)
Wodajo Bulti	(Eth)	Kozo Akutsu	(Jap)
Jean-Louis Prianon	(Fra)	Arturo Barrios	(Mex)
Takeyuki Nakayama	(Jap)	Werner Schildhauer	(GDR)
Paul Kipkeoch	(Ken)	Carl Thackery	(UK)
Hansjorg Kunze	(GDR)	Ezequiel Canario	(Por)
Martti Vainio	(Fin)	Steve Binns	(UK)
Haji Bulbula	(Eth)	Andrew Lloyd	(Aus)
Xolile Yawa	(SA)	Masanari Shintaku	(Jap)
Paul Arpin	(Fra)	Martin Vrabel	(Cze)

3000 METRES STEEPLECHASE

Francesco Panetta	(Ita)	Bruno Le Stum	(Fra)
Hagen Melzer	(GDR)	Henry Marsh	(USA)
William Van Dijck	(Bel)	Patriz Ilg	(FRG)
Julius Korir	(Ken)	Alessandro Lambruschini	(Ita)
Raymond Pannier	(Fra)	Hans Koeleman	(Hol)
Brian Diemer	(USA)	Roger Hackney	(UK)
Patrick Sang	(Ken)	Jose Regalo	(Por)
Fethi Baccouche	(Tun)	Boguslaw Maminski	(Pol)
Peter Koech	(Ken)	Joshua Kipkemboi	(Ken)
Graeme Fell	(Can)	Brian Abshire	(USA)

110 METRES HURDLES

Greg Foster	(USA)	Jack Pierce	(USA)
Tonie Campbell	(USA)	Javier Moracho	(Spa)
Mark McKoy	(Can)	Stephane Caristan	(Fra)
Rod Woodson	(USA)	Carlos Sala	(Spa)
John Ridgeon	(UK)	Jiri Hudec	(Cze)
Arthur Blake	(USA)	Vernon George	(USA)
Colin Jackson	(UK)	Eric Reid	(USA)
Igor Kazanov	(USSR)	Andrew Parker	(Jam)
Sergey Usov	(USSR)	Roger Kingdom	(USA)
Cletus Clark	(USA)	Liviu Giurgean	(Rom)
Keith Talley	(USA)	Arto Brygarre	(Fin)

400 METRES HURDLES

Ed Moses	(USA)	Toma Tomov	(Bul)
Danny Harris	(USA)	Kriss Akabusi	(UK)
Harald Schmid	(FRG)	Athanassios Kalogiannis	(Gre)
Amadou Dia Ba	(Sen)	Aleksandr Vasilyev	(USSR)
Kevin Young	(USA)	Tranel Hawkins	(USA)
Sven Nylander	(Swe)	Shem Ochako	(Ken)
Winthrop Graham	(Jam)	Jose Alonso	(Spa)
Henry Amike	(Nig)	Nat Page	(USA)
Reggie Davis	(USA)	Andre Phillips	(USA)
Dave Patrick	(USA)	Craig Calk	(USA)

HIGH JUMP

Patrik Sjoberg	(Swe)	Lee Balkin	(USA)
Carlo Thranhardt	(FRG)	Aleksandr Kotovich	(USSR)
Igor Paklin	(USSR)	Andrey Morozov	(USSR)
Gennadiy Avdeyenko	(USSR)	Roland Dalhauser	(Swi)
Javier Sotomayor	(Cub)	Brian Stanton	(USA)
Jim Howard	(USA)	Sorin Matei	(Rom)
Jan Zvara	(Cze)	Clarence Saunders	(Ber)
Dietmar Mogenburg	(FRG)	Jake Jacoby	(USA)
Jerome Carter	(USA)	James Lott	(USA)
Gerd Nagel	(FRG)	Gennadiy Martsinovich	(USSR)
Hollis Conway	(USA)		

POLE VAULT

Sergey Bubka	(USSR)	Vladimir Polyakov	(USSR)
Joe Dial	(USA)	Tim Bright	(USA)
Ferenc Salbert	(Fra)	Zdenek Lubensky	(Cze)
Rodion Gataullin	(USSR)	Doug Fraley	(USA)
Earl Bell	(USA)	Hermann Fehringer	(Aut)
Thierry Vigneron	(Fra)	Atanas Tarev	(Bul)
Mike Tully	(USA)	Brad Pursley	(USA)
Philippe Collet	(Fra)	Grigoriy Yegorov	(USSR)
Billy Olson	(USA)	Nikoli Nikolov	(Bul)
Aleksandr Obizhayev	(USSR)	Aleksandr Zhukov	(USSR)
Kory Tarpenning	(USA)	Veleriy Ishutin	(USSR)
Marian Kolasa	(Pol)		

LONG JUMP

Robert Emmiyan	(USSR)	Vernon George	(USA)
Carl Lewis	(USA)	Yussuf Alli	(Nig)
Larry Myricks	(USA)	Gordon Laine	(USA)
Jaime Jefferson	(Cub)	Vladimir Ochkan	(USSR)
Giovanni Evangelisti	(Ita)	Khristo Markov	(Bul)
Mike Conley	(USA)	Vadim Kobylyhanski	(USSR)
Sergey Layevskiy	(USSR)	Jens Hirschberg	(GDR)
Vladimir Bobylov	(USSR)	Mike McRae	(USA)
Mike Powell	(USA)	Andreas Steiner	(Aut)
Marco Delonge	(GDR)	Ron Beer	(GDR)
Paul Emordi	(Nig)		

JAVELIN

Jan Zelezny	(Cze)	Brian Crouser	(USA)
Klaus Tafelmeir	(FRG)	Einar Vilhjalmsson	(Ice)
Mick Hill	(UK)	Duncan Atwood	(USA)
Viktor Yevsyukov	(USSR)	Dag Wannlund	(Swe)
Lev Shatilo	(USSR)	Mike Barnett	(USA)
Kazuhiro Mizoguchi	(Jap)	Detlef Michel	(GDR)
Roald Bradstock	(UK)	Gerald Weiss	(GDR)
Seppo Raty	(Fin)	Sergey Gavras	(USSR)
Sead Krdzalic	(Yug)	Marek Kaleta	(USSR)
Tom Petranoff	(USA)	Nicu Roata	(Rom)

TRIPLE JUMP

Khristo Markov	(Bul)	Nikolay Musiyenko	(USSR)
Mike Conley	(USA)	Vyacheslav Bordukov	(USSR)
Aleksandr Kovalenko	(USSR)	Ray Kimble	(USA)
Oleg Protsenko	(USSR)	Jacek Pastusinski	(Pol)
Aleksandr Yakovlev	(USSR)	Charles Simpkins	(USA)
Al Joyner	(USA)	Ivan Slanar	(Cze)
Willie Banks	(USA)	Frank Rutherford	(Bah)
Jorge Reyna	(Cub)	Volker Mai	(GDR)
Aleksandr Leonov	(USSR)	Vassif Asadov	(USSR)
Oleg Sokirkin	(USSR)	Peter Bouschen	(FRG)

SHOT

Alessandro Andrei	(Ita)	Vyacheslav Lykho	(USSR)
John Brenner	(USA)	Mikhail Kostin	(USSR)
Werner Gunthor	(Swi)	Randy Barnes	(USA)
Udo Beyer	(GDR)	Ame Pedersen	(Nor)
Ulf Timmermann	(GDR)	Saulis Kleisa	(USSR)
Remigius Machura	(Cze)	Ron Backes	(USA)
Sergey Gavryushin	(USSR)	Lars Arvid Nilsen	(Nor)
Sergey Smirnov	(USSR)	Helmut Krieger	(Pol)
Greg Tafralis	(USA)	Klaus Bodenmuller	(Aut)
Klaus Gormer	(GDR)	Grigoriy Todorov	(Bul)

DISCUS

John Powell	(USA)	Imrich Bugar	(Cze)
Stefan Fernholm	(Swe)	Vestein Hafsteinsson	(Ice)
Jurgen Schult	(GDR)	Art Burns	(USA)
Mike Buncic	(USA)	Vaclavas Kidikas	(USSR)
Luis Delis	(Cub)	Juan Martinez	(Cub)
Alwin Wagner	(FRG)	Goran Svensson	(Swe)
Svein-Inge Valvik	(Nor)	Kiril Georgiev	(Bul)
Randy Heisler	(USA)	Romas Ubartas	(USSR)
Rolf Danneberg	(FRG)	Dimitri Kovtsun	(USSR)
Vladimir Zinchenko	(USSR)	Knut Hjeltnes	(Nor)

HAMMER

Sergey Litvinov	(USSR)	Heinz Weis	(FRG)
Juri Tamm	(USSR)	Viktor Apostolov	(USSR)
Igor Nikulin	(USSR)	Vasiliy Sidorenko	(USSR)
Ralf Haber	(GDR)	Jorg Schafer	(FRG)
Gunther Rodehau	(GDR)	Johann Lindner	(Aut)
Igor Astapkovich	(USSR)	Ken Flax	(USA)
Benjaminas Viluckis	(USSR)	Plamen Minev	(Bul)
Christoph Sahner	(FRG)	Jud Logan	(USA)
Sergey Alay	(USSR)	Ivan Tanev	(Bul)
Yuriy Sedykh	(USSR)	Donatas Plunge	(USSR)

DECATHLON

Torsten Voss	(GDR)	Christian Schenk	(GDR)
Siggi Wentz	(FRG)	Sergey Zhelanov	(USSR)
Pavel Tarnavetskiy	(USSR)	Pedro da Silva	(Bra)
Simon Poelman	(NZ)	Alain Blondel	(Fra)
Tim Bright	(USA)	Gary Kinder	(USA)
Valter Kulvet	(USSR)	Uwe Freimuth	(GDR)
William Motti	(Fra)	Ivan Babiy	(USSR)
Andrei Nazarov	(USSR)	Aleksandr Areshin	(USSR)
Christian Plaziat	(Fra)	Thomas Fahner	(GDR)
Aleksandr Nevskiy	(USSR)	Sergey Popov	(USSR)

WOMEN'S EVENTS

100 METRES

Anelia Nuneva	(Bul)	Juliet Cuthbert	(Jam)
Silke Gladisch	(GDR)	Diane Williams	(USA)
Merlene Ottey	(Jam)	Marina Molokova	(USSR)
Marlies Gohr	(GDR)	Nedezhda Georgieva	(Bul)
Heike Drechsler	(GDR)	Sheila Echols	(USA)
Florence Griffith	(USA)	Gwen Torrence	(USA)
Angella Issajenko	(Can)	Kerstin Behrendt	(GDR)
Angela Bailey	(Can)	Evelyn Ashford	(USA)
Gail Devers	(USA)	Jeanette Bolden	(USA)
Alice Brown	(USA)	Nellie Cooman	(USA)
Pam Marshall	(USA)		

200 METRES

Silke Gladisch	(GDR)	Maria Pinigina	(USSR)
Florence Griffith	(USA)	Nadezha Georgieva	(Bul)
Anelia Nuneva	(Bul)	Vineta Ikauniece	(USSR)
Pam Marshall	(USA)	Pauline Davis	(Bah)
Merlene Ottey	(Jam)	Mary Onyali	(Nig)
Heike Drechsler	(GDR)	Ewa Kasprzyk	(Pol)
Valerie Brisco	(USA)	Evelyn Ashford	(USA)
Grace Jackson	(Jam)	Angella Issajenko	(Can)
Lillie Leatherwood-King	(USA)	Randy Givens	(USA)
Gwen Torrence	(USA)	Marina Molokova	(USSR)

400 METRES

Olga Bryzgina	(USSR)	Dagmar Neubauer	(GDR)
Petra Muller	(GDR)	Aelita Yurchenko	(USSR)
Maria Pinigina	(USSR)	Denean Howard	(USA)
Lillie Leatherwood-King	(USA)	Yuliana Marinova	(Bul)
Olga Nazarova	(USSR)	Ute Thimm	(FRG)
Valerie Brisco	(USA)	Sandie Richards	(Jam)
Ana Quirot	(Cub)	Larisa Dzhigalova	(USSR)
Kirsten Emmelmann	(GDR)	Vineta Ikauniece	(USSR)
Jill Richardson	(Can)	Sabine Busch	(GDR)
Diane Dixon	(USA)	Katya Ilieva	(Bul)

800 METRES

Sigrun Wodars	(GDR)	Tatyana Grehenchuk	(USSR)
Christine Wachtel	(GDR)	Kathrin Wuhn	(GDR)
Lyubov Gurina	(USSR)	Ella Kovacs	(Rom)
Ana Quirot	(Cub)	Gabriela Sedlakova	(Cze)
Slobodanka Colovic	(Yug)	Martina Steuk	(GDR)
Andrea Lange	(GDR)	Kirsty Wade	(UK)
Doina Melinte	(Rom)	Heike Oehme	(GDR)
Lyubov Kiryukhina	(USSR)	Delisa Walton-Floyd	(USA)
Jarmila Kratochvilova	(Cze)	Sandra Gasser	(Swi)
Mitica Junghaitsu	(Rom)	Shireen Bailey	(UK)

1500 METRES

Tatyana Samolenko	(USSR)	Liz Lynch	(UK)
Hildegard Korner	(GDR)	Diana Richburg	(USA)
Sandra Gasser	(Swi)	Svetlana Kitova	(USSR)
Doina Melinte	(Rom)	Mitica Junghiatu	(Rom)
Cornelia Burki	(Swi)	Elly Van Hulst	(Hol)
Andrea Lange	(GDR)	Regina Jacobs	(USA)
Ulrike Bruns	(GDR)	Kathrin Wuhn	(GDR)
Kirsty Wade	(UK)	Birgit Barth	(GDR)
Paulo Ivan	(Rom)	Sue Addison	(USA)
Yvonne Murray	(UK)	Ilinca Mitrea	(Rom)

3000 METRES

Ulrike Bruns	(GDR)	Mary Knisely	(USA)
Tatyana Samolenko	(USSR)	Margareta Keszeg	(Rom)
Paula Ivan	(Rom)	Doina Melinte	(Rom)
Maricica Puica	(Rom)	Wendy Sly	(UK)
Liz Lynch	(UK)	Lesley Welch	(USA)
Cornelia Burki	(Swi)	Lynn Williams	(Can)
Yelena Romanova	(USSR)	Olga Bondarenko	(USSR)
Yvonne Murray	(UK)	Annette Sergent	(Fra)
Elena Fidatov	(Rom)	Martine Fays	(Fra)
Elly Van Hulst	(Hol)	Marie-Pierre Duros	(Fra)

10 000 METRES

Ingrid Kristiansen	(Nor)	Anne Audain	(NZ)
Yelena Zhupiyeva	(USSR)	Sue Lee	(Can)
Katherine Ullrich	(GDR)	Martine Oppliger	(Swi)
Olga Bondarenko	(USSR)	Marleen Renders	(Bel)
Liz Lynch	(UK)	Lieve Sleghers	(Bel)
Lynn Jennings	(USA)	Yekaterina Khramenkova	(USSR)
Albetina Machado	(Por)	Nancy Rooks-Tinari	(Can)
Wang Xiuting	(Chi)	Carole Rouillard	(Can)
Angela Tooby	(UK)	Zoya Ivanova	(USSR)
Kerstin Pressler	(FRG)	Maria Curatolo	(Ita)

100 METRES HURDLES

Ginka Zagorcheva	(Bul)	Stephanie Hightower	(USA)
Yordanka Donkova	(Bul)	Anne Piquereau	(Fra)
Gloria Uibel	(GDR)	Tatyana Reshetnikova	(USSR)
Cornelia Oschkenat	(GDR)	Heike Theele	(GDR)
Mihaela Pogacian	(Rom)	Aliuska Lopez	(Cub)
Kerstin Knabe	(GDR)	Florence Colle	(Fra)
LaVonna Martin	(USA)	Natalya Grigoryeva	(USSR)
Claudia Zaczkiewicz	(FRG)	Yelena Politika	(USSR)
Laurence Elloy	(Fra)	Sophia Hunter	(USA)
Jackie Joyner-Kersee	(USA)	Olga Sinutina	(USSR)
Eva Sokolova	(USSR)		

400 METRES HURDLES

Sabine Busch	(GDR)	Nawal El Moutawakil	(Mor)
Cornelia Ulrich	(GDR)	Anna Ambraziene	(USSR)
Debbie Flintoff	(Aus)	Yelena Filipishina	(USSR)
Judi Brown King	(USA)	Marina Stepanova	(USSR)
Sandra Farmer	(Jam)	Nicoleta Carutasu	(Rom)
Tuija Helander-Kussisto	(Fin)	Yelena Goncharova	(USSR)
Schowonda Williams	(USA)	Sophia Hunter	(USA)
Margarita Khromova	(USSR)	Linetta Wilson	(USA)
Gnowefa Blaszak	(Pol)	Helene Huart	(Fra)
LaTanya Sheffield	(USA)	Gudrun Abt	(FRG)

HIGH JUMP

Stefka Kostadinova	(Bul)	Gabriele Gunz	(GDR)
Tamara Bykova	(USSR)	Charmaine Gale	(SA)
Susanne Beyer	(GDR)	Albina Kazakova	(USSR)
Louise Ritter	(USA)	Marina Degfyar	(FRG)
Emilia Draguieva	(Bul)	Coleen Sommer	(USA)
Desiree du Plessis	(SA)	Heike Redetzky	(FRG)
Lyudmila Avdeyenko	(USSR)	Gabriela Mihalcea	(Rom)
Svetlana Issaeva	(Bul)	Silvia Costa	(Cub)
Lisa Bernhagen	(USA)	Larisa Kositsina	(USSR)

LONG JUMP

Jackie Joyner-Kersee	(USA)	Eva Murkova	(Cze)
Heike Drechsler	(GDR)	Yelena Kokonova	(USSR)
Yelena Belyovskaya	(USSR)	Shelia Echols	(USA)
Galina Chistyakova	(USSR)	Heike Grabe	(GDR)
Irina Valyukevich	(USSR)	Mariet Ilcu	(Rom)
Helga Radtke	(GDR)	Irina Ozhenko	(USSR)
Yelena Ivanova	(USSR)	Carmen Sirbu	(Rom)
Valy Ionescu	(Rom)	Ludmila Ninova	(Bul)
Niole Medvedyeva	(USSR)	Anke Behmer	(GDR)
Svetlana Zorina	(USSR)	Jennifer Innis	(USA)

SHOT

Natalya Lisovskaya	(USSR)	Grit Haupt	(GDR)
Claudia Losch	(FRG)	Ilona Briesenick	(GDR)
Natalya Akhrimenko	(USSR)	Li Meisu	(Chi)
Katrin Neimke	(GDR)	Michael Loghin	(Rom)
Ines Muller	(GDR)	Sona Vasickova	(Cze)
Heike Hartwig	(GDR)	Marina Antonyuk	(USSR)
Larissa Peleshenko	(USSR)	Valentina Fedyushina	(USSR)
Svetlana Mitkova	(Bul)	Danguole Bimbaite	(USSR)
Heidi Krieger	(GDR)	Gordula Schulze	(GDR)
Helena Fibingerova	(Cze)	Lyudmila Voyevudskaya	(USSR)

DISCUS

Diana Gansky	(GDR)	Irina Shabanova	(USSR)
Tsvetanka Khristova	(Bul)	Gabriele Reinsch	(GDR)
Martina Hellmann	(GDR)	Mariana Lengyel	(Rom)
Ilke Wyludda	(GDR)	Galina Yermakova	(USSR)
Svetla Mitkova	(Bul)	Florenta Craciunescu	(Rom)
Zdenka Silhava	(Cze)	Yu Houren	(Chi)
Silvia Madetzky	(GDR)	Irini Khval	(USSR)
Irina Meszynski	(GDR)	Franka Dietzsch	(GDR)
Hilda Ramos	(Cub)	Larissa Korotkevich	(USSR)
Tatyana Byelova	(USSR)	Anne Khorina	(USSR)

JAVELIN

Petra Felke	(GDR)	Maria Colon	(Cub)
Fatima Whitbread	(UK)	Natalya Yermolovich	(USSR)
Trine Solberg	(Nor)	Ivonne Leal	(Cub)
Ingrid Thyssen	(FRG)	Irina Kostyuchenkova	(USSR)
Susanne Jung	(GDR)	Natalya Shikolenko	(USSR)
Beate Peters	(FRG)	Regine Kempter	(GDR)
Sue Howland	(Aus)	Svetlana Pestretsova	(USSR)
Anna Verouli	(Gre)	Zhou Yunxiang	(Chi)
Tiina Lillak	(Fin)	Katalin Hartai	(Hun)
Tessa Sanderson	(UK)	Anya Reiter	(GDR)

HEPTATHLON

Jackie Joyner-Kersee	(USA)	Heike Tischler	(GDR)
Anke Behmer	(GDR)	Tatyana Shpak	(USSR)
Svetlana Buraga	(USSR)	Cindy Greiner	(USA)
Larisa Nikitina	(USSR)	Yelena Davydova	(USSR)
Jane Frederick	(USA)	Svetlana Filateva	(USSR)
Marion Reichelt-Weser	(GDR)	Nadezhda Miromanova	(USSR)
Marianna Maslennikova	(USSR)	Nadine Debois	(Fra)
Chantal Beaugeant	(Fra)	Svetlana Chistyakova	(Cze)
Jane Flemming	(Aus)	Zuzana Lajbnerova	(Cze)
Liliana Nastase	(Rom)	Vera Malotetnyeva	(USSR)

* Source: *Athetics Weekly*, October 3rd 1987.

Population (in millions) for countries included

Country	Pop.	Country	Pop.
Algeria	22.2	Kenya	20.2
Australia	15.8	Mexico	79.7
Austria	7.5	Morocco	24.3
Bahamas	0.2	Netherlands	14.5
Belgium	9.9	New Zealand	3.4
Brazil	138	Nigeria	91.2
Bulgaria	8.9	Norway	4.2
Burundi	4.6	Poland	37.3
Canada	25.4	Portugal	10.3
China	1042	Romania	22.8
Cuba	10.1	Senegal	6.7
Czechoslovakia	15.5	Somalia	6.5
Ethiopia	36.0	Soviet Union	278
Finland	4.9	South Africa	32.5
France	55.0	Spain	38.5
German Democratic Rep.	16.7	Sudan	21.8
German Federal Rep.	61.0	Sweden	8.3
Greece	10.1	Switzerland	6.5
Hungary	10.7	Tanzania	21.7
Iceland	0.2	Trinidad	1.4
Ireland	3.5	Tunisia	7.2
Italy	57.4	United Kingdom	56.4
Ivory Coast	10.1	United States	239
Jamaica	2.4	Venezuela	17.3
Japan	121	Yugoslavia	23.1

Source: Population Reference Bureau, *World Population Data Sheet*, 1985.

AUTHOR INDEX

Page numbers in *italics* indicate a full reference.

SUBJECT INDEX